Seeking the Hiding God

A Personal Theological Essay

Arnold Eisen

Ben Yehuda Press
Teaneck, New Jersey

Published by Ben Yehuda Press
122 Ayers Court #1B
Teaneck, NJ 07666
http://www.BenYehudaPress.com

To subscribe to our monthly book club and support independent Jewish publishing, visit
https://www.patreon.com/BenYehudaPress

Ben Yehuda Press books may be purchased at a discount by synagogues, book clubs, and other institutions buying in bulk.

For information, please email markets@BenYehudaPress.com

Cover art from the painting, "Seeing Sinai" by Jill Nathanson, from the collection of the Jewish Theological Seminary of America.

ISBN13 978-1-963475-44-94 hc   978-1-963475-45-6 paper 978-1-963475-46-3 epub

Library of Congress Cataloging-in-Publication Data

Names: Eisen, Arnold M., 1951- author.
Title: Seeking the Hiding God : a personal theological essay / Arnold
   Eisen.
Description: Teaneck : Ben Yehuda Press, [2024] | Series: Jewish arguments
   | Summary: "Seeking the Hiding God" by Arnold Eisen examines the
   elusive nature of God and the significance of divine encounters through
   the lens of Jewish rituals and traditions. The book explores the
   responsibilities of humans as God's partners and the personal and
   communal implications of faith and doubt"-- Provided by publisher.
Identifiers: LCCN 2024023214 (print) | LCCN 2024023215 (ebook) | ISBN
   9781963475449 (hardback) | ISBN 9781963475456 (paperback) | ISBN
   9781963475463 (epub)
Subjects: LCSH: God (Judaism) | Faith (Judaism)--Meditations. |
   Judaism--21st century. | Conservative Judaism--United States. |
   Jews--United States--Identity. | Commandments (Judaism)--History of
   doctrines. | Eisen, Arnold M., 1951---Religion.
Classification: LCC BM610 .E445 2024 (print) | LCC BM610 (ebook) | DDC
   296.4--dc23/eng/20240604
LC record available at https://lccn.loc.gov/2024023214
LC ebook record available at https://lccn.loc.gov/2024023215

24 25 26 / 10 9 8 7 6 5 4 3 2 1   20240829

To my children and my students

Preface

The theological essay that follows represents an entirely new direction for me as a Jew and scholar of Judaism. It might well differ in style and substance from any work about faith that you have read. Let me explain at the outset what I want to accomplish in *Seeking the Hiding God*, and why I chose to write the book in the way I did.

We've all been changed by the multiple upheavals that have overtaken America and the world during the past few years. The combination of the COVID-19 pandemic, unparalleled polarization in our nation's politics, heightened attention to poverty and racism, the arrival of AI, and increasing evidence that global warming will soon prove catastrophic for much of humanity, has altered the way we think about a host of matters great or small. Faith has been sorely tested. In my case, the transformations that convulsed our lives with the onset of the pandemic were superimposed upon a professional transition that significantly altered my life's course. In 2020, I stepped down after thirteen years as the leader of a major religious institution—the Jewish Theological Seminary of America (JTS)—and began a year-long sabbatical. Leaving behind a calendar filled with appointments six days a week from morning to night, I found myself with unscheduled time in which to read, think, write, and dream. I decided early on—even before turning the page in my career—that what I most wanted to do in the year before reaching the age of seventy was to give myself an accounting of what I believe about God.

The irony of that decision was not lost on me. I had been studying other people's thoughts about God for nearly half a century. I had just led an institution that trains rabbis, cantors, and educators to guide congregants and students of all ages in reflecting on and encountering the divine. I had been living a life marked by regular prayer and ritual observance since childhood. Sustained thinking about God, however, had never been a feature of my religious practice. This is not unusual among Jews, it seems, or among Americans of other faiths. Most people don't talk a lot about God these days, even—or especially—with life partners, adult children, and close friends. A person might sit beside fellow worshippers in church or synagogue for years without holding a single conversation about what one is doing or experiencing. Similarly, a person might worship without conducting an internal audit of what one does or does not believe.

American Jews have long been among the least religiously observant and believing of all major religious groups. Jews engage in sustained or fervent God-talk much less than Americans of other faiths; in fact, it is often argued that theology has never been central to Judaism. A recent article on the subject by a noted authority opens with the disclaimer that "the word 'theology' is not part of the vocabulary of most Jews, even of [the] most religiously learned." When Jews *have* engaged in theology over the centuries, their God-talk usually focused less on God's nature or workings than on how to seek and serve God. Unlike Christians, who are asked to take a leap of faith for belief in God, Jews—in the words of Rabbi Abraham Joshua Heschel, the American Jewish thinker who has had more impact on me than any other—are asked to take a "leap of action."

I, too, generally make the action leap more often than the faith leap, in part because I believe that human beings simply are not equipped to know or say much about God. For contemporary individuals and communities, theology is rendered more difficult by the shadow of the Holocaust and the utter disjunction between religious assumptions and claims about ultimate reality and what scientists tell us about the origin and nature of the universe. What can one say credibly from our little spot on a planet that circles a sun that is one of billions of stars in the universe? Can anything cogent be said of God's involvement in a world that has known multiple genocides in recent memory? What wisdom can an age-old religious tradition contribute that won't be outstripped by worldviews and technology that change at the speed of light?

I write about God in this book nonetheless, as theologians plagued by ignorance and doubt have done for many centuries. Like them, I feel impelled to write what I think can be said about the Unsayable, and to do so humbly and truthfully. Unlike many other writers about faith, however, I do not claim special insight into the divine realm. I have little knowledge of God and what I do have is uncertain. I instead offer testimony to a religious life of *yearning and desire*. I seek a relationship with the God who is far beyond my understanding and bear witness to intuitions of God's presence in, and impact upon, my life. There are times when I have a strong sense that God is both hiding and seeking—looking for me, as well as for every one of us. I realize in those moments that I, like many other human beings in this and every age, can often not be found when I am needed.

What could it mean to "love the Lord [my] God," I wonder, let alone to do so with all my heart, soul, and might, as the Torah commands? I'm not sure, but I try to do so anyway. Unable to affirm many of the truths about God and history stated almost matter-of-factly in the prayer book and in texts such as the Passover Haggadah—and quite certain at times that these claims are false—I nonetheless utter the prayers and observe holidays faithfully. I could not imagine my life without them. Week in and week out, the Sabbath provides meaning, succor, and challenge without demanding doctrinal knowledge or belief in return. I gratefully enter its embrace.

This lifelong pattern of behavior calls for explanation that I have never before forced myself to provide. After five decades of adulthood, four decades of published scholarship on Judaism and other faiths, thirty-plus years of marriage and parenting, and hundreds of speeches delivered as the Chancellor of JTS, the time has come. None of us knows how much time we have left on earth. At age seventy, procrastination seems especially perilous.

* * * * * *

Once I decided to face the matter squarely, the question became what form theology could and should take in our day. What could a Jew like me honestly say about God? What truths *do* I hold? I resolved that four principles would guide my thinking and writing.

First, my theological reflection would be *honest*—free of pretense or false pieties—and *true to my personal experience* of life in the world. I believe that all great works of Jewish theology have been personal in this way, whether or not their authors admitted that fact. In the twenty-first century, it seems more necessary than ever to declare to the reader where one comes from and why. This essay, while by no means a memoir, draws on memories of transformative encounters and events: for example, the birth of my first child, my one-on-one meeting with Rabbi Heschel, or the first Yom Kippur that I marked in Jerusalem. I engage in confession to make the point that theology arises in the midst of life, emerging—in my case at least—from boundary moments and life-altering journeys.

Second, theology *responds to history*. Think of the impact on biblical authors of the Exodus and the destruction of Solomon's Temple. Consider the way that the destruction of the Second Temple by the Romans and the subsequent far-flung dispersion of Jews exercised the rabbinic imagination for many centuries. In our time the impact of history on religious thought is no less obvious. I was born in 1951, three years after the State of Israel and six years after the end of the Holocaust. As a child in an observant Jewish family, I could not help but ponder the juxtaposition of these events with my own existence. As a scholar of contemporary Judaism, the Holocaust and Israel often occupy my mind. I began to write the first draft of these reflections in the months when the world awoke each morning to the latest count of COVID-19 cases, hospitalizations, and deaths. History seemed to be banging on every door, provoking questions about God's care or indifference that could not be avoided. The knock of history is sounding again as I make final corrections to the galleys of the essay. War between Israel and Hamas continues, eight months and tens of thousands of deaths after it began. What should a religious person think and do about the grave matters that relentlessly confront us?

What does God think of these matters? What, if anything, is God doing about them?

Third, theology *should be a pursuit open to every human being* rather than, as it so often is, an esoteric domain that requires the equivalent of a PhD in philosophy or religion. Moses Maimonides, perhaps the greatest Jewish theologian of all time, made the reasonable case that one could not make sense of metaphysics or theology, and should not try, without firm grounding in physics and mathematics. If he was right, I am excluded from the theology game, and chances are that you are too. But I refuse to believe serious reflection about God must be limited to a specialized elite. This cannot be what God intended. The Torah speaks repeatedly of God's desire to be known by us and to have us join with God in covenant. The command to "love the Lord your God" presumes the ability to think seriously about the God we love, even if accurate knowledge and actual comprehension of God are out of the question.

Therefore, I have sought a conversational voice for my theological reflection—the sort of voice used to discuss complex matters with spouses and friends—and I found that voice by writing letters to and from friends with whom I have talked about everything from religion and politics to children and careers. These letters comprise the prologue to the book and set the stage for the chapters that follow. The epilogue of this essay is a letter addressed to my wife. I imagine myself sitting across the table from trusted conversation partners as I reflect upon the meaning that I find in holidays or themes that are well-known to Jews and non-Jews alike: Passover and redemption; covenants of love and commandment with God and one another; and atonement and forgiveness at Yom Kippur in the face of ritual encounter with sin and death. I believe this is how most people do theology: conversationally, episodically, sometimes with urgent force and at other times with musing curiosity, but never with a finality that puts the question to rest or arrives at answers worthy of formulation in a creed.

Reading *Seeking the Hiding God* requires no specialized knowledge. It presumes no Jewish birthright or affiliation and expects no commitment to particular beliefs or behavior. I ask only that readers be willing to join me in thinking seriously about matters that we tend to avoid.

Finally, I want my theological reflection to contain *multiple voices*. Almost every major work of the tradition in which I live and think resounds with multiple perspectives, from the Bible and the Talmud, through the great medieval collections of mystical teachings and scriptural commentary, to the outpouring of modern Jewish thought that is my scholarly area of expertise. Philosophers who have attempted to offer exclusive truth about God or Torah have quickly been challenged by other philosophers putting forth different truths. Judaism has thrived on such disagreement and diversity, which will be in full view in my citation of biblical and rabbinic sources that have shaped both my thinking and my life. The prayer books used by every denomination are anthologies, not creeds. Every synagogue includes worshippers who bring a range of belief and doubt much wider than the spectrum represented by the individuals whose voices fill the prologue of this book. Friends, students, and family members holding diverse views have long made essential contributions to my wrestling with belief, doubt, and ritual observance. So, too, have the religious thinkers of multiple traditions whose works I have studied and taught over the decades. The hundreds of Jews who engaged me in honest conversation as I travelled around North America as Chancellor of JTS have left their mark on my thinking as well. I trust that they and other readers of varying conviction and practice will find echoes of their own questioning and doubt in these pages, and perhaps derive benefit from the resolutions at which I have arrived.

✽ ✽ ✽ ✽ ✽ ✽

One question from my travels around North America has occupied me more than any other as I tried to understand what I think about God and how I should live in God's world. It came during the Q&A following a talk about Jewish tradition and community that I gave one evening at a synagogue in Baltimore soon after assuming the role of Chancellor. From the back row of a very large sanctuary, a teenager quietly but firmly demanded to know something that I too had struggled with since I was his age. "But Professor Eisen," he asked, "what is true?"

I do not remember what I said in response. I hope that I had the presence of mind to pass on the words of reassurance and summons that Moses gave in his final address to the Children of Israel, as reported near the end of the Book of Deuteronomy. The good that we are called to do in this life is not beyond reach, even though answers to the ultimate mysteries are not in our hands. We are commanded to choose blessing, choose the good, and choose life—and the ability to make these choices *is* in our hands. God remains in hiding much of the time, but we sense God's presence in our lives in any number of ways, including study, prayer, ritual observance, and the performance of good deeds. The work to which we are summoned is more than enough for the time on earth that has been granted us and will require the best effort that each one of us, and all of us together, can bring to it. The Torah points the way. Pursue justice. Practice compassion. Love your neighbors. Stay close to those whom you love and who love you.

We get by with the help of our friends. *Seeking the Hiding God* starts and concludes with the voices of people who have taught me for nearly half a century how to hide, seek, and be found.

Prologue
Correspondence with Friends

from: Arnie
to: Adam

You asked me a few months ago why I don't stop complaining about evangelical Trump supporters who invoke God's name to justify bigotry, Haredi Jews who wouldn't wear face masks at the height of the COVID-19 pandemic because they believed God would protect them from the virus while they studied Torah, and New Agers of all faiths who consider God their best friend and are sure that—unlike my friends, thanks goodness—God never asks them for anything or judges them for wrongdoing. You pointed out that these views of mine are in keeping with what you consider a general grouchiness that expresses itself in dissatisfaction with biased journalism, bad service in restaurants, chitchat at wine-and-cheese parties, and a hundred other things you could name. Then you paused for effect, looked me in the eye as you rarely do, and said: "So why not show us what you think good talk about God should sound like? How about writing your own theology?"

I've been obsessed with that challenge ever since you issued it. Many opening paragraphs have occurred to me in the shower, often following frustrating dreams that don't seem to be the wish fulfillment that Freud said dreams should be. Last night, for example: I dream that I am expected to chant a portion from the Torah in synagogue that morning. However, nobody told me ahead of time, and I am not good enough at chanting Torah to do it without reviewing the words and musical notation in advance. I go home to get the practice book that includes vowels and notes but realize that my sports jacket has chalk all over it and my pants are sloppy, so I must change my clothes for synagogue. I can't find an outfit that is suitable. I finally find one and hurry to the subway but I don't have a Metro card, there is a long line to buy one, but how would I do that in any case, as I don't spend money on the Sabbath or ride the subway? I woke up greatly relieved; there was no need to stand in line or find clean clothing (the wish fulfillment that Freud promised?). No Torah portion to learn—just this book on theology to write, important relationships and commitments to attend to, and praises and thanks to utter to God. Silence to contemplate in fear and trembling. Am I prepared for any of this?

Søren Kierkegaard, who has left his mark on me ever since I first encountered his book *Fear and Trembling* in my freshman year at Penn, wrote thousands of words about the difficulty of writing about God in the modern age, given the particular fear and trembling to which human beings have been subject over the past two centuries. That sentiment is widely shared among writers about God in recent decades, whether Christians like Kierkegaard or Jews like me, though my experience has been that books about faith tend to circle round the matter of fear without facing it squarely. I certainly don't think Kierkegaard got the Torah's frightening story of the Binding of Isaac right in *Fear and Trembling*—perhaps because he was estranged from his father, felt guilty about that for the rest of his life, and therefore read that story in the light and shadow of that cloud.

I, by contrast, idolized my father in all his incredible ordinariness. (The fact that you knew him well, Adam, heard him play piano, laughed good-naturedly at his jokes, and treasured the fact that he was alive into his nineties, will help both of us understand what I write about God, Genesis, and much else in this book.) Unlike Kierkegaard (and most ancient and modern Jewish commentators), I never thought that Abraham went up the mountain that day with the equipment needed for sacrifice intending to kill Isaac at God's command. He loved his son dearly and had received a promise from God that the Covenant would be transmitted through him to future generations. My dad too was named Abraham until he changed it to Alan and shortened Eisenstein to Eisen, at the suggestion of a piano teacher who thought his musical career would advance further with a name that did not sound so Jewish. I am his only son, his "Isaac," whom he loved dearly. Even as a kid, I knew that he and my mother had both faced numerous tests and trials. More than once they had encountered the angel of God who—unlike the one who tells Abraham to put down the knife—did not come to save.

Even in moments of hot Oedipal anger, when any excuse to hate my father—as Kierkegaard apparently hated his—would have been welcome, I never believed for a minute that my dad would do such a thing to me. Or would want to. I did not experience him (or God) as hungry for the sacrifice of human life, including mine. So, I have never read the biblical story that way. Abraham would not be asked to sacrifice his blessing and his future in a barbaric act of sacrifice. His God and mine, whatever else He was, would not be that petty or that trite. The God portrayed in Genesis knew well the plots that entertained ancient Near Eastern deities and had entirely new story lines in mind. Abraham was not lying when he told the servant boys in Isaac's presence, as the two of them prepared to ascend the mountain, that "we will return to you." Kierkegaard must have thought Abraham lied at that point to spare Isaac from the knowledge that his "Father in Heaven" and his father on earth were about to kill him. I believe Abraham was telling the truth; indeed, the entire Book of Genesis tells truths about the human situation that, if anything, offers more cause for trembling than Kierkegaard.

I read that story and many others in the Bible as a kind of boulder that blocks the path of anyone who thinks they can ascend to the heights where the secrets of God and Torah might be found. (Jewish tradition identifies the mountain on which Abraham did not kill Isaac as the place where the Children of Israel would one day worship God in the Temple built by Solomon—worship that involved the routine slaughter of thousands of animals.) Far more of God is concealed than revealed on that holy site. Our God often seems to be in hiding and doesn't want to be found. Fear and trembling remain the lot of human beings, whether God is absent or present. If you think God intervenes to help couples in their nineties bear a child—as He did for Abraham and Sarah—think again. That intervention is as unlikely as God coming down from heaven to destroy a city because the inhabitants are overwhelmingly evil. There's little chance of averting such an outcome if ten righteous residents can be identified. These stories will not happen in the real world.

I received that message loud and clear in Hebrew school—a gift that probably prevented the sort of disillusionment with childhood belief that many suffered in early adulthood. The teaching I received continues to preclude any theological claim to have definitive answers to ultimate questions and keeps me from speaking with overconfidence about God. I was not surprised, given my upbringing and experience, to learn that God had not intervened to prevent the Holocaust. I would not have expected God to disarm the gunman who killed my next-door neighbor at the office where he worked, or to save my cousin from drowning at age thirteen. Nor did I feel entitled to explanations of such inaction on God's part.

But I was taught by my parents and teachers that there is, nonetheless, Meaning (the capital M became affixed to the word early in my life and has not disappeared) to be found in a life guided by the Torah. An abundance of Meaning, and of pleasure, too, could be derived from studying the Torah's laws and narratives year after year amid a like-minded Community. (The capital C signifies the seriousness of mutual relation that common study and practice creates among its members.) Accompanied by Jewish commentators from across the centuries and by careful non-Jewish readers of the biblical text like Kierkegaard, one could take part in a conversation that offered great reward in this life and held out the possibility of life in a world to come. That conversation with Torah forms a major part of this essay. I also learned during high school that Jewish theologians had shuttled between faith and doubt long before modern science and the Holocaust posed new challenges to belief and supplied new armories for skepticism. In the company of fellow students and teachers across many generations, I could chart a similar path.

My final thought at this point in our correspondence concerns the balance of fear, trembling, and faith at which I have arrived after fifty years. I confess that Freud does make it harder to read the Torah without irony or suspicion of self-deception. I can't separate meat from dairy dishes assiduously, as I do, without hearing the words "obsessive-compulsive neurosis" in my head. There are times when I try to address God in prayer in the traditional formulation—"Blessed are You"—and am interrupted by the authoritative voice of the learned doctor with the cigar, scolding me for indulging in tragic "illusion." It turns out, though, that Freud had his own father issues to contend with and, being Freud, did not entirely hide them from the reader or deny their impact upon his thinking about religion. I'm grateful to our teacher Philip Rieff for demonstrating how a person can resist Freud even while appreciating his undeniable insight into our modern selves and our reach for faith. If you are going to be a religious believer today, you have to resist the voices of numerous modern Western authorities who maintain that one cannot, in good faith, maintain faith in God.

You must also be comfortable with a significant degree of uncertainty—a quality of mind to which believers, and especially theologians, are usually averse. Faith is not a yes-no matter, belief or non-belief, God or atheism, truth or heresy, tradition or modernity, religion or science. As with so much else in life, one takes what one can get in the domains of truth and Meaning. If you are wise, as the rabbis taught two millennia ago, you learn from everyone you can—and learn to be satisfied with your portion.

I think a person of faith must believe that what you most *want* to be true, what you most desperately *need* to be true, might actually be the case.

Anyway, that's what keeps me going. That and the people I love. Be well.

Arnie

from: Adam
to: Arnie

Thanks for your letter. Happy Presidents' Day. You got me thinking. I'll try to respond with as much consciousness as I can muster for the task early in the morning of a day off from work, sipping the first of what will be many cups of coffee. Let's cut to the chase: I don't know whether I believe in God or not, as you have heard me say many times during our half century of friendship. No doubt you remember me whispering that disclaimer more than once as I sat beside you at Yom Kippur services. What I do know is that thinking about God as you are determined to do—even *trying* to think about God—brings to the surface a riot of swirling feelings and associations of the sort I spend my professional life helping people to untangle, clarify, and overcome. Maybe in this exchange of letters I can do a bit of that for myself.

You talked a lot about your father Abraham, but not much about your mother. It was, of course, my father's death during my first year of college—just before you and I met—that sent me into therapy for the first time and propelled me into my career as a psychiatrist. But it was probably my mother—ever-present, loving, combative, gorgeous, and extremely needy—who furnished much of the content for my own therapy sessions over the years and who nourished the empathy I've brought to the sessions I have with my patients. It occurred to me, contemplating your project, that I could not entertain the hope of thinking constructively about "Our Father in heaven" until I had clarified my feelings toward my father, mother, and siblings. I have little patience with philosophers who write as if their command of pure reason is adequate to scale the fortress of truth even though they do not have a clue about why they screamed at their kids or spouse at breakfast. The theology business seems pretty hopeless to me, therefore, though it may shed light on why God becomes so angry with the Children of Israel—no doubt a projection, in part, of our anger with our parents and with Him.

Really, though, shouldn't God's expectations have been lower after prior experience with human beings? He did create us after all. We are what we are. And shouldn't *our* expectations be lower, both about what God is likely to do for us and about the chance of knowing much about God? (I assume that at some point in your book you will deal with the issue of the Bible and Jewish prayers using only male pronouns to talk to God or about God. "Father in heaven" language is a real problem, and not only for women. I'm using it in this letter to make the point, from personal experience, that Freud was onto something.)

Therapy sessions, whether I'm on the couch or by my desk, are humbling when it comes to knowing anything about God. It's so hard to comprehend *ourselves*, let alone the universe. This morning an op-ed piece called "Aliens Must Be Out There" appeared in the *Times*. The first piece of evidence it cites for that claim is that our sun is "one of an estimated 100 billion to 400 billion [stars] in the Milky Way galaxy alone. And the Milky Way is itself just one galaxy among hundreds of billions or perhaps trillions in the observable universe." The author uses that data to argue that other life shares the universe with us. We've talked about this and how we think calculations are cause for sheer terror. Remember the image of the young Woody Allen unable to sleep at night because the sun is due to burn itself up in a few billion years? We laugh at that, uncomfortably, because we share little Woody's anxiety at some level. The fact of infinity—ungraspable, inconceivable, unimaginable—does not help me feel at home in the universe. It does not help either one of us sleep soundly. Fear and trembling run wild whenever astronomers present their wondrous reports about the universe. What do they do to your attempt at theology?

I combat the terror by filling my days with reassuring matters such as work and the people who do it alongside me. I've felt real gratitude lately for the team of physicians and nurses with whom I spend my days. During the COVID-19 pandemic, they did everything in their power to provide care to patients and their families, despite the odds. There's so much trauma out there right now and so many good people who go out every day and confront it.

Acts of service work as an antidote to fear, as does the love we experience when we return home from work. The fact that Becky loves me is barely less inexplicable than the lack of communication between alien beings and earthlings. She loves me despite failings in me that are so obvious no therapy is required to expose them. Remarkably, I manage to love her too, despite those same failings. Add to these wonders the fact that I love our kids with a ferocity that is greater than my anger or my fear and feel a connection to them that science has yet to explain.

There is a lot in that category, I think; I seem to place more there the older I get. I am sometimes amazed at consciousness itself; the fact that I can sit here on a Monday morning and write these words to you is amazing to me. I'm almost tempted to say that existence itself smacks of miracle, much as I resist that kind of language. But surprise at being here makes it hard to dismiss out of hand the notion of a de-signing deity, in whom on some days I almost but never quite believe.

I've learned from experience that a threat to the well-being of some-one you love can wring belief out of the most confirmed agnostic. It got me to pray last year when Becky was ill. None of us is a mere observer where God is concerned. I seem to always need the divine forgiveness I have ritually prayed for on Yom Kippur year after year. I also seem to need to give things freely to others, including forgiveness, even when that is the very last thing in the world I *want* to do. This need too, it turns out, is one of the things that puts me in mind of God.

One more thought about the ultimate mystery before I close. I've taken up painting again, and there have been moments—putting paint on canvas and watching a landscape or still life emerge, stroke by stroke—when I have had a sense that there is something in the world resembling *wholeness*. Why, I do not know. But I feel the same way sometimes—another illusion?—when a particular chord progression that I've played on the guitar seems especially haunting, somehow *right*. The music comes together, and I do too. You were correct in suspecting that I would identify with some of the sensations attributed to Cezanne in the book you gave me for my birthday. I do have a sense of painting as an "instrument of order," or of a "feeling for harmony." Your attempt to do theology, Arnie, is perhaps not entirely unlike my attempt to paint something decent. I don't know if I will ever experi-ence what the Cezanne book called "a mystical immersion in nature's hidden depths." Is that what you are wont to call God? It may come, it may not. I will let you know.

I have to stop now and go to the store, which means putting on a mask for safety's sake, even after getting the vaccine. The pandemic can either serve as proof for the amazing intelligence of a divine Creator— the virus' ability to spread and reproduce itself is truly brilliant—or as additional evidence for the already-extensive case against intelligent design. You decide.

Adam

from: Josh
to: Arnie

Adam shared your theology correspondence with me. The first thing that came to me was a book you and I talked about when we met in college: *I and Thou*. Martin Buber got me with its opening line—"The world is twofold, in accordance with our twofold attitude toward it"—and held me straight through to the end of the book, despite all the baffling paragraphs about "The Eternal Thou." You and I pondered those paragraphs for hours without figuring out what they mean. I've been holding on to Buber's sense of what is possible in this world ever since.

Community has always been one of the most important words in my vocabulary, as it was in Buber's. I've tried to follow Buber's advice that we focus on what happens *between* people rather than what goes on inside them. The conviction that "actual life" is given and received in the "relation of an I to a Thou" is probably what caused you, me, and Adam to put so much energy into our friendship ever since. It's also a major reason I became a doctor; I wanted to practice medicine in a way that addressed the whole person rather than a set of symptoms or a disease. That has become a cliché over the past few decades, but it's still far from the usual practice where I've worked. Much of the good that I think I do for patients comes from the words and eye contact I exchange with them. Do you know what it's like to tell a patient that his bladder cancer might prove fatal? You don't rush through a conversation like that. Nor do you hurry when providing assurance that the cancer is treatable. The meds and surgery that I prescribe are not the only remedies that help patients, and their families, heal.

Life is given and received in this way. I know that for a fact. Buber deserves some of the credit for my knowing it.

What I don't know is how this translates into truth, let alone theology. You and I shared I-Thou relationships with our friends. We bonded over shared love for my dog, aware that Buber had written about having an I-Thou relationship with a cat. Neither of us doubts that these connections were profound. (I do not know if human beings have souls. I have no doubt that my dog did.) From time to time, we imagined an I-Thou community of the sort Buber described. We wanted to raise families and work for social justice together, and vowed to stay close no matter what happened. We were serious about this, however naïve it seems today. One by one, though, each of us pursued personal ambitions, romances, and careers after college that ended any chance of us staying together. You were the first to betray the dream; you finished college and went abroad for five years of grad school. You were sheepish about departing from the plan but unapologetic. I eventually came to accept a more realistic I-Thou relationship that, while less intense and fulfilling, was still loving.

But tell me how you think the "lines of relation extended" can be said to "meet in the Eternal Thou," as Buber claims. I think I understand how the lines of relation "meet" in some fashion. Love grows despite distance in time or space. The lines joining two people hold firm even if they are broken or blurred. And we know that loving relationships can take a hundred different forms, none of them less or more loving than the others. The lines all "meet" in the sense that they all partake in love, but I'm not sure about the "Eternal Thou" piece. Buber must have had in mind the mathematical truth that parallel lines meet in infinity and I, like Adam, find the concept of infinity to be beyond anything I can grasp. The best I can make of what Buber is saying is that God has everything to do with love. This makes a lot of sense to me.

It occurs to me as I write this letter that part of what I love about medicine is that real human beings sit opposite me in the examination room—flesh and blood individuals, body, and spirit. No metaphysical abstraction is needed to understand them. No imagination of infinity gets in the way. Just empathy for what ails, threatens and inspires them. I don't know if the Eternal Thou is present in the room with us, but I do believe there is something sacred in the lines of relationship that bind me to the people who come to me for help. They are suffering, and I can assist them. I also learn from them. This is one of the truest things I know.

Then there is my newfound passion for photographing birds, which is the most surprising turn my life has taken so far. Nancy began by indulging me, tolerating the obsessiveness I've displayed and the thousands of dollars I've spent on cameras, but she's since come around. My love of birds, like other loves, is not easy to explain. I'll just say that the soaring ospreys you spent hours searching for in Scotland come to rest almost daily in the tallest tree in our backyard. When hummingbirds or blue jays hover at the birdfeeder on the fence outside our window, the delicate perfection of their bodies sometimes brings tears to my eyes. Afterward, I marvel at the images captured in the photographs that I've taken and feel both inadequate and grateful—the same way I feel when a patient I've become close to makes it through surgery. The lines of relation meet.

Does God have anything to do with these sensations, or with the intimations of wholeness that Adam said he occasionally feels? You tell me. I've lost too many patients, some of them too young, to believe in divine providence, and I've read too much science to believe in the Bible's account of creation. Much remains beyond human understanding and probably always will. Can any credible theology venture there? I count on you to write theology that is credible.

The "realm of the between," the "lines of relation"—that is where theology should focus, I think, for I'm sure that is where, if anywhere, God is to be found.

Love you.

Josh

from: Arnie
to: Adam and Josh

It's hard for me to believe that we never really had this conversation before, despite having gone through what close friends face together over 50 years: good, bad, and blissfully ordinary. How many funerals and shivas have we attended? How many bar and bat mitzvahs? (Too few weddings for my liking: the readiness for romantic commitment seems to come even later in 21st-century America than it did for us.) Having the God conversation is not something normal adults do, I guess. The fact that we're having it now makes me feel connected to you as never before. It also makes me feel a bit lonelier.

Adam: you confessed that, sitting beside me at Yom Kippur services, you were not always sure that God is out there, let alone that God hears prayers for forgiveness and sometimes answers them. I've occasionally had that doubt too (we've talked about this, between services), but it usually passes in a matter of days or weeks, and sometimes dissipates during Yom Kippur itself. I'll try to explain how and why that happens in the chapters that follow this exchange of letters. The words and music somehow invite me to put aside doubt about whether God is there to hear or answer prayer. It helps that many of the most important parts of the Yom Kippur liturgy are sung in three-quarter time. The waltz offers comfort. I sway to it contentedly, as Jews have done for centuries.

Ironically, my doubt is assuaged by the knowledge that sacred Jewish texts from the Bible to our own day are filled not only with testimonies of faith but with expressions of protest and despair about God's failure to answer when called upon or to save when needed. These works affirm God's presence in the world and in all our lives even when they bear witness to God's distance. "He who speaks," Buber wrote, "is incomprehensible, irregular, surprising, overwhelming, sovereign." No "regular contact" with this God can be had "in fixed places and at fixed times." No "I-Thou" encounter can be relied upon, even on Yom Kippur. There is no surety in anything. That's the nature of faith. Abraham Joshua Heschel taught this lesson in his book, *Man Is Not Alone*, which I first read as a teenager. At the end of Chapter

Nine, the most pious, learned, and courageous Jew I will ever meet lyrically describes what can only be a personal experience of God's presence. When you turn the page, you immediately encounter the title of the following chapter, printed in large boldface letters: **Doubts**. Heschel's progress from faith to doubt and back again has more than once saved my own faith.

Witnessing people doing acts of justice and kindness in God's name has helped sustain me in my periodic struggles with doubt. I've held onto those experiences for dear life ever after, fearing they would somehow disappear from memory if I spoke or wrote about them. I have rarely shared them until now even with good friends like the two of you.

Theology takes shape in moments like these, which interrupt our daily routines and propel us in unforeseen directions. I will try to describe some of those moments and chart the impact they have had on me in the chapters that follow. I will also record the effect of experiences as routine—and spectacular—as those you and Josh have described: staring at a particularly brilliant sunset, for example, or watching birds fly and our kids grow. There won't be what Buber called "demonstrable assertions" in this book; I have few of these to offer. But I do hope to point toward the "hidden realm of existence" that you too have glimpsed and the sense of rightness or wholeness that you have tried to articulate.

Josh: you wrote, "I'm sure that is where, if anywhere, God is to be found." Those words called to mind the teaching of a great Hasidic master, in turn based on the work of earlier Jewish mystics, that God had to remove God's self from the universe at the Creation to make room for other beings. God had to "contract" to a point so small that the "Being without End" (a favorite kabbalistic term for God) virtually disappeared into No-Thingness (another one of the mystics' names for God). Rabbi Nachman of Bratzlav was convinced that if he felt God's absence from the world so keenly despite fervent prayer and practice, it was because God was not here to be found. God had no choice but to hide so that human beings would be free to seek, act, think, love, and dream. The tragic result is that human beings are free to do a host of things that run counter to God's intentions and our own instinct to do good.

This teaching has reassured me on many occasions when, despondent at God's palpable absence from my life, I have blamed myself for God's hiddenness or considered abandoning my search. Similar assurance comes my way every Saturday morning in synagogue. At one of the liturgical high points of the service, I join in chanting the words of the Kedushah, "God's glory fills the earth, His glory fills the world"—words followed by: "His angels ask one another: Where is the place of His glory?" The angels don't know where God is any more than we do, it seems. So we say together, "Blessed be the glory of the Lord from His place"—*wherever that may be*. You said in closing your letter, Josh, that God must be found in relation, if anywhere. In other words, in love. That sounds right to me too. The question bothering me has never been *whether* God exists, but rather whether, where and how God can be found by us, by me.

I do not have a definitive answer to that question, of course. But I believe that if we keep looking for God, guided by reason, experience, and tradition; if we walk a path marked by justice and compassion; and if we are fortunate, God will find us on occasion. In my case, this sometimes happens when I am not looking or do not want to be found. I refuse to believe that one must be a great philosopher like Maimonides or Plato, or a great mystic like the Baal Shem Tov, to embark on the search for God. One need not be meticulous in observance of the commandments, let alone an ascetic who goes beyond even that high standard. Nor must you attain a level of faith so pure that no doubt can sully it. All these restrictions would preclude a life of faith for 99% of humanity, including me.

The Bible itself bears witness that faith is always more a matter of seeking than of finding God, who is at once more present and more distant than we can grasp. God will never be available at our beck and call—that's the definition of idolatry. The life of faith is one of yearning for God, calling out again and again in hopes of hearing an answer that is not an echo. You trust that your steadfast search will be rewarded one day, and you hope you will have what it takes to respond when God calls back. Buber was right, I think—and thoroughly in accord with Jewish tradition—to insist that an encounter with God, if and when it occurs, grows from the sort of loving relations that you both wrote about in your letters. I wish we and other adults expressed love, and talked about love and about God, a lot more than we do.

* * * * * *

The two of you have often asked me how I came to sit on the believers' side of the aisle, as it were, while you, despite intimations of divinity, are unable to sit there comfortably. No doubt the reason starts with upbringing. When I was a boy, I could not have said what the Torah means by God "causing His name to dwell" in the "House of the Lord" in Jerusalem. But I recognized that God's name was present in my house in Philadelphia all the time, so I felt that God was there too. I suspect that my memories of childhood are typical for an American Jewish kid raised by observant parents in the fifties. You've met my parents and have been to the home I grew up in, so you easily can imagine the scene: my mother lighting Sabbath candles, covering her eyes with her hands as she blessed "the Lord our God, Sovereign of the Universe." My father reciting the priestly benediction: "May the Lord bless and keep you." He'd put his hands on my head as he did so and, invariably, he would cry. I recall the synagogue halls where I ran around with my friends during Sabbath services, from the back stairs outside the rabbi's study on the top floor to the boiler room and kitchen in the basement. Every step confirmed that the place belonged to us, and we to it. I was at home in this building that had God's name inscribed in giant letters over its door. I'm not sure what I believed about God then except that I knew I did not have to be sure about what I believed. It was clear that Judaism—and God—played a major part in my life.

Years later, during a break from an academic conference in New England, the Jewish theologian Richard Rubenstein suggested to me that those childhood experiences were what enabled my faith, unlike his, to survive confrontation with the Holocaust. He had come to belief in God as an adult, he said—and the Holocaust had taken his newfound faith away soon afterward. "Your faith rests on powerful emotional bonds formed early on. That's what has kept it strong."

He may have been right; certainly, the bonds of my faith were reinforced as a teenager—when rebellion is most expected—by exposure to a tradition of study of ancient texts that encouraged questioning and creativity. My fellow students and I sat around a table, Hebrew texts and medieval commentaries open before us, and grew accustomed to the fact that the commentators did not agree on what the words in the Torah meant. "In the beginning God created heaven and earth, and the earth was formless and void." Or is it, "In the beginning of God's creation of heaven and earth, the earth being formless and void?" Was creation *ex nihilo* or not? Another major question: What did it mean to proclaim, "Hear O Israel, the Lord our God is One?" One, and not two or three? Unique? Uniquely whole? To this day, the Torah and its interpreters fill my head with ideas and my soul with inspiration. I cannot think, or live, without them.

Students who grew up in religious homes but did not have the benefit of that sort of experience with interpretation of text were perplexed when they encountered the Hebrew Bible in the courses that I taught at Columbia or Stanford. How could there not be agreement on the correct translation of the opening verses of Genesis on which essential tenets of faith depend? I warned them that they would not receive satisfactory answers in my classroom to age-old questions about the meaning of life. Judaism offered a variety of answers—or no answer at all. Why does evil so often hold sway in the world created by a good God? Will love one day conquer the forces of injustice and hate? What awaits you and me, if anything, after death? The point of the religious tradition to which I introduced students was to assist reflection on these matters and to guide its adherents in living a life of ultimate meaning, marked by acts of justice and love, in the absence of answers to the ultimate questions. I hope to do that in this essay as well.

The teachers who most influenced me as a teenager—some of them rabbis—were far more radical than I was in their departures from what I thought Judaism believed, but also far more observant of the Torah's commandments than I was or wished to be. My fellow students and I got the message: the tradition was inviting us to take part in its responsibilities and pleasures, including reinterpretation of the texts and practices that we had inherited. Moreover, the tradition *needed* us to undertake this work, the prerequisite for which was commitment to both study and practice. At fifteen or sixteen, reading Heschel under the guidance of a young rabbi, I welcomed the authoritative judgment that religion had declined in the modern world because it had become "irrelevant, dull, oppressive, insipid." That had been my experience of synagogue worship exactly! Heschel was summoning us to do something about the situation. Religion needed to be reworked, along with society and politics. The Christian friends I made at Penn, and the Christian theologians I began reading in college and grad school, testified that this religious situation was not limited to Judaism.

That is why I spent so much time talking through questions of faith with you and other friends and focused on those questions in almost every class I took. I wanted to understand how the rich Jewish tradition of text and ritual had become "irrelevant and dull." I *needed* to know how the Judaism I treasured could be made to speak more meaningfully to me, to you, and to the communities that we—and so many other members of our generation—were determined to fashion. You may remember how shocked I was in Rieff's seminar during senior year when I encountered the condescending assurance from sociologist Max Weber that "the arms of the old churches [were] opened widely and compassionately to receive" people of faith like me, as long as we were ready to "bring [our] intellectual sacrifice." I made a vow to myself that I would not purchase adult faith, whatever form it took, at the price of intellectual integrity.

I'll share more of the journey that tested and refined that commitment in other sections of this essay. Five years of graduate study in England and Israel proved crucial to the development of my religious beliefs and practices. Here I recount two particularly powerful memories.

The first was an event that took place as my two years at Oxford were coming to an end. My thesis work focused on Weber, Puritans, and the secularization of religion in the modern West. Tutorials and seminars had provided in-depth exposure for the first time in my life to Islam and Buddhism. Attendance at evensong services in the four-teenth-century chapel of my college had constituted my first sustained encounter with worship amid statuary and stained glass. Shortly be-fore I was to leave Oxford for doctoral work in Jerusalem, I went to synagogue on Shavuot and had the honor of lifting the Torah after the chanting for that day. I held the scroll on my lap as its cloth cover was replaced, and I continued to hold it for another fifteen minutes or so during the chanting of the *haftarah* and the reciting of prayers for the congregation, for Israel, and for the Queen. At some point in that interval, I felt a strong sense of connection to the Torah I was holding, and, through the Torah, to God. The feeling was no doubt influenced by the biblical verses that I knew would be chanted in front of the open ark as soon as the Torah was lifted from my lap: "It is a tree of life to them that hold fast to it." I could not have explained to myself or anyone else at the time what I felt as I held the Torah tight, but I think a large part of it was trust, *emunah,* a word often translated mistakenly as *faith.* I trusted that I would be okay during the next stage of my journey. As long as I had Torah with me, I would not get lost, and would not lose myself.

The second experience took place in Jerusalem, a city that—after my work on secularization at Oxford—struck me immediately as suffering from too much religion rather than too little. I had never met so many people of faith, of so many persuasions, crammed together in one small place. It was obvious that I was not alone in maintaining religious commitment in a secular age. Concern with doing God's will was so intense, so passionate and pervasive that it was frightening at times. Men and boys dressed in black seemed to rush by on almost every street, bound for study or prayer that was not of this century. I did not feel at home in Israel any more than I had in England. It was hard to find one's place, to stretch oneself and breathe deeply, in close quarters so charged with intensity.

One day—marveling at this fervor from my usual observation post near the Western Wall, and unable to participate in the supplications taking place there with the required sincerity of belief—I nonetheless felt immense gratitude that I could be there at all. My maternal grandfather, who became quite pious at the end of his life, never made it to Israel; I'm not sure that my father's father, who was not observant, would have cared. I did care, and I was there—where Jews had worshipped as long as three thousand years ago. But I sensed no particular aura of holiness at the Wall that day; indeed, I noted that I felt no closer to God there than I had at Oxford or back home in America. I decided to respond to that lack of feeling in a way I had never done before: to pray with all my heart for a prayer. I asked God for words that had not come to mind. Seconds later, a fragment of paper flew toward me and landed in my hands. It was a page torn from a prayer book: "*Ashrei*"—Psalm 145. I knew the words by heart. "Happy are they who dwell in Thy house. They will ever praise Thee." I prayed the prayer and put the paper in my pocket. I still have it in a box in the top drawer of my bureau.

Did God send me that prayer? I do not know. I will never know. Do I now believe, did I believe then, that—as the psalmist promised—"The Lord is near to all who call upon Him, to all who call upon Him in truth"? No, I did not and do not believe that in an uncomplicated way, though it is often my hope. I learned during those years in Israel, spent writing a doctoral dissertation about twentieth-century American Jewish thought, that "simple" and "uncomplicated" are not adjectives appropriate to modern theological reflection, certainly not to any that I take seriously.

My search for God having been altered and intensified by these and other formative experiences, I came back to the United States, with PhD in hand and a job at Columbia awaiting. Multiple voices of faith and doubt resounded in my head daily at this point in my life. They comprised a sort of background music to the pleasure of hearing your voices once again in person rather than imagining them while reading closely written aerograms. I brought back with me a texture of faith that was largely unknown among our circle of friends (but shared by members of the newly formed *minyan* I joined on the Upper West Side and the woman I soon met and married). I had a strong sense that

God is here with us in the world, though not necessarily to be found by you or me or anyone else—not even by the holy men and women of the three faiths whom I had met in Jerusalem.

One thing seemed utterly certain—God should not be searched for *alone*. As my colleague Serene Jones wrote recently in her personal essay about faith, "Theology is not a [strictly] personal endeavor; it is about truths that pertain to the whole of reality. With truths that big, conversation and openness are not just good, they're a theological necessity." That's why I want your voices and those of other friends in this book, and I will keep your views of the matters at hand—and your friendship—in mind throughout. On this matter, as on so many others, I need the help of the people whom I love and who love me.

To be continued. It's almost time to light Shabbat candles, so I must stop. Take good care.

Arnie

from: Liz
to: Arnie

I was happy to see you demonstrate in your letters to Adam and Josh that the personal is not only political, as feminists have declared, but is theological as well. It is certainly so for feminist theologians, male or female, among whom I would like to count you. The references to God as "He" and "Him" in the sources quoted in your correspondence with male friends point to theological and political matters that go far deeper than mere pronouns.

I cannot think of what it means to be a person without paying attention to the fact (in my case) of having been born and raised a girl rather than a boy, a daughter and not a son, and having become a female student who reads books written almost entirely by men. Even today I sit in synagogue, often with a woman officiating as rabbi, and another as cantor, but nonetheless pray from a liturgy that refers to God almost exclusively as He/Him, never as She/Her or They/Them. Personal experiences of Jewish womanhood have shaped my politics and my parenting. They have set a very different course than yours for my thinking about God and religion.

That does not mean—lest we become overly essentialist here—that the thinking I do about matters of faith is *determined* by my gender or my feminism. It does mean that prominent aspects of my experience, connected to my gender, play a major part in the way I reflect, for example, on the balance between transcendence and immanence in God's relation to the world. Or the legitimacy of law and hierarchy. Or the virtues of making changes in a historical (and therefore patriarchal) religion as opposed to starting a new one that is free of gender bias. As you argue in the exchange of letters, theological reflection does not take place in ivory-tower isolation or wilderness retreats from civilization's discontents, even when it claims to do so. The place to think about faith is during life (and history) and only there. I know that my ideas about Judaism, like yours, were first formed inside my extended family, at school, and in interaction with close friends. My faith grew in, and out of, experiences very different from the ones you had in Oxford and Jerusalem, including political and sexual experiences. Gender is a big part of what has made my experiences unlike yours. So is the fact that I am from a generation younger than yours.

Not to belabor the point, but just to state the obvious: I would have been at a woman's college at Oxford had I been there in the 1970s. If I had met Israelis there when you did, I would have likely become close, for the most part, to women who had not been on the battlefield in the Yom Kippur war but rather mourned or nursed brothers and partners who had. (Of course, by the time I got to graduate school, Oxford colleges—like so many in America—had become coed, and Israel was no longer seen as the alleged victim of Arab aggression and intransigence but as the Goliath holding sway over Palestinians and denying fulfillment to their national aspirations.) When I stood at the Western Wall for the first time, it was on the women's side of the barrier; if a prayer had flown into my hands, it surely would not have referred to God in feminine or gender-neutral language. If it *had* done so, the event truly would have been still more miraculous than the one you recounted!

Sadly, you missed out during your formative years on the stories and insights of women jurists and commentators. Jews have for too long gone without the biblical and rabbinic narratives (and legal rulings) that women did not have the opportunity to write. Feminist discourse is still marked by demands for equal access to roles long denied to Jewish women. In the Orthodox world (and not only there), these roles are withheld from women even today. We don't seem able to escape from that "stage one" focus on equality and to progress to experiences and insights of women that will radically reshape the tradition. Many dozens of women rabbis, scholars, and legal authorities are now contributing to that effort, thank goodness. Their work has added to the repertoire of possibility from which women can draw, today and in the future. My generation of Jewish women has been profoundly affected by it.

Speaking for myself, I must say that the most important experience in my life, theologically and in other respects, was carrying two persons-to-be in my womb. I labored for many hours to bring them into the world and thanked God profusely when they emerged from inside me; I nursed each of them at my breasts for nearly two years, joyfully or contentedly and sometimes painfully, often sleep-deprived or manic with adrenaline. I worried about them as they grew as I had never worried before, paid attention to every gesture and need, marked every milestone. Day by day, wisely or foolishly but always with abundant love, I raised them to adolescence, standing close by them at times of need. It often felt to me that I was at their disposal; no doubt it felt to them that I needed to step back and let them be. Nothing in my life—not the classes I've taught or the books I've read—has compared to the awesome responsibility of helping them grow. Parenthood has shaped every thought I have, or will ever have, about God.

So, when Moses complains to God at one point as a mother would, "Did I give birth to this people or raise it up, that you say to me, carry it in your bosom as a nurse carries one who suckles?" I know what he means. For once, there is no need to translate the biblical metaphor from male to female, or to think about whether the image used for God is one to which I can relate. I still cringe when the prophets (Hosea is the worst) describe Israel as a wayward wife who is unfaithful to

God, the husband who loves her, or when Book of Lamentations pictures God chastising, beating, or abandoning "the daughter of Israel" in punishment for "her" sins. The insult to women is immediately felt.

I know that the theology behind these images is problematic for you too, Arnie. One does not have to be a woman to feel pain when the Bible describes God as abusive. But I'm reasonably sure that your problem with such texts is not the same as mine. It can't be. Your connection to Judaism, and so to God, is strengthened by easy identification with biblical heroes such as Abraham and Moses, whereas I cannot identify with either one of them unless I first abstract from their gender and mine, which of course takes away the immediacy that readers of the Torah's narratives are meant to feel. Nor can I be at ease in the presence of the biblical God, for whom, with good reason, male pronouns come naturally. I don't know the source of the quip that Judaism's God is a "relatively genderless male deity." From my experience, the God in our tradition is rarely genderless, and in His maleness bears major responsibility for men's domination of women through much of history in much of the world.

Thankfully, women like me have drawn closer to God in recent decades—or at least to Judaism—with the help of *midrashim* that fill gaps in the Torah's narrative with stories about female characters and new rituals that express what it is like to be wives, mothers, grandmothers, daughters, sisters—and female judges, teachers, and prophets. I hope that Jews will soon grow comfortable using feminine and non-gendered as well as masculine pronouns to describe the "genderless" God.

The issue goes beyond pronouns. A more feminine deity would likely be more immanent. She would chafe at not being involved up close in the affairs of the children she birthed herself. Those children would still be part of her in a palpable way. The creation narrative in Genesis imagines a totally transcendent God who creates and orders things from afar. Much of the Bible pictures a God Who comes onto the scene from a distance, or comes down upon it from above, intervenes briefly in human affairs, and then departs, leaving "His" name or a mysterious cloud behind. God's periodic encounters with the peoples of the world don't seem all that satisfying to them or to "Him." Both sides are left disappointed and wanting more.

I personally relate more easily to the kabbalists' imagination of creation, according to which God births a cosmos that had been latent inside God all along. Human beings are the furthermost layer of divine emanation, and not necessarily the climax of the process—one part of an outpouring from God's self that will continue to all eternity. This way of telling the story makes more sense to me than the concept of absolute divine transcendence that appears on virtually every page of the prayer book.

I must admit that I do not move comfortably in the domain of speculative theology. The paragraph I just wrote did not come easily to me. Like you, Arnie, I don't think anyone knows God as God really is. Theology is written by human beings out of their own fears, desires, and experience. I can tell you that in the delivery room the biblical character most on my mind was Rachel, who died giving birth to Benjamin. I had a great-aunt Rachel who died giving birth to my uncle. His father insisted on naming him Benjamin, of course, and Benjamin went on to name his daughter, my cousin, Rachel. This is how the losing fight with death works, I guess: a battle that, even more than gender, stands behind a great deal of theological reflection.

One final thought occurred to me as I read your exchanges with Adam and Josh. Just as you found comfort as a teenager, and perhaps a calling, in Heschel's description of religion as "irrelevant and dull," I found reassurance and direction in the open letter that Franz Rosenzweig sent to Martin Buber a century ago. A tradition remains vital, he wrote, when people committed to its survival make the leap from "path" to "pathlessness," that is, from what the tradition has been until then, in all its varieties, to what those who "leap" need it to be, as Rosenzweig put it, "at any price." I realized that was true of my emerging relation to Judaism. I needed to be a faithful Jew without sacrificing my feminist commitments, and I needed to keep faith with feminism without sacrificing my Judaism. Otherwise, I could not have remained the person I was and wished to be. Judaism had to leap with me from a patriarchal past to a future that my generation of women would help to shape. Like you, I made a vow of intellectual integrity that has inspired me to re-interpretation of Torah, in the name of Torah and in service to my faith.

I hope with all my heart that my daughter and son will someday make a similar leap. It means a lot to me to have your company and that of other friends on the path to pathlessness.

Be good.

Liz

from: Karen
to: Arnie

To me, at least, the exchange of letters so far proves one thing: gender does not absolutely determine the way a person thinks about Judaism. Or feminism. Or faith.

Liz lost me when she moved from her feminist awakening, which reminded me of my own a generation earlier, to talk about God's workings and attributes. My life took me in a very different direction, before and after childbirth. I remember a political science professor in college saying that the two most important disciplines one could study were politics and theology. *Politics:* because we need to make the world much better than it is, and we need to figure out what changes should be made and how to accomplish them despite the efforts of people who see things differently than we do. *Theology:* because if there is a God, we should want to live in relationship and obedience to God, and to do that we need to know God's nature and will as best we can. I remember saying to myself as I left class that day that I had better learn all I could about politics because religion was not for me and probably never would be. I have been wrong about a lot of things in the decades since college, but not about that. I knew myself well enough to be sure that I would not get to know God.

My Judaism has been about two subjects that have not received much attention in your correspondence: the Jewish people and social justice. The only God who ever holds my attention is the one who freed the Israelites from Egypt and has been inspiring movements of liberation from oppression ever since. The Jewish thinker of the past

century who speaks to me most directly is Mordecai Kaplan, who had
the honesty to declare a hundred years ago that Judaism should not
be understood as a religion, by definition focused on relation to God,
but as the "civilization" of a people, the Jews. Religion is just one part
of that culture, Kaplan insisted, along with history, literature, social
organization, and all the rest. He knew that religious belief and ritual
are not for everyone, any more than poetry or music is. A person's
Judaism might not include God at all.

That's me. I felt, when I first heard about Kaplan in my twenties,
years after I began to think seriously about feminism and became
active in political movements of the day, that I had finally come across
a Jewish thinker whose vision of Judaism had room for me.

I must confess (sorry, Arnie) that I was never much interested in
what Kaplan or anyone else thought about God. I'm not sure he was
all that concerned with the subject either. Here was a man—a rabbi,
no less—who declared that he did not believe in a supernatural God
who hears prayer, revealed the Torah, and would one day send a messiah to save the world. I found it fascinating that Kaplan nonetheless
prayed three times a day, an activity that has never interested me.
You've written about how God, to Kaplan, was a "trans-natural" force,
or a unified set of forces, pushing the cosmos forward in the direction
of beauty, order, and goodness. To me, that description sounds a bit
like something from *Star Wars*—too much so to take seriously or get
excited about. And yet it seems to me that there is some truth there.
When human beings heal the sick, feed the hungry, or free those who
are enslaved, the Force is with us, and we are with It.

On the rare occasions when I do go to synagogue—usually on the
High Holidays—I regard the prayers, in which I sometimes join, as
Kaplan did. The community is summoning collective resolve to help
one another advance the cause of justice and recommitting ourselves
to doing it. That's what matters for me: the work for justice, and not
the nature of the God who, in a way that no one understands, perhaps
assists and guides us in this work.

Passover for obvious reasons has always been the Jewish holiday
that means the most to me. No other holiday even comes close. The

Haggadah instructs us to invite those who are hungry to share our meal and reminds us that none of us are free even today because not all of us are free. The lesson I always take away from the seder is that it's our duty to help others achieve the freedom that our ancestors gained when they left Egypt. When I learned as a child how the story of the Exodus had kept hope alive among African-American slaves for generations and later inspired leaders of the civil rights movement in the United States such as Martin Luther King, I was proud to be a Jew as never before. The Exodus story remains one that I feel obligated to transmit and emulate, both as a Jew and an American. The effort to redeem those who are oppressed brings my Judaism, my feminism, and my politics together.

You made a vow in college to cleave to Judaism without sacrificing intellectual integrity. Liz vowed not to surrender either her Judaism or her feminism. My promise to myself at that point in my life, or just afterwards, was to work for justice inside the Jewish community and beyond it. Theology played no role in that pursuit. Politics—and a Jewish community committed to justice—meant everything.

Like you and Liz, I first learned about this Judaism at home. My father used to shake his head when he'd read the *New York Times* and encounter fresh evidence of evil in the world, which happened almost every day. "God has a lot to answer for," he'd say. He and my mother seemed to feel real pain when they witnessed suffering first-hand or heard about suffering far away. "Genocide did not begin with the pharaoh and won't end with Hitler," my mother said solemnly at one memorable seder when I was a girl. "Poverty and injustice will break your heart if you let yourself feel them too deeply," she advised on another occasion. My parents marched for civil rights, protested the Vietnam War, and campaigned for the release of Soviet Jewry. "There are so many people in pain, every second of every day," my mother would sigh. "If God knows about it, I don't understand how God's heart does not break." My daughter said something similar one day, upon hearing that the number of deaths from the pandemic in America had surpassed half a million. "How can God allow this?" she asked. I replied, without hesitation, "How can we?"

You see, I had come to understand by the time I graduated from college that injustices like poverty, racism, and unequal access to health care are systemic problems that require determined political action and far-reaching institutional change. I decided in my twenties to devote my career to such action and change. That has been the way I enact my commitment to Judaism. The strategies I deploy and the vocabulary I use do not come from the Torah or the Talmud, but I am obeying the Torah's command: "Justice, justice, you shall pursue." That is what Judaism means for me. One does not need to believe in God to practice this Judaism.

I don't know how these thoughts fit into your project on theology, Arnie. For Jews like me, the relevant religious inquiry does not concern the nature of God but how to do God's work in the world. Theology will always be a guessing game. We have so little to go on. But there is no need to guess or speculate where poverty and injustice are concerned. The evidence of suffering is all around us. Love for the God we will never understand should take the form of concrete action to help God's creatures.

I admit there's a major paradox here: I'm not sure I believe in a divine Commander, but I feel obligated by the command to "love thy neighbor." That neighbor need not be a Jew. I'm frequently asked by non-Jewish friends and allies why I take a special interest in what happens among Jews, and I am asked just as often by Jews why I devote so much effort to political activism in American society, and sometimes to global issues like immigration or climate change, rather than focusing on "my own community." These are not hard questions to answer. All human beings are created in God's image, which to me means they deserve lives of dignity and respect. I also believe that Jews are here to make a difference in the world for good. If the extended family of the Jewish community were stronger, more united, and more devoted to the social and political ideals set forth loud and clear in the Torah and the prophets, it could accomplish a lot more good for humanity. American Jews at our best are generous philanthropic donors and are overrepresented in all sorts of social and political causes. This is true of Jews both individually and as an organized community. Israel likewise can boast significant achievements. It also has major failings, of course. I do not apologize for them. Quite the contrary. Jews there and here are not always at our best. No group or nation is. We need to work hard to do better. Judaism demands this, and the world cries out for it.

It's frustrating to me that Jews are so often pulled to the extremes of exclusivism—concern for Jews alone—or the opposite: concern for humanity in general but not for Jews. Chauvinism disgusts me, but I'm also troubled when people tell me that progressive politics forbids special allegiance to my community and my people. I refuse to choose. Modern Jews have been having these arguments with one another and with other groups for more than two hundred years, so I suppose the challenge will not disappear anytime soon. Neither, apparently, will antisemitism or other forms of prejudice. It's sad, though. There is so much work to be done, inside and beyond the Jewish community; so many alliances to be built among different kinds of Jews and between Jews and other groups. The work is difficult, as the rabbis said long ago, and time is short, but the reward is great.

What gets in the way of these alliances much of the time? Religion! Theology! The voices of hate and intolerance that seem to be the loudest call upon believers in the name of God! What a waste! How self-defeating. Perhaps theologians of every religion should take a vow of silence for a while, the better to perform God's service. Maybe John Lennon was right. I sometimes wonder if we shouldn't stop talking about God altogether, in the name of peace. In the name of God! That's a religious movement I would join with a full heart.

Go well.

Karen

from: Arnie
to: Karen, Liz, Josh, and Adam

Friends: What strikes me more than anything else, reading over our correspondence, is the range of beliefs you hold concerning God and the role God plays, if any, in bringing more justice and compassion to the world. As you know, I think Judaism thrives on honest conversation like this about what God and Torah want from us, leaving no hard questions unasked. I'm more and more convinced that good God talk is just as essential to the task of building alliances among different religious communities. If friends like us cannot talk civilly about their religious convictions, who can? Is it unreasonable to hope that such discussion can extend across wider and wider circles, and bridge more substantial disagreements than ours? In the scary polarized politics of this moment, with global warming proceeding apace, and much of the world's population faithful to one of the major religious traditions, it does not seem an exaggeration to say that the survival of humanity depends on those traditions moving from mutual suspicion and intolerance to dialogue and cooperation.

I wanted the readers of *Seeking the Hiding God* to hear the harmony as well as the dissonance among your voices firsthand, and to learn about the personal experiences that gave rise to all our diverse views. It's clear from your letters and mine that individual backgrounds and situations have shaped the way we think about, and respond to, matters great and small. That is true not least when it comes to the possible presence of God among us. The most important of the formative events and experiences that we have recounted have grown out of, and flowed into, love.

Reflection on love and *mitzvah* (commandment) is the subject of the central chapter of this book. I want and need to know what it means to love my neighbor as myself, and to love God; I want and need guidance in following God's commandments, as set forth in Jewish tradition—a well-traveled path of loving neighbors and God. Love and mitzvah together comprise the work of covenant—partnership with God and human fellows—that stands at the very heart of Judaism. Covenant defines the work of justice and compassion to which the Torah calls Jews. Like Karen, I feel personally called by that work. Unlike her, I think the call ultimately comes—in a way I cannot define—from God.

That said, I must admit that I was stopped in my tracks by one point in our correspondence more than others: the question from Karen's daughter about how a compassionate and just God could accept the fact that, as of that day, half a million Americans had died of COVID-19.

Another half million would die in the coming months in America alone. It was truly awful. Every one of us knows families left scarred by the disease. The wounds have not yet healed. No words are adequate to the suffering, and certainly no theology. The plague evoked prayers in many communities of faith for a saving intervention by God; in some of those communities, the plea for divine assistance was accompanied by defiance of the danger, expressed in the refusal to take reasonable precautions against contagion. It was as if they were raising a finger to protest the authority of government—and perhaps against the sway of the angel of death as well. I appreciated Karen's answer to her daughter's query. The question is not how God could permit the pandemic to wreak havoc, but how we could do so.

I wonder, taking her response one step farther, whether now is the best time for reflection about God. Aren't there more pressing matters on our individual and communal agendas—obligations that we avoid by looking upwards to heaven instead of focusing on the suffering and injustice all around us, here below? God has been in and out of hiding for ages, after all, and so have we. It's hardly a surprise that God has not visibly answered the call for miracles lately. Or that some human beings refuse to take responsibility for humanity's collective well-being. This too is not new. Couldn't theology be put on hold while we attend to more pressing business? I confess that, especially at moments of crisis, the ambiguity and doubts that for me are the very stuff of theology compete to be heard inside my head against the shouts of militant atheists who urge us to forget about God once and for all and attend to pressing business on earth. The "still small voice" of God is drowned out on other days by the strident voices of religious leaders who are sure they know exactly what God wants from humanity. Some of these leaders, remember, were so confident of God's wishes at the height of the pandemic that they directed their followers to crowd into houses of worship and study halls where the virus was known to spread like wildfire. "It's called faith," the spokesmen for God said derisively to critics of their course. "We trust in salvation from the Lord!"

I will reflect on God's role in nature and history in the chapter of this essay that immediately follows the prologue. Suffice it to say at this point that the Bible's views on these matters are the very opposite of simple, and the same is true of rabbinic thought on the subject. They do not lend support to militant atheists or overconfident believers. The presence or absence of divine providence has vexed Jewish theology for millennia and still does. It has come up at almost every Passover seder I have attended. The Haggadah emphasizes that the Israelite slaves in Egypt were redeemed by God—not by an angel, not by human liberators, but by God alone—thereby eliciting questions about God's action or inaction in our own time. Where was God during the Holocaust? Did God play a role in the Jewish people's return to Israel after two millennia? Was it foolish to ask for divine assistance in the battle against the COVID-19 epidemic? Shall we pray for salvation from climate catastrophe?

These questions point to the most difficult theological matter of all—the crux of all thought about providence and covenant—which you have challenged me to address directly, honestly, and credibly: How do I conceive or imagine God? More specifically: How and why do I pray? What does it mean to me to stand before God, seek God's blessing, ask God's forgiveness, and plead for God to come out of hiding? You are right to demand answers to these questions from me. It's one thing to say, as I do over and over again in this book, that no human being can say very much about God, whose proper name Jews are forbidden to pronounce and whose image we are forbidden to depict. The Unknowable must remain Unsayable. And yet I address this God almost every day, silently or aloud, and I am writing a book with the word "theology" in the title. What am I doing, and why am I doing it? These questions resounded, vocally or silently, in every one of your letters. The challenge is one that I will not ignore.

The third chapter of the book reflects directly on what it means to stand before God in service or prayer. It is built around the observance of Yom Kippur, the day on which ultimate matters of life and death are confronted by Jews more frontally than at any other point on the Jewish calendar. I confess that I have another reason for structuring the chapter around Yom Kippur. Year after year, Adam sent quizzical looks my way as he stood beside me at High Holiday services, venturing glances that seemed to ask what exactly his good friend Arnie was thinking and doing at that moment. I have been asking myself that question for a long time, quite often at Yom Kippur services. I love the day, love the liturgy which shapes my words and directs my thoughts for most of twenty-five hours—and find major themes in that liturgy alienating, disturbing, and unacceptable. I will do my best to provide cogent and honest answers in Chapter Three to Adam's questions and my own.

I am writing this book, in part, to urge you, myself and my readers not to abandon our attempts at relation with the Lord of the universe because accurate knowledge of the Creator is far beyond reach. Let's not shut down theological inquiry—or prayer from the heart—because we cannot make sense of addressing God from our station on a planet that orbits one of billions of stars in the known universe. Theological muscles should not be immobilized by the fact that we cannot fathom the absence or silence of God in the face of relentless evil and incalculable suffering. We are called to keep our side of the Covenant—to keep seeking and not hiding—no matter what happens from God's side of the relationship. While difficult to comprehend, it is true that God needs us. For sure, the world needs us. A lot of hungry children need us—with God's help—to bring forth bread from the earth.

That for me is the bottom line. The rabbis had the good sense to warn long ago not to "inquire into four things . . . What is above? What is below? What came before? And what will be hereafter?" They worried that our thinking would be paralyzed by inability to answer such questions, and our practice led astray. But they used every legitimate tool available to try to fathom what God wanted them to do: reason and imagination, tradition and experience, law and ritual, the wisdom of their own tradition and insights derived from other cultures. They learned, not least, from encounter with God and relationships to other human beings.

* * * * * *

So here I am, my friends, about to join the believers and teachers of all the world's traditions who have ventured over the years onto the uncertain terrain of theology, determined to walk there without sacrifice of intellectual integrity. I am driven by longing to speak *to* God and *about* God despite lack of knowledge of what God is really like. Your voices accompany me on the path, whether or not you "believe in God" or see the value of theological inquiry. Either way, you remind me that the path to the Eternal Thou goes through "I-Thou" relations with other human beings and must aim at fashioning a world where relations of love are the rule.

You know, because you've heard me belt out the song on multiple occasions, that I believe the Rolling Stones affirmed a profound religious truth when they asserted that we can't always get what we want—no, we can't always get what we want—but if we try sometimes, we just might find that we get what we need. The mysteries belong to God, the Torah says, but the revealed things belong to us: all we need to do the work of love and justice that most needs doing.

To which the Beatles added the piece of wisdom that underlies this Prologue and makes possible all the chapters that follow. We get by with help from our friends. With your help, and God's, I will engage in theological reflection that is both honest and worthwhile.

Passover and
the Work of Redemption

The Seder

The Hebrew month of *Nisan* had just begun when I sat down to write a first draft of this chapter. Passover was two weeks away—barely enough time for Ace and me to start preparing for the seder. Happily, this one would be held in person rather than on Zoom. COVID-19 had twice robbed us of the opportunity to sit around the seder table for hours with family members and good friends, engaged in lively discussion prompted by the ritual symbols set before us and the provocative text of the Haggadah. These evenings have been a highlight of the year for me for as long as I can remember—a major source of joy, satisfaction, and faith. The presence of our three-year-old grandson at the table this year will significantly alter the meaning and rhythm of the evening; so too will news of the day, which always influences discussion of the major theme of Passover: redemption. It's not often one has a chance to talk about matters of such importance for hours at a time, let alone with people who matter greatly to each other. Ace and I had a lot to do in the next fourteen days to get ready. The time could not pass fast enough for me; I love this holiday.

The Haggadah itself urges seder participants to discuss the reasons for observing the holiday. Why the fanatical scrubbing of oven, fridge, and countertops, the exchange of bread and rolls for matzah, and the ritual reading of a text that we know so well we could almost recite it by heart? "You do this," the Haggadah seems to say, "because God redeemed your ancestors from Egypt, and has redeemed you as well. You need to remember that you are now obligated to help redeem others." The question shifts from "Why are we here?" to "What should we be doing when we leave the seder table?" What should change in our society—and how should *we* change—between this Passover and next Passover because of lessons learned and commitments made in the course of the evening? As a bonus to those lessons, I invariably discover things about my kids or my friends at the seder that I did not know before. A holiday that I have celebrated since childhood takes on new meanings every time I observe it, summoning me to new and old responsibilities.

The pleasures of the day—and the meaning it carries for me—do not end there. For one thing, our seder features turkey that I roast and stuff in accordance with my mother's handwritten recipe, carefully preserved on a piece of paper that is removed from its plastic covering for this occasion. That places her and my dad with me in the kitchen as I prepare for the holiday. Having kids at the table is a pleasure in itself, of course, and has the added advantage of providing adults with an occasion to ask questions, ostensibly on their kids' behalf, for which they have long wanted answers. Then, too, there is the satisfying ritual requirement to drink four cups of wine during the evening: good wine by common custom, with a predictable effect on the spirits of those assembled. The after-dinner hunt for the hidden piece of *afikomen* matzah gives adults license to look under pillows, inspect cabinets, and get silly as it conjures memories of how the search went when we or our children were little, and our parents distributed the finder's reward. Finally, there are the songs chanted during the seder and at its conclusion, some of them boisterously: a welcome release from the utter seriousness of discussion about the chances for achieving redemption or bringing it near.

Inside the ritual time and space of the seder, such talk comes almost naturally; I say "almost" in recognition of the fact that contemporary American Jews live much of our lives to the rhythms of a different calendar and surround ourselves most of the time with very different images and symbols. Like other adult members of our culture, Jews rarely pause to take stock of the big questions of life, and almost never discuss them with our children. This above all, I think, is what makes "this night different from all others." Symbols on the table, a familiar text in hand, and a great meal just ahead, one sits down to confront difficult matters that are otherwise avoided. I gladly seize the chance to face them.

* * * * * *

I have made Passover the entry point to this essay for another reason as well. Theological discussion requires the equivalent of a seder for its setting if it is to fulfill its promise. I'll be raising matters that are best discussed in a *communal* setting, and will therefore imagine that you are participating with me throughout in the way that friends and family participate at the seder table. Those who hold back from honest, face-to-face conversation, resist hard questioning or stifle doubt cannot make the Passover story their own. Recognizing this, the Haggadah pointedly calls a child who declares that the seder means nothing to them "wicked" and announces that "whoever enlarges [on the story being told] is to be praised." The rabbis who set forth the ground rules for Passover observance two thousand years ago understood that little that is truly important in life can be learned alone, and nothing significant can be learned without questioning and challenge. That certainly holds true for theological reflection. The more you and I come together as a virtual community united by shared ultimate concern, the more we will be able to confront eternal mysteries with the openness that the task requires.

That is perhaps why the rabbis mandated discussion among those around the table instead of simple recital of the Exodus story. The four "children" who are described in the Haggadah—wise, wicked, simple, and one who "knows not how to ask"—hold radically different attitudes toward the evening program and the redemption from Egypt that it recalls. Versions of all four are usually present at our table.

There are people who know, or want to know, every detail of what the ritual expects of them. Others signal their disdain for the proceedings and their desire to get past the conversation quickly and move on to dinner. Attendees new to the seder confess that they "don't get it" and request a basic explanation of what is going on. A few are so removed from the events taking place—their minds clearly on other things—that they have no notion of what to ask and perhaps no interest in listening to an answer.

Participants who do give full attention to the meaning of the seder are likely to find that the Haggadah poses serious questions about faith. It certainly does so for me. As the evening gets underway with recital of the blessing over wine, I ask myself whether I really believe, or in what sense I believe, that God "chose us from among the nations," "creates the fruit of the vine," and "has sanctified us by His commandments." These core affirmations of Judaism are stated matter-of-factly in the *kiddush*; each has occasioned endless dispute and commentary through the centuries and continues to do so among Jews today. The rabbis who formulated the blessing held divergent views on what it means that God chooses, creates, and commands. How could participants at a twenty-first century seder *not* question these claims?

I have found that doubts raised at a seder are different in kind from those that arise during private contemplation or public debate. I hear or recite *kiddush* at a table that is home ground to me, surrounded by family and friends whom I trust. An evening to which I have looked forward for weeks has just begun. Questions, including doubts about the point of being there, are a cherished part of a holiday celebration that features not only vigorous discussion but chicken soup, gefilte fish, turkey and/or brisket, sweet potato and carrot *tzimmes*, and the ritual consumption of four cups of wine. God is not a subject to be formally investigated this evening but the leading character in a familiar story and in songs chanted before and after the meal. In that context, I put aside the theological reservations that occur to me and resolve to wait and see how things develop during the evening. Who knows? I may think differently by the time the seder ends. This has happened more than once—another reason that Passover continues to hold my attention and elicit my gratitude.

Ritual does that. It makes things possible that rational discourse in other settings cannot. The sense of community nourished around the table is vivid and strong, and it elicits an equally strong sense that ultimate Meaning resides in our midst and that such Meaning can be found outside and beyond the sacred precincts of the holiday as well. Having glimpsed it during the ritual, one watches for it afterwards with a more open mind and heart.

Solomon Schechter, the founder of JTS, wrote at the start of his book on rabbinic theology that Jews over the centuries did not concern themselves with theology very much because, living in integral communities, they had no need for it. They left the Seder for a time and space no less Jewish than the ritual that had just surrounded them. Pre-modern Jews knew exactly who they were, Schechter suggests, and therefore did not have to know exactly what they believed about God. The situation today is quite different for the great majority of American Jews, who thankfully play an integral part in the larger culture of their country but are not part of an integral Jewish community. Many know little about Jewish history or tradition. On the rare occasions when such American Jews engage in religious reflection, they do so in isolation from one another, and at a distance from Judaism. The lack of shared religious practice outside the Orthodox world makes theological inquiry among Jews more difficult than it otherwise would be.

Occasions for such inquiry do arise for almost everyone at some point, and in that sense none of us is *entirely* alone when we engage in theological reflection. When serious illness or death strikes someone close to us, it is hard not to consider matters of ultimate significance, however briefly; one may resolve at such moments to live in a way that leaves the world better than we found it. Even in this secular age, America remains one of the most religious societies in the West, though decreasingly so in recent years. Religiously affiliated or not, the bulk of the American people have not only considered whether a relationship to God is possible but engaged in such a relationship in some form. A slight majority report that they pray regularly, in or out of church, synagogue, temple, or mosque. I suspect that the pandemic that we went through and the threat of disaster from climate change that awaits us have given theology new urgency and made many people more receptive to religious ideas that they had previously dismissed.

Passover is a time-tested framework of response to the human predicament and to the questions it renders inescapable. More: it points beyond both questions and answers to action that needs to be undertaken to advance the project of redemption. The Haggadah does not recount the biblical story of the Exodus in any detail. For the rabbis who designed it, the point of the seder was not to get the history right but to get our *lives* right, that is, to inquire into the *meaning* of the Exodus here and now. We come together at Passover to consider the consequences and implications that the story holds for us—and then to act on those lessons. Our responsibility to work for the redemption of humanity does not depend upon the amount of historical credence that we give to the biblical account of the Exodus or upon the meaning we find in matzah, bitter herbs, and the recital of the *kiddush*. Nor should it stand or fall with any particular theological stance. For the world is in turmoil. We ourselves are in turmoil much of the time. Yet there is joy and blessing in our lives. With luck and grace, there is love as well. Essential work awaits each of us. We must find our bearings and find a way forward and join the project of redemption.

I wish I could discuss these matters with each of you in the company of others who are similarly committed to the project that we are undertaking. Ideally, I would do this during a communal practice resonant with the purposes of our work. The best I can do under the circumstances is to ask you to *imagine* this sort of setting along with me. I do so now.

✳ ✳ ✳ ✳ ✳ ✳

The themes of the seder are foregrounded powerfully in a brief paragraph that introduces the telling of the Exodus story. That passage can serve as a fitting introduction to theological inquiry as well. "This is the bread of affliction that our ancestors ate in the land of Egypt. Let all who are hungry come and eat. This year, [we are] here. Next year, [may we be] in the Land of Israel. This year, [we are] slaves. Next year, [may we be] free."

I read the passage as saying something like the following:

By all means, debate what it means that matzah is the "bread of affliction"—this is important—but do not fail to feed those afflicted with hunger while you are debating. Make sure that your Judaism, and your seder, invite them in. Theology has its place, but action is required.

Ponder whether the references to Egypt and the Land of Israel should be taken literally and, if not, what they might symbolize for us. Where you are now? What does your present situation require of you? Where you would like to be—and how would you like the *world* to be—next year and the year after? What does it mean to be free or enslaved, literally and metaphorically, in Egypt or the Land of Israel?

Think about the "we" of which you are a part, the "we" that is "enslaved" this year, but next year perhaps "free." Enlarge that "we" beyond your seder table, your community, your neighborhood. Hope for the redemption of those included in the expanded concentric circles of your "we." Work for it.

There is one final directive in the passage, I believe, discernible between the lines and communicated in what is *not* said. During the seder and afterward, think about what it means to share the world with God—a major player in the Passover story Who is not mentioned in this opening paragraph of the Haggadah. Could that omission be a call for us to speak and act in the way that Passover commands, and take on the work of redemption that God performed in Egypt? If God remains in hiding when redemption is needed, human beings must stand up and be counted.

"Stand By" and "Get Moving"

My favorite lines in the Torah's narrative of the Exodus from Egypt do not appear in the Haggadah. They come in a passage that begins with an expression of delicious sarcasm on the part of the Children of Israel—humor born of suffering and fear. Caught between the sea looming in front of them and Pharaoh's army approaching from behind, the people say to Moses, "Was it for lack of graves in Egypt that you took us out to the wilderness to die?"

Moses responds sternly and piously to this dark humor. Having been schooled by the ten plagues to expect help from God, he instructs the people to "stand by and witness the deliverance, which the Lord your God will work for you today." The Lord will fight for you, he tells the Israelites. "You will be silent." God has other ideas, however; I believe that the response God makes to Moses at this crucial juncture of Israel's history carries major consequences for Jewish theology ever after. "What are you crying out to me for?" God demands. "Tell the Children of Israel to get moving!"

God reverts to form immediately afterward, telling Moses about all the wonders that He will perform to secure the deliverance of which the Israelites had despaired. The sea will split. The Children of Israel will cross safely to the other side on dry land. Pharaoh's army will drown as the waters return. But God puts the people on notice that He will not do everything for them while they stand by and watch. Human initiative and courage will be required to reach the Promised Land. A well-known rabbinic midrash in that spirit claims that the sea did not begin to split until the first Israelite plunged into its waters.

Jewish theologians, like those of other religious traditions, have long debated the balance between human and divine action—"works" and "grace"—in the scheme of redemption. The question has come up in some form at almost every seder that I can remember. Isn't the human situation so bad that it will take direct action by God to change the course of history? Will human effort ever be enough to improve matters decisively without divine assistance? Isn't it more likely that, left to ourselves, human actors will make matters worse? On the other hand, whatever the truth about the Israelites' escape from Egypt, it seems that God has often failed to send help when it has been most needed. Shouldn't humanity take on the messiah's work ourselves? Can we afford to keep waiting in vain for God?

My response to those heartfelt queries—the lesson that I take away from the Passover story—falls somewhere in between those two positions. Given the difficulty that human beings always have in discerning God's role in nature or history, and God's apparent lack of involvement on the stage of history, a threefold strategy seems in order.

(1) We should continue to hope for God's help, which may come—and perhaps does come—in a form that we do not recognize.

(2) We are encouraged to trust that a larger force is at work in the world, perhaps in part through human beings like you and me.

(3) We are commanded to act as if the world depends on us— on *all* of us, individually and together. Whatever God's part in reducing suffering and countering evil, our role in mitigating suffering and combatting evil is indispensable.

I am pleased to report that there is nothing particularly modern about this stance. The issue of God's presence in (or absence from) history is especially salient for contemporary Jews because we live in the shadow and light of two events in the recent past that have significantly altered Jewish history and Jewish theology: the Holocaust and the creation of the State of Israel. But we are not the first generation of Jews to probe God's activity in the world or to stress the importance of human effort and initiative alongside divine activity. Recall that Joseph, according to the Torah's account, interprets Pharaoh's dreams, secures food for his family and all of Egypt during a seven-year famine, and leads his brothers to repent their sins against him and their father—all of this without a single reported encounter with God! Joseph sincerely believes that God is the key player in the drama in which he figures: the author of his dreams as well as Pharaoh's; the source of his brothers' journey to Egypt. Joseph can find no other plausible explanation for the fact that salvation has repeatedly and miraculously come his way, and readers of his story may come to the same conclusion. It is striking, however, that the Torah describes no call from God to Joseph like those reported in the stories of his ancestors, nor do we ever see Joseph praying to God or offering God thanks.

Joseph's story is therefore one with which many modern readers can identify. His God is distant. God's actions, if such there be, are unseen.

God is also famously absent from the Purim story. Mordecai warns his cousin Esther that if she does not risk her life to save her people from the wicked Haman, "help will come from some other place." The phrase likely refers to divine providence, but it may not—and the Book of Esther contains no word to or from God. Despite this absence, or perhaps because of it, the tale was included by the rabbis in the biblical canon. It is as if the author of the book and the editors of the Bible turn to the reader with a knowing glance and say: "Be prepared! Redemptive action may be expected of you too at some point. It will take courage and brains to do the work required. You should not count on direct assistance from God any more than Mordecai and Esther did."

I think that is exactly the strategy recommended by the rabbis who compiled the biblical canon and created the blueprint for the Passover seder. They undertook this work in the years following the destruction of the Temple by Rome in 70 CE and the failure two generations later of a rebellion against Roman rule. Leading rabbinic sages had believed the revolt would usher in the messianic age—but it did not. Rome was victorious, and the Jews were once more sent into exile. As a result, I think, the rabbis had to walk a fine line where issues of divine providence, human initiative, and hope for redemption were concerned. On the one hand, despite all that had occurred to Jews of their generation, they clung to the belief that God continued to supervise human history. If the Jewish people proved worthy, God would save them from enemies who, the rabbis recognized, were far too powerful for Jews to defeat on their own. The belief that God would prove a redeemer one day was strengthened every day by ritual reminders of God's saving acts in the past, and further reinforced by the sense of God's saving presence in their personal lives. Sicknesses were healed. Dangers were averted. There was ample occasion for gratitude and celebration.

It therefore did not seem unreasonable to interpret the tragedies that had befallen Jews as divine punishment or chastisement. The people had fallen woefully short of God's expectations—and that recognition gave grounds for hope that one day, if Jews were faithful, God would forgive and redeem them. God had not ceased to play a part in the life of their community—and never would.

However, at the same time, and to the same degree, the sages wanted Jews to exercise agency: to maintain communities, defend Jewish interests, and work for the betterment of the world. Individuals and communities disheartened by oppression and defeat needed to have confidence in *themselves,* not only in God. The Sinai covenant required human beings who possessed good minds and unbroken spirits. Jews waiting passively for God to act might not do all they could to ensure that they would be alive for God to save when the time came.

A fine balance needed to be struck. Despite their faith that God on occasion intervenes directly in history—indeed, as we see, *because* of that faith—the rabbis held fast to the conviction that what human beings decide and do matters greatly. You and I are not mere puppets on a string controlled by God or fate. We can and must consider pros and cons, plan for the future, devise strategy, organize and carry out projects, build and maintain communities, develop businesses, and govern states. Individual decisions to cultivate friendships, love our partners, raise children, keep or break promises, love or disobey God—all these decisions are our own and not subject to fate or divine power. When the Torah instructs its readers to "choose blessing, choose goodness, choose life," it validates the conviction that human beings *can* and *do* exercise a meaningful degree of agency.

"All is foreseen—but freedom is granted," the rabbis declared, embracing the paradox that determined the course of Jewish existence. "All is in the hands of heaven except the fear [or awe] of heaven," they taught, believing that moral action is part and parcel of that fear. The ethical choices that we make are real and consequential. Moral judgment and responsibility would make no sense otherwise. Passover seders would be pointless.

There are days when the choices available to humanity seem as painfully limited to me as they were in the eyes of the rabbis. We stand confounded in the face of natural or historical events that bear down on us with inexorable force and render human effort inadequate or futile. Our technological prowess does not spare us from disasters that we cannot predict or control. The sea, as it were, roars in front of us with the might of a tsunami. An enemy army approaches suddenly from behind, leaving defenders without a route of escape. A building collapses, or a regime; jobs and industries that had been secure for generations disappear overnight; an entire city is ravaged by fire or flood. Sometimes the forces that overpower us seem to strike at random, while other events appear to be effects of discernible causes or recompense for wrongdoing. It is often hard to tell which is which; either way, people suffer and cry out for salvation. One must think clearly and act decisively.

The paradox embraced by the rabbis suits the situation in which we find ourselves. So does their complex counsel. Accept full responsibility for righting as many wrongs as we can, for covenants with God and fellow human beings demand that wrongs be righted and injustice curbed. Answer God's call for partners who exercise initiative and intelligence. Do not wait for God's Messiah to make things right in the world, but do not give up on divine assistance or ignore the help that comes to us, indirectly and invisibly, "from some other place." Do not lose faith that a more sweeping redemption will come one day, most likely in a form that we cannot at present imagine. The eye of faith discerns divine activity that cannot be demonstrated empirically. The Messiah will come, ushering in future redemption that will draw upon the efforts at redemption, large or small, that we ourselves have made.

This view of the matter is beautifully articulated in the classic Jewish joke about the man who is drowning and prays fervently to God to save him. When a rowboat pulls up alongside him, he thanks the rescuers inside it but says he is waiting for God to perform a miracle on his behalf. A luxury yacht approaches and sends the man a motorized raft. Again, he declines the offer of help. When a helicopter circles overhead and lowers a ladder, our hero once more remains in the surging waves to wait for God. He soon drowns. When he reaches heaven, the man demands to know why God did not save him. "Idiot!" God replies. "I sent the rowboat, and the yacht, and the helicopter.

What more of a miracle do you want?"

That, to me, is Judaism's best word about waiting versus moving: an eloquent statement of Passover's timeless message about redemption.

Seeking God in History

The issue of God's role in human history, and particularly in Jewish history, moved to the forefront of Jewish theology in the last third of the twentieth century, driven by the pressing need to come to terms with the Holocaust. Consideration of God's role in the destiny of Jews and other peoples was given further impetus by the miracle of restored Jewish sovereignty in the Land of Israel. The Haggadah gives God the sole credit for Israel's deliverance from slavery; the rabbis, following in the footsteps of the biblical prophets, similarly ascribed the destruction of the Second Temple to God's will. Had God also been responsible for the destruction of European Jewry by the Nazis, and the renewal of Jewish statehood after two millennia? The question was inevitable for many Jews and received commensurate attention by theologians. Emil Fackenheim gave poignant expression to the stakes involved in a landmark essay entitled "God's Presence in History" (1970). It was not clear, he wrote in a footnote, "whether, and if so how, the contemporary religious Jew" could continue to recite the passage in the Haggadah affirming that "in every generation [enemies] rise up against us and seek our destruction, but the Holy One, blessed be He, saves us from their hands." For six million Jews, salvation had not come.

Fackenheim's answer to his own question was not straightforward. Earlier in the essay he had explained how the rabbis managed to affirm God's majesty and power in the face of historical catastrophe. Their "midrashic strategy"—telling stories rather than proclaiming truths— had enabled the sages to hold contradictory positions without letting go. Fackenheim recommended a similar strategy to contemporary Jews. We are morally bound to observe a "614th commandment" in addition to the traditional 613, he declared. "Jews are forbidden to hand Hitler posthumous victories." Believers must not allow Hitler to take away their faith, whatever their doubts about God's saving power; those who do not believe in God must remain attached to the Jewish people. Whether or not one is comfortable with unconditional avowals of divine salvation like the one in the Passover Haggadah, the Covenant must not be abandoned. Jewish history was bound to leave a lasting mark on Jewish faith in our time, as it had after the destruction of the Jerusalem Temple, but both Jewish history and Jewish faith must continue.

The resolve not to award Hitler posthumous victories continues to speak powerfully to Jews today, I believe, even if the Holocaust no longer dominates Jewish theological discussion as it did a generation ago. I suspect too that the full impact of the Nazis' murder of one-third of the Jewish people and their destruction of the world that Ashkenazi Jewry had inhabited for a millennium will continue to be felt for a long time to come. Jewish belief and practice have never remained unaffected by the awesome events of Jewish history, and the Holocaust will surely be no exception. One wants to preserve the faith that sustained the ancestors for many centuries, while being careful at the same time to safeguard intellectual integrity. I feel both imperatives keenly. The rabbis taught that "the seal of God is truth." One does not want that seal to be broken.

I urge us to proceed cautiously in this treacherous theological terrain. Jewish individuals should not say words *to* God, or hold beliefs *about* God, that they cannot utter in good faith. The Holocaust has made faith in the Lord of history even more difficult than it was already in a scientific age that shunts religion to the side of culture and denies God a role in the explanation of nature or history. But I am not persuaded by the argument—famously associated with the theologian Richard Rubenstein—that belief in a God Who supervises human history is no longer tenable. "After Auschwitz," Rubenstein declared provocatively in a book of that name, the God of the Bible is dead. In the wake of renewed Jewish sovereignty in the Land of Israel, he suggested, pagan gods of the earth might soon be resurrected by Jews who once again worked the soil of the Holy Land. To me both assertions are suspect.

The Nietzschean claim that God is dead is blasphemous to my ears, even if it refers only to loss of belief in God rather than the end of God's existence. In my view, it is also unwarranted theologically. The only valid reason for a Jew to question God's presence in history in the wake of the Holocaust—while *not* doing so in response to the many tragedies in Jewish history before and since, and in the face of the numerous crimes, catastrophes, and genocides visited upon *other* peoples—is that Jews hear the "commanding voice of Auschwitz" from up close. *That* horrific voice speaks to us directly, loudly, and unambiguously. We cannot silence its awful roar or plug our ears to escape its annunciation of mass death. Running away from this confrontation is not possible (though many people try to do so). Doubts about God's role in the world, already raised in modern Western minds by post-Enlightenment notions of science and history, are reinforced by graphic images of the death camps. Contemporary Jews, even if (like me) they are not personally descended from victims or survivors, know that they too would have been among them but for accidents of birth-cohort and geography.

What is more, the reality of "Auschwitz" has long been well-nigh inescapable for Jews and non-Jews alike. Europe and the Americas have been bombarded with information about the Holocaust for the past five decades. TV, movies, and school curricula work to ensure that the subject is not forgotten. It has been observed that many people in the world (including a fair number of Jews) know a lot more about how Jews died in Europe between 1933 and 1945 than about how Jews lived anywhere, at any time, or about the sorts of Judaism to which the murdered Jews adhered. The Holocaust now serves as the epitome and definition of human evil, cited in countless moral arguments where lesser offenses would have sufficed to make the ethical point in question. Whether this balance of ignorance and knowledge works to increase or decrease antisemitism is not clear; one often hears it said that for a time the Holocaust tamped down expressions of hatred toward Jews, but that time has now passed. I worry that placing the Holocaust in the foreground of Jewish and general consciousness has strengthened the erroneous conviction—a staple of some Christian theology—that Jewish history has been one of unending suffering. That view does not promote affiliation with the Jewish community or increase interest in Jewish religious and cultural traditions. Quite the opposite.

Whatever the *historical* uniqueness of the Holocaust (a subject of continuing debate among scholars), I think it is important that we not regard the Nazis' systematic murder of European Jews as *theologically* unique. God's providence and justice are (or are not) in question whether six, six hundred, or six million innocent Jews are murdered, and regardless of the manner in which the crime occurs. What is more, no Jewish theologian to my mind can credibly hold the belief that God cares more about the murder of Jewish children than about the murder of other children, or (worse still) that God *should* care more. That belief is abhorrent. Heschel made the point succinctly: a God who cares about me but not about you is an idol.

I hope that Jews (and other religious seekers) will find their way around the formidable obstacle that the Holocaust, like all unjustified suffering, places in the path of relation to a good and caring God. That relationship is hard to sustain in any age, and it's arguably harder still in an overwhelmingly secular culture that makes faith a matter of individual choice rather than a communal norm. I do not think commitment to Judaism or attachment to the Jewish people can or should be secured by spite against Hitler. Here Fackenheim erred theologically, whatever the emotional power of his appeal. There are many grounds for commandment, as I will argue in Chapter Two, but "Auschwitz" is not one of them. The Holocaust itself, as Fackenheim well knew, has no real "commanding voice." We feel obligated to respond to its horrors because of commitments accepted for other reasons: familial, communal, ethical, or religious. The source of our felt obligation to choose life, do good, and spread blessing as a Jewish human being should be based on knowledge of what Jews have stood for and achieved over many centuries, and still achieve and aspire to today.

✳ ✳ ✳ ✳ ✳ ✳

How then should we address the vexing question of God's presence in, or absence from, momentous events of human history? Can we do so in a way that does not shut down questioning—a fatal blow to intellectual integrity, and one that will sap energy from Jewish faith—but also does not permit the shadow of the Holocaust to keep Jews from working for redemption and searching for divine encounter? It's clear to me, as I have already indicated, that two roads should *not* be taken: belief that Auschwitz utterly disproves the existence of a God Who is present in history, and the opposite (and appalling) claim that God blessed or carried out the Nazi slaughter.

Let's begin our consideration of alternative paths by recognizing that every theological claim about ultimate truth encounters intractable problems at some point. Sooner or later, the attempt to speak about the Unsayable or reason one's way to the realm of the infinite is bound to fail. That is particularly true in the matter of theodicy: justifying the good God in the face of the suffering of innocents. No matter which route one travels, at some point the smooth road ends. One finds the way forward blocked, and one must stop well short of the intended destination. Some questions cannot be answered. Some contradictions cannot be resolved or must be accepted as paradoxical. Max Weber's warning about the "calculation of consistent rationalism" applies with even greater force to the reasoning of theologians: as in long division, the arguments rarely come out even with nothing left over. In the case of the unanswerable question of how a good God could have allowed the Holocaust to happen, the remainder is especially large. The path to theological coherence is blocked. Detours are unavoidable.

The Psalmist bore witness to that conundrum in the plaint, addressed to God, that "You have made us like sheep to be eaten and scattered us through the nations….You made us a shame to our neighbors, derision and mockery to those around us…For Your sake we are slain all day long, we are counted as sheep for slaughter. Awake, why sleep, O Master! Rouse up, neglect not forever." Another psalm asks "Why, O God, have You abandoned us forever? Your wrath smolders against the flock You should tend!" Although the author of this psalm works their way back to expression of confidence that God will not forever "draw back Your hand, and Your righthand hold in Your bosom," disappointment with God's inaction has been forcefully articulated. The plea for divine assistance remains unanswered. "Arise, God, O plead Your cause…Forget not the voice of Your foes, the din of those against You perpetually rising." Western literature has rightly pointed to the challenge made by the book of Job to God's justice as a high point of biblical achievement. Job's so-called friends and comforters tell him over and over that he must have done some really terrible things to merit the suffering that has come his way, but he refuses to see it that way—and God finally appears on the scene, rebukes the friends, and instructs Job that a mere mortal, a creature of dust and ashes, cannot possibly understand the way of the Creator of the universe. God's answer is no answer—but, the book seems to say, it will have to do.

The Jewish theological position on the matter that I find most cogent confesses implicitly that its answer is no answer. Abraham Joshua Heschel, Martin Buber, and the Modern Orthodox theologian Eliezer Berkovits all laid major blame for the Holocaust (and the rest of human history) squarely on the individuals, groups, and governments involved. Whatever God's part in human affairs, it was not God Who set up and ran the death camps. Nazis did that. What then *was* God's role? All three theologians in effect throw up their hands in lack of understanding by invoking the Deuteronomic notion of *hester panim*, "the hiding of God's countenance." For me, as I wrote in the Prologue to this essay, that concept forms the core of the entire theological enterprise.

Recall the declaration by Moses that, even in the best of times, "hidden things belong to God" and not to us. The "revealed things" include what we need to know to do God's will and perform God's commandments. In some biblical passages, the hiding of the countenance is said to be a divine punishment for Israelite disobedience. "Truly you are a God Who hides Himself, O God of Israel," the prophet Isaiah declares. Elsewhere the notion refers to a situation with which human beings sadly must contend at *all* times, or a condition that particularly afflicts the modern age. This is how Buber used the phrase. God's light has been "eclipsed" in recent centuries. God is there, as always, or rather *here*, but God's presence is hidden from us and out of view. The founder of Hasidism, the Baal Shem Tov, helpfully distinguished between the hiding of God's countenance from humanity, a situation hard enough to endure, and *the hiding of the hiding*—an uncanny description of the situation of many would-be believers in our time.

This answer to the question, "Where was God during the Holocaust?" is not entirely satisfying, of course. It may block the avenue to faith that it seeks to keep open. We all know people—you may be one of them—who have grown so frustrated at the impossibility of discerning God's presence in history that they have given up on God altogether. Having concluded that God is nowhere to be found, they have stopped looking. Heschel himself complained that God hides, and we do not seek, thereby precluding renewed experiences of God's presence. I imagine that Heschel suffered from God's hidden countenance for years, waiting in Cincinnati for news of his family members trapped in Poland during the Holocaust, fearful of learning news of their fate that eventually reached him. But Heschel's work overflows with testimony to God's overwhelming presence at other moments of his life. That is what enabled him to follow the rabbis of old and picture God mourning the innocent victims of evil and injustice along with us rather than presiding over the events that caused their suffering.

Rabbi Joseph Soloveitchik, the leading Modern Orthodox thinker in America during the second half of the twentieth century, likewise urged his readers to believe that God's countenance can be unaccountably hidden at one point and unmistakably visible at another. Unlike Heschel, Soloveitchik asserted that the divine countenance that had been hidden during the Holocaust came into view once more when the United Nations voted in 1947 to partition Palestine, and when Israeli forces began defeating Arab enemies on the battlefield the following year. That theological route courts serious danger, in my view. Its specificity and certainty about God's absence and presence, though perhaps effective pastorally, are unwarranted. Blessing and curse often alternate in a person's life, or a nation's, with dizzying speed. Shall theology turn its head back and forth just as quickly to track God's comings and goings?

I prefer to state unequivocally, as Heschel did after the 1967 war—a moment of great rejoicing among Jews, when one might have expected Heschel to make an avowal like Soloveitchik's—that in good times or bad, "the presence of God in history is never conceived to mean His penetration of history. God's will does not dominate the affairs of men." This utterance is blessedly unequivocal. Having lost most of his family in the Holocaust, Heschel refused to lay responsibility for what happens in the world upon God—but he would never state categorically that God is *not* involved in human history. "History may form a vessel for God's action in the world and provides the material out of which man's doing in time is fashioned." That is the point. God wants human beings to respond to the divine call. "The Spirit of God speaks intermittently through the events of history, and our life is a continual wrestling with the Spirit." Providence, he wrote, refers to our sense of God's presence in history rather than the fact or location of that presence. What we call "sacred history" is "the collecting of the threads of His promise": events that seem to support the divine promises to Israel reported by Moses and other biblical prophets. As to where God is or is not, and where or when one can legitimately assign God blame or credit for historical events, Heschel wrote else-where—another one of my favorite lines in the corpus of modern Jewish thought—"none of us pretends to be God's accountant."

One cannot and should not say more. Berkovits, who made great-er theological use of the notion of the "hiding God" than any other twentieth-century Jewish thinker of my acquaintance, wrote that Jews in the concentration camps never received the visitation from God that was eventually granted to Job. "No such denouement to the dra-ma of faith took place [there]. To the very end, God remained silent, and in hiding. Millions were looking for him in vain." Martyrs went to their deaths in sanctification of God's name and God all the while "is silent, and God is hiding his face." In the aftermath of the Holocaust, faithful Jews should "reason" with God about this silence, "and, if need be, wrestle with him," but they must not give up on the conviction that God cares for humanity and intervenes in human history. Indeed, Berkovits argues, God always cares for us, but we generally do not recognize that care—in part because God must hide in order to make room for human freedom, and to enable mere mortals to survive encounter with the God of infinite majesty. Berkovits summarizes his theory this way in *Faith After the Holocaust*: "The hiding God [*El Mistater*] is present; though man is unaware of Him, He is present in His hiddenness. Therefore, God can only hide in this world. But if this world were altogether and radically profane, there would be no place in it for Him to hide. He can only hide in history. God hides in human responsibility and human freedom."

I confess that Berkovits loses me here. It is one thing to admit that human beings are not equipped to penetrate the divine mystery, and another to speculate about God's intention in establishing this order of things through "hiding," "absence," and self-limitation. Perhaps Berkovits wishes to suggest that God is not content with the distance from humanity that has been forced upon both parties by the realities of their disparate natures. Like Heschel, he invokes the "hiding of the countenance" to safeguard belief in divine concern for humanity. The emphasis in Berkovits's thought falls on the human search for God, rather than the reverse, but his aim too is to defend the covenantal partnership against the assault of disbelief in the goodness of both God and humanity. To that end, Berkovits takes care to highlight acts of nobility and altruism that took place during the Holocaust. "If man's ability to perpetrate incomprehensible crimes against his fellow bespeaks the absence of God…what shall we say of his equally incomprehensible ability for kindness, for self-sacrificial heroism, for unquestioning faith and faithfulness? Is that all man's doing?"

Once again, theology fails to "come out even," making redemptive action by human beings imperative. I come back once again to the rabbinic imperative to feed the hungry while one tries to figure out why God has not done so. Whether we make peace with the fact of God's apparent absence from some of the most terrible and epochal events of human history—or refuse such peace—we must not stop caring about one another, lest history furnish still more testimony that God has ceased caring about us. There are moments when, amid human care, divine caring may come into view. We will never experience these temporary interruptions of God's hiding if we do not believe that they are possible.

* * * * * *

There is a second reason why the question of God's role in human history arises ineluctably for contemporary Jews, this one largely celebratory rather than mournful: the restoration of Jewish sovereignty in the Land of Israel after two millennia of prayer and longing. The State of Israel seems a miraculous fulfillment of divine promise, one that Jews alive at this moment in history are fortunate to witness. As Haggadot composed in Displaced Persons (DP) camps after the Second World War had no trouble identifying Hitler's death with the drowning of Pharaoh in the Reed Sea, so Haggadot composed at Israeli kibbutzim carried the story of the Exodus forward to the Israelites' entry into the Promised Land. The existence of the State seemed to furnish clear evidence, three years after the shuttering of the death camps, that God *does* care about the Jewish people. Israel's creation led many unbelieving Jews to speak of miracle and divine redemption.

Israel's victory over Arab enemies in 1967 made the matter of God's role in history still more consequential; suddenly the subject took on divisive *political*, and not only *theological*, import. Some of the Israeli Jews who built settlements and towns in areas of the West Bank conquered (or re-conquered) in 1967 did so in the belief that Israel's return to these areas of the biblical Land of Israel marked a historical stage required for the coming of the Messiah. Indeed, some settlers pronounced Israelis' return to "Judea and Samaria" a reliable sign that the Messiah's arrival was imminent. For many centuries Jews everywhere had ended the Passover seder with the words, "Next year in Jerusalem!" That expression of hope for ultimate redemption changed for many residents of modern Israel. The goal henceforth was "rebuilt Jerusalem." Was return to Hebron and the Temple Mount the first stage—or perhaps the decisive stage—of the redemption for which we and our ancestors have been waiting?

I think caution is required regarding this matter, no less than about God's hiding during the Holocaust. When I recite the prayer that asks God's blessing for the State of Israel, I interpret the phrase that calls Israel "the beginning of the flowering of our redemption" as hope rather than fact. That formulation, adopted by the official rabbinate of Israel, accords with the mystical theology of Abraham Isaac Kook, the first chief rabbi of Palestine and the leading influence on nationalist Orthodoxy in Israel to this day. Kook based his messianism in part on a passage in the Kedushah prayer that I too recite with passion. "Appear from your place and rule over us, O Sovereign, because we await You. When will You rule in Zion? Soon, in our days, [please] dwell there [again and] forevermore." I do not have Kook's confidence that divine activity in the upper worlds has become visible here below in the return of Jews to the Land of Israel. I hesitate to avow that the State marks even the "beginning" of redemption's "flowering." To me the words express aspiration and resolve. May Israel prove to be a further stage in the progress of the world toward redemption. May we do all we can to make it so.

Kook's son, Zvi Yehudah Kook, took his father's teaching one step further and in doing so directly inspired the settler movement in Israel. Z. Y. Kook's ride in a jeep just behind Israeli soldiers advancing on the Old City in 1967 offers a telling snapshot of the intersection between theology and politics in contemporary Jewish history—and the dangers of that intersection. Some of his followers went so far as to say that in the present moment of messianic fulfillment, signaled by conquest of Jerusalem, the Land of Israel took priority over the people of Israel and the Torah of Israel. They had no hesitation about defying Israel's democratic government or trampling the rights of Palestinians who stood in their way. I have met several of these people, and they scared me to death.

There are too many imponderables in recent Israeli history—in *any* history, of any nation, in any age—to say with certainty that God has taken sides with one party to the conflict. These imponderables give ample reason for not pronouncing any set of facts on the ground a revelation of divine action or intent. Jews should know better, after a long history of ups and downs, one diaspora giving way to another, friends and foes sometimes exchanging places. The gripping narratives of the biblical books of Samuel and Kings—utterly realistic in their depictions of the complex motives of political actors and the machinations of people in power—make this clear. Good kings sometimes do bad things—and vice versa; kings who "did what is good in God's sight" may enjoy short reigns, while those who "did evil in God's sight" may sit on the throne for decades. God's doings and motives are often indecipherable.

The news in our day is similarly too messy, the details too murky, the actors too numerous, to draw lessons about divine approval or involvement. Lines of cause and effect are rarely clear. Israelis who were quick to regard the victory of 1967 as a sure sign of divine favor struggled to make sense of the reverses on the battlefield, and the eventual costly triumph over enemies, six years later. Was God sending a more complex message than it had seemed? What was it? On this matter, I agree with ultra-Orthodox rabbis who maintain that Jews should wait for God's Messiah and not presume to take the work of ending history as we know it—or proclaiming its end—into our own hands. Do not try to "force the end," they plead. Do not proclaim yourself sole agent of God's redemption.

A fervent adherent to that view hosted me in his apartment one afternoon in the ultra-Orthodox Jerusalem neighborhood of Me'ah She'arim. As we stood on his balcony, which offered a picture-postcard view of the churches, mosques, and *yeshivot* of the Old City, he expressed a reading of history that decades later retains its ring of truth. "Either the world's religions will learn to live in peace here in Jerusalem," he said quietly, "or this will prove to be Armageddon."

"But wait a minute," adherents of Z. Y. Kook might say in response to that warning and other objections to the messianists' reading of history. (Some have said words similar to the following to me and to others, publicly and privately.) "You believe that we cannot depend on God to save Jews or anyone else. Fair enough. You urge Jews to do what is needed to assure deliverance from our enemies and to help

PASSOVER AND THE WORK OF REDEMPTION 67

secure redemption for all humanity. Good. But when we do precisely that—trade "passive" for "active messianism"—you hang back from history, condemn us for our fervor, and urge us to slow down and wait to see what develops. Are Jews who enjoy sovereignty over the Land of Israel supposed to behave like you do in the Diaspora? You must tread warily, secure alliances with other groups and get the approval of the powers that be before moving to obey the injunctions of the Torah. We do not. For us, Passover is not merely a lesson in ethical theory but an impetus to action. Is theology a hypothesis about what God wants from us, or shall we apply theory and put theology to the test by doing what God wants us to do?"

I will address these questions at length in the following chapter, for they go to the heart of my conception of the covenant that spells out what partnership with God requires of Jews and other human beings. But I want to respond briefly here as well to the challenge that I have paraphrased. Like the settlers who issued it, I too want my theory of Judaism to shape Jewish practice. Theology must be tested by its application in society, politics, and culture. My quarrel with the followers of Z. Y. Kook is not that they act in history, and believe that God does too, but that *they act wrongly*, and their beliefs about God's role are presumptuous. They do not promote justice and compassion, the twin purposes of covenantal partnership with God. Nor do they "walk humbly with God," as the prophet Micah commanded. They rather presume to know exactly what God wants at this historical moment and have the arrogance to believe that God's political program conforms in every detail to their own.

We know how unjustified such readings of history are when we view them from afar. Jill Lepore reports in her recent history of the United States, *These Truths*, that "it became commonplace among the French, the Dutch, and the English, to see their own prosperity and good health and the terrible sicknesses suffered by the natives [of North America, brought with them by the Europeans!] as signs from God." It "appears visibly," one French settler wrote, "that God wishes that they yield their place to new peoples." Up close, skepticism about such claims seems to disappear. I noted that Israelis quick to draw conclusions about God's politics and plans after the 1967 war were forced to rethink matters after 1973. Yet some of the faithful even today rush to draw conclusions about God's preferences and interventions, unable to stop themselves, perhaps, because the very existence of Israel, defying all sorts of historical odds, seems so miraculous. (In the weeks immediately following the Hamas attack of October 2023, a religious Israeli whom I respect wrote that he could not help but wonder whether the terms of the "covenant of fate" binding the Jewish people to God in history had just been altered. I understand the fear, pain and hope that drive the question, but the writer himself knows that his question cannot be answered. No definitive theological conclusion should be drawn from this event or any other.) Attempts to decipher the marks God leaves in history set us on a path that leads away from, rather than toward, redemption.

* * * * * *

The Passover story insists that on at least one occasion—the Exodus from Egypt—God *did* intervene in history. As we have seen, it was important to the rabbis who gave us the Haggadah that Jews not abandon this belief, even as the sages insisted that Jews exercise initiative and assume responsibility for their side of the Covenant with God. I've come to understand their position better with the help of Abraham Lincoln's masterful Second Inaugural Address. The President humbly observed, as the Civil War raged, that North and South both "read the same Bible and pray to the same God." He confessed that it seemed strange to him that Southerners asked God to assist them in the oppression of other children of God. "But let us judge not, that we be not judged." Neither side in the conflict was blameless. God could not answer the prayers of the two sides as they wished. Neither North nor South controlled the outcome of the war in any event. That was up to God.

"The Almighty has His own purposes . . . If we shall suppose that American Slavery is one of those offences which, in the providence of God, must needs come, but which, having continued through His appointed time, He now wills to remove, and that He gives to both North and South this terrible war as the woe due to those by whom the offence came, shall we discern therein any departure from those divine attributes which the believers in a Living God always ascribe to Him? If God wills the bloodshed continue, it must be said now as ever that 'the judgments of the Lord are true and righteous altogether.'"

Rarely does one witness a political leader puzzling aloud over a profound theological quandary as if in colloquy with a biblical prophet. We know that Lincoln took the responsibility he bore for sending men into battle with utmost seriousness. He did not see himself or his troops as mere puppets of fate, history, or the Almighty. Lincoln believed the decisions that he made were his—and that he would be judged for them in the world to come. But he did not believe that the carnage taking place on the battlefield was unrelated to God's purposes and commandments. The war was a reckoning and bore imperatives for moral action. Free human choices and judgment by God were both involved in determining the course of history.

It is telling, I think, that the Haggadah at its most decisive juncture turns away from the story of God's work in Egypt and finds a lesson in Israel's history like the one that Lincoln would draw from the American Civil War. In every generation Jews should express gratitude for the blessings they enjoy and the redemptions that they have experienced. These blessings—freedom from slavery first among them—obligate us to "thank, praise, and glorify" God; presumably, we should not do so in words alone. Everyone who enjoys a measure of freedom is urged to accept responsibility for helping to redeem those who are not free.

Laurence Thomas, a contemporary African-American philosopher, teaches that the importance of a narrative such as the Exodus story lies in the "affirming cooperation" that it makes possible. "A people with a narrative identify both with one another and with shared positive goals. Moreover, they take enormous delight ... [and] great pride in contributing—contributory pride, as I shall call it—to the realization of these goals." The work moves a person or a group beyond "the mere endeavor to overcome social hostility," which on its own is never "an adequate basis for the self-identity of a people."

I'd put it this way. Had redemption *not* occurred in Egypt and on numerous occasions since (although not always when it was needed!), and had you and I not remembered those instances of redemption and told their story again and again, we might lack confidence that redemptive events can take place in our day and in the future. In the absence of that confidence, we might lack courage to perform redemptive acts that are within our power to achieve. Evidence of non-redemption is all around us every day, making the reminder that we have seen and benefited from redemptive actions all the more essential. We must believe that redemption is possible in order to work for it. And we need to know, if our efforts fail, that we were in the right.

The Power Who Gives Courage

As we turn to other ways of thinking about God's role in history, I want to share a Talmudic story about divine action and human responsibility that has inspired me since I first encountered it in Jerusalem in 1975. Israel was still suffering the trauma caused by the Yom Kippur War two years earlier; many who had seen God's hand in victory in 1967 were working hard to interpret what had happened in the second round of fighting. Was the war a warning, perhaps, or a chastisement, or a divine message that had yet to be interpreted? All around me, people seemed to be peering closely at recent events in search of lessons about the meaning and direction of history. In tractate *Baba Batra* of the Babylonian Talmud, the sages warned against that course.

The scene is this: A Roman general named Tinaeus Rufus is putting Rabbi Akiba and other sages to death for the crime of teaching Torah, which Rome had outlawed during the Bar Kokhba rebellion as an act of political subversion. Before executing Rabbi Akiba, the general asks a good Talmudic question, a Passover question if ever there was one. "If your God loves the poor so much, why does He not take care of them?" Akiba's first response does not satisfy us any more than it satisfied Tinaeus Rufus. "So that through them we may be saved from the punishment of Gehinnom [hell]." (What? God sentences the poor to suffer so that others can be rewarded with eternal life for giving them charity? This makes no sense! The discussion cannot end there.)

"On the contrary, this is what sentences you to hell," the general replies. In good rabbinic fashion, he offers a parable. If God got angry with a servant and put him in prison and ordered that he not be fed, and someone came and gave the servant food and drink, would God not punish that person? And you are called God's servants! The Roman then cites a relevant biblical text to prove the point. Note that the true subject of the debate, ostensibly about feeding the poor, is now shown to be something else. Tinaeus Rufus maintains that just as the poor are meant (by God or fate) to be poor, else why would they be poor, the Jews are meant (by God or fate) to be the losers in this moment of history—else why would he, Tinaeus Rufus, be putting Akiba to death rather than the reverse? The Jews in his parable are not the ones bringing food to the servant in prison, as we might have expected, but the servant! God has put Jews and the poor where they are, the Roman maintains, and there they should remain.

Akiba offers a counter parable. If God became angry with His son, put him in prison, and ordered that he not be fed, would God not rejoice in the person who brought the son food and drink? "And we are called God's children." Akiba too cites the relevant prooftext. When you obey God, the general replies, you are called children, and when you don't, you are called servants. Right now you are not following God's wishes (or you would not be bound for execution!). Akiba knows that is not the case. Jews are the ones caring for the poor and the stranger as God had commanded. His prooftext is the chapter from Isaiah that is chanted on the morning of Yom Kippur. "Undo the bands of the yoke and let the oppressed go free . . . share your bread with the hungry, and bring the poor that are cast out into your house." Akiba asks rhetorically in conclusion: "When must we do this?" The answer is, "Now." In other words: always.

Akiba believes that God somehow stands behind the events of history. He believes that the First Temple was destroyed as punishment for idolatry, and that the loss of the Second Temple was just as surely God's doing, although the reason for that punishment was as yet unclear. He dare not conclude, however, that Rome's victory validates its paganism—and he will not give up the core Jewish conviction, reiterated countless times in the Torah (and soon to be placed at the heart of the Haggadah) that the poor must be fed, the naked clothed, and the oppressed freed from bondage. Tinaeus Rufus, probing into the area of divine mystery, draws a self-serving lesson from what he finds. Akiba, unable to explain God's workings, sticks to the revealed words that Jews of every generation are commanded to obey. He will teach those words until he dies, as he now does.

The wisdom of the rabbis' position on doing the right and good thing, in the absence of understanding God's action and inaction, was articulated beautifully by the philosopher Hannah Arendt in a reminiscence about W. H. Auden that praises the poet for realizing, before many other intellectuals in the West did, that goodness cannot be equated with success. "History does not tell you who is right." During the 1920s and 1930s, Arendt writes, adherents of socialism or communism often argued that they were in step with the inevitable progress of history, and therefore correct in their critiques of fascism and capitalism. Opponents of history's inexorable march forward were wrong. Then came the Hitler-Stalin pact, and in the decade that followed, many intellectuals refused to abandon the belief that history declared moral winners or losers. They merely "switched trains" to "Capitalism or Freudianism or some refined Marxism, or a sophisticated mixture of all three. Auden, instead, became a Christian; that is, he left the train of History altogether."

Arendt connects this move on Auden's part to the emphasis he placed on gratitude and love, citing testimony by poet Stephen Spender, who knew Auden well, that love had been the major theme throughout Auden's work. "Had it not occurred to Auden to change Descartes' 'Cogito ergo sum' by defining man as the 'bubble-brained creature' that said 'I'm loved therefore I am?'" I do not know if Arendt and Spender were correct in this characterization of Auden's poetry, but it strikes me that, at several junctures in key poems, Auden articulated a point of view that follows the lesson taught by the rabbis and the seder. Memorializing Yeats, Auden famously wrote that "poetry makes nothing happen." We might say the same of sacred ritual or theology. But the poem concludes with a prayer that captures well the hope or aim of the seder: "In the deserts of the heart/Let the healing fountain start/In the prison of his days/Teach the free man how to praise." Auden's sober meditation upon the outbreak of the Second World War expresses similar hope for the vocation of the poet and again brings the rabbis to mind: "May I, composed like them/Of Eros and of dust/Beleaguered by the same/Negation and despair/Show an affirming flame."

Arendt speculates that Auden's faith provided him with "time-honored coherent meaningfulness that could be neither proved nor disproved by reason ... an intellectually satisfying and emotionally comfortable refuge against the onslaught of what he called 'rubbish'; that is, the countless follies of the age." Auden did not attempt an explanation of history's tortuous course. He focused instead on words that he could speak and actions that he could take. The poet moved, as the Haggadah does, from history to blessing, thanksgiving, and resolve.

******

One of the most helpful responses I know to the question of God's part in human history was offered by the American religious figure of my lifetime who most embodied the combination of humility and determination, the mix of faith and activism, that the rabbis believed is required for redemptive work. Martin Luther King, Jr. responded to the demands of the biblical prophets, and to Jesus's reiteration of those demands, in a way that allied him both theologically and politically with Heschel. The son of a Baptist minister and the son of a Hasidic rebbe thought about God's role in their own lives in a way that points to yet another dimension of redemption.

In an oft-cited sermon from 1957 entitled "Our God is Able," King ponders God's apparent failure on many occasions to act in history when human beings cried out for salvation. He notes the resulting suspicion among the faithful that God is not able to intervene, and then tells the story of a time when he feared for his life and that of his family after receiving a death threat on the phone. Unsure if he had the strength and courage any longer to lead his community's struggle, he "bowed over the kitchen table and prayed aloud" for God's assistance. "At that moment I experienced the presence of the Divine as I had never before experienced him." His fears passed. "I was ready to face anything." Three nights later the family home was bombed. No one was hurt, and King got through the ordeal calmly. He does not say in the sermon that God sent the bomber, acquiesced in the bombing, or made sure that King and his family would survive. Rather he thanks God for the courage, born of faith, that enabled him to carry on. "Let us notice . . . that God is able to give us interior resources to confront the trials and difficulties of life. . . . God is able to give us the power to meet [the] weighty problems and staggering disappointments of life."

Another sermon included in the *Strength to Love* collection, "A Knock at Midnight," describes the moment when King and his supporters learned that the U.S. Supreme Court had declared unconstitutional the segregation on buses in Montgomery, Alabama. Someone in the crowd, King reports, cried out that "God almighty has spoken from Washington." King neither affirms nor denies that interpretation of the event. He would have agreed with Heschel, I think, that "belief in Providence" does not mean that God's will "dominates the affairs of men." The sermon rather recounts what Heschel called the community's "collecting of the threads of [God's] promise"—the way that Heschel thinks the notion of providence should be understood. King famously believed that the arc of history bends toward justice—and that the arc is painfully long. God surely plays a role in its trajectory, in his view, but what that role is exactly, and why progress toward the goal is slow—this King could not and did not say.

King's humility about divine intentions did not stop him from speculating about the reason for God's failure to intervene directly in history. Perhaps God's desire for "responsible human beings, not blind automatons; persons, not puppets," precluded regular interference in human affairs. Human freedom is apparently part of God's ultimate purpose for the world. God will not defeat that purpose through the exercise of omnipotence. Like Heschel and Berkovits, King saw strength rather than weakness in God's decision to tolerate human evil rather than curtail human freedom. He too pictured a compassionate God Who stands with human beings in suffering that God for some reason does not intervene to end.

The focus of vision zooms in, as it were, from God's role in the fate of nations to God's part in sustaining the faith and courage of individuals. God's work on this personal level, as King describes it, takes various forms: the "daring faith" that God stands with those who march for freedom and "dwells with us in life's most confining and oppressive cells"; the support of family, friends, allies, and community that gets a social movement, and the individuals who take part in it, through difficult times; the guidance provided by religious leaders and teachings; the help of experts and leaders; or—as in King's story of his midnight prayer—direct experience of God's saving presence.

* * * * * *

It was apparent to our ancestors, as it is to us, that there is rarely a clear one-to-one correspondence between an individual's action and the good or bad fortune that comes their way. Human beings often pay the price for decisions made by parents, grandparents, or societal ancestors. History, if not God, visits the sins of one generation upon those that follow. It is a fundamental psychological truth that we bring baggage from upbringing to the dynamics of our adult relationships. Individuals also routinely suffer the consequences of policies adopted by governments or leaders over whom they have little or no influence. That is the price one pays for being part of a family, a community, or a nation-state. Each of us enters the course of history—of life itself— midstream. Suffering in any human community befalls innocent and guilty alike, sometimes with a measure of cruelty out of proportion to the sins that those most guilty might have committed. It is painfully obvious that "fathers eat sour grapes and children's teeth are set on edge" all the time.

Ezekiel's teaching that this will no longer be the case—that henceforth every person will be rewarded or punished according to their own good or evil doings—satisfies our desire for divine justice, but stands in blatant contradiction to our experience of the world. I regard many of the books that comprise the third section of the Hebrew Bible, "The Writings," as eloquent testimony to the difficulty of making sense of God's role in history in the way that—according to the Bible's second section, "Prophets"—rulers, prophets, priests, and ordinary Israelites routinely tried to do. Ecclesiastes and Job openly call into question—or reject absolutely—the claim that sickness and health, poverty and prosperity, life and death, can be understood as divine judgment. Other books—including Ruth, Proverbs, the Song of Songs, and the Psalms—immensely complicate that notion and decisively shift focus from collective to individual well-being. The Book of Esther gives us a political world ruled by scheming, prejudice, greed, sexual desire, drunkenness, and sheer accident—a world we easily recognize, and one that is the very opposite of a historical drama that testifies to God's redeeming power.

Martin Luther King, Jr. thus stood on firm biblical ground when he raised, but did *not* attempt to solve, the age-old theological problem of divine justice. Instead, he turned attention to the experience of God's assistance and care in individual lives. King addressed his congregation as a pastor rather than a theologian, offering his flock—and participants in the civil rights movement, many of whom put their lives on the line—needed reassurance that God would stand with them in their struggle and give them courage to continue. When King cited the prophets in his "I Have a Dream" address, it was to assure the crowd that God was marching with them and someday would grant victory to their cause. The struggle for justice was not theirs alone, and they did not face their enemies alone. What is more, they could point to progress along the way, from the days of the prophets through the end of slavery in 19th-century America, and to our own day. Those who stand with prophets and God in any age can rest confident that they stand on the right side of history.

Heschel's point was similar when he proclaimed in his "Religion and Race" address—delivered in 1963 to a conference on that subject where he first met King—that the participants at the first conference on religion and race were Pharaoh and Moses. "The outcome of that summit meeting has not come to an end. Pharaoh is not ready to capitulate. The exodus began but is far from having been completed." Heschel's rhetoric was powerful, not only because gospel hymns sung by African-American slaves and their descendants identified their oppressors with Pharaoh and themselves with the Children of Israel in Egypt. Denouncing segregation in terms that brooked no moderation and declaring that "it is not within the power of God to forgive the sins committed toward men," he left no doubt about which side God was on in the struggle for civil rights then underway in the South. God's hand might not be visible in present-day events, but right and wrong were clearly marked. The prophets had taught that "God himself is concerned with 'the transitory social problems'. . . . Our tragedy begins with the segregation of God . . . the bifurcation of the secular and sacred."

The iconic picture of Heschel marching by King's side in Selma in 1965 meant everything to me as a teenager. It was living proof that Judaism mattered, that religion mattered, that God mattered. I could not expect God to intervene to prevent violent attacks on civil rights demonstrators. But I could and did believe that God, Who is just and merciful, was standing with the marchers in their struggle for justice. They could be confident of this because they were standing with God, Whose will was unambiguously expressed in the Torah and the books of Israel's prophets.

This, I believe, is how God figures in history, shaping the lives of individuals, communities, and movements. We are impelled to action by the words of the prophets and strengthened in our conviction by those who, like Heschel and King, bring the prophets to life. Moved and strengthened, individuals perform acts of redemption that alter the world and may prove one day to help save it.

✳ ✳ ✳ ✳ ✳ ✳

King's story about his prayer at midnight points to the fact that theology, when it arises amid personal practice and takes its place in the flow of everyday activity, is an entirely different matter than in reasoned exposition or debate. The latter can be highly abstract and theoretical, especially when it aims to be systematic and proceeds by accepted academic standards of argument and evidence, or when it contrasts one dogma or creed against another. This kind of theology generally takes the form of third person "God-talk"—that is, talk *about* God. The debate over whether, how, and when God is or has been present in history—yes or no, true or false, certified by revelation to this prophet or that prophet—is a good example of this sort of theological inquiry. Its currency is certainty; its aim is the establishment of truth versus falsehood.

By contrast, applied theology (Heschel called it "depth theology") often arises out of a boundary moment in personal life and is expressed in second-person address *to* God. "Tell me, God, how could You let my family die in the camps?" Or, "I prayed to You with all my heart that You not let my child die, God, and You did not answer my plea—so there is no way I will be praying to You again anytime soon." (I cannot count the number of people who have approached me after talks at synagogues to say they no longer believe in God because prayers of this sort went unanswered.) The tone of this sort of theological inquiry is humbler, even when it announces impatience, anger, or rejection. It pretends to no final word or system, proceeding rather in what my late colleague at JTS, the philosopher Neil Gillman, called "sacred fragments." The currency of this theology is uncertainty. Its driving force is longing. Its aim is a relationship of trust.

Seen from this vantage point, the plane on which God acts in the big events of history, is not the only one. God acts as well—and perhaps more often—in the personal lives of human beings. Although it is true that beliefs regarding the two planes are logically connected, such that one cannot with certainty maintain that God is present on one plane but absent on the other, exercising general providence but not individual providence, or vice versa, it is also true that in practice theology does not work this way. Nor is this the only domain in which the "theo" and the "logy" in "theology" are out of sync. As I have noted more than once during this inquiry, human beings cannot hope to attain accurate knowledge of God or understand the workings of God, yet a person can with good reason trust—as I do—that they walk on a path where God can be encountered from time to time. Some people are unable to live with that apparent contradiction. Others call it paradox, settle for "fragments," and believe they have no choice but to take life, and God, on these terms. I am one of them.

A rabbi once told me about a congregant who would not recite *kiddush* at his Sabbath dinner table because he could find no scientific justification for calling God "the Creator of the fruit of the vine." His story brought to mind Heschel's observation that many people who have experienced God's presence in their personal lives do not allow themselves to trust that experience or to label it as a divine encounter because their beliefs about science or history do not allow it. "The issue that emerges before us is . . . not whether God exists, but whether we are intelligent enough to advance adequate reasons for affirming it. The problem is: How do we tell it to our minds?"

I belong to a modern community of faith that is not discouraged from the search for God or dissuaded from the attempt to do God's will despite inability to explain religious experience to our minds in a manner acceptable to standards set by reason. It's important to the well-being of our families—and I think, with King and Heschel, to the character of our nation—that we hold fast to experiences of God that have been granted us, as we do to experiences of love and of so much else for which we cannot rationally account. We go on with life together in good faith, nonetheless. As the world lurches from crisis to crisis, I hope that we will not allow doubt or disbelief concerning God's redemptive activity—or the redemptive power of love—to interfere with our own work on behalf of redemption. I am not recommending that we "believe because it is absurd," as the church father Tertullian advised, or that we walk through the open doors of religion at the price that Max Weber feared was required, that is, sacrifice of intellectual integrity. The beliefs that we hold and the actions that we take must at some point pass the triangulated test of reason, tradition, and experience that I will discuss at length in Chapter Three. But one can test both belief and action *in the midst of commitment*, just as we learn about love from loving and about friendship by being a friend.

Debate the meaning of the Passover seder, argue about the meaning of matzah and bitter herbs, but be sure to feed the hungry, and to do it now.

The Politics of Redemption

Heschel looms large in this essay in part because he was the thinker who first made me care about theology. He did so by writing books like *Man Is Not Alone* and *God in Search of Man* that wrestled honestly, from inside a lifelong commitment of faith, with the doubts that assail faith. No less important, and probably more so, was the knowledge that this pious and learned Jew had not only partnered with King in working for civil rights but had joined with Catholic and Protestant colleagues in founding and leading a major anti-war organization, Clergy Concerned about Vietnam. Theology and politics were allied. The latter flowed from the former. The former was pressed by the latter into service.

When I interviewed Heschel one day in 1971 for my college newspaper, I asked him about the link he saw between theology and politics. I politely but insistently demanded to know what gave him the authority to say that the war in Vietnam was evil—not just wrong on balance, or ill-advised, but actually evil. By the same token, on what basis did he declare that religion in our time had become "irrelevant, dull, oppressive, [and] insipid?" At first Heschel tried to duck the question (perhaps taken aback by the cheek of the 20-year-old reporter sitting in his office). He said, in effect, that he had as much right as anyone else to an opinion on these subjects. Then, perhaps realizing how much was at stake in the matter for me personally, Heschel gave an answer that has guided my thinking ever since. He was the heir to a great religious tradition, Heschel said, and as such it was not only his right but his duty to speak in the name of that tradition as best as he could, knowing full well that others would speak in its name differently.

Religious leaders have the obligation to speak in this way, I believe.

They serve congregations or movements that stand in service to God and represent venerable religious traditions that insist that God cares about justice. As such, they must care about politics but cannot pledge loyalty to particular parties or candidates for office. Those who speak in the name of Scripture also must be careful to respect the limits inherent in the task of applying age-old sacred texts to present-day circumstances. If the sources give explicit and unambiguous instruction that speaks directly to issues or policy debates on the current agenda, rabbis and other clergy must convey that message loud and clear. Racial injustice is such a case: one set of God's children exploiting another because of a difference in skin color. Poverty is another case. Perversion of justice is a third.

Even in such cases, Scripture usually tells us that the evil cited must be remedied—the poor must be fed, for example, and the stranger protected—but leaves it to us to figure out the best way of doing so in existing circumstances. Even when the Torah or the rabbis prescribe specifics of care or practice, reams of commentary and disputation ensure that subsequent authorities will approach the matter at hand with due regard for its complexity. There are mandates for action, but those mandates—if the process works in the way intended—contain a degree of nuance that matches that of the issue requiring action. My complaint with the Israeli followers of Tzvi Yehudah Kook was not that they applied the Torah and the prophets to present-day disputes but that they did so simplistically, with little appreciation for opposing arguments, and with too much confidence that they and only they understood what God had in mind. Justice and compassion were cast aside.

Nonetheless, there are times when morality and Torah demand a specific political stand and/or systematic change to end a pattern of injustice. My friend Karen made this point in our correspondence, as did Heschel in the "Religion and Race" address. Just as it was wrong for Pharaoh to order that newborn male Israelite infants be drowned in the Nile, it was wrong to lynch Black men, women, and children. If Pharaoh "is not ready to capitulate," and his evil practices are carried on by contemporary despots, our duty to act is clear. The war in Vietnam was a more difficult call for Heschel, I suspect, although after he made that call he declared his stand with prophetic hyperbole and zeal. In his judgment, the suffering our country was causing far outweighed any good that victory in the war might achieve. I am certain that were Heschel alive today, he would elect to stand on solid moral and religious ground and call for concerted action to mitigate the effects of climate change caused by fossil fuels. He titled his 1947 eulogy for the world of Eastern European Jewry that the Nazis had destroyed, "The Earth is the Lord's." Human beings hold God's earth in trust and are obligated to be faithful stewards. The planet, like life itself, is not ours to do with as we please. We have obligations to protect our fellow bearers of the divine image and the earth on which each of us is privileged to dwell for a time. On this matter more than many others, Heschel's well-known dictum holds true: "Some are guilty, but all are responsible."

That application of theology to politics is reinforced—and complicated—by a long tradition of Jewish political wisdom that regards human beings as governed by both good and evil urges. One cannot depend on people to do the right thing, or to know what the right thing is, just as one cannot presume that they will always, or as a rule, act selfishly, cruelly, or thoughtlessly. Rousseau famously declared at the start of *The Social Contract* that he would "take men as they are, and laws as they might be." That seems to be what God is doing, according to the Torah, when God makes a covenant with Noah and his descendants after destroying the world by flood. The DNA of humanity was not altered by the flood, meaning that the nature of the human beings who repopulated the earth and rebuilt its cities remained as it was before Noah and his family entered the ark. At several points in the Torah, God threatens to destroy the Children of Israel and start over with another people but is dissuaded each time by Moses. What good would that do, given that any new progenitor of humanity would possess and transmit the same proclivities to wrongdoing as well as to virtue? And how would the world interpret or misinterpret God's action?

Jewish political theory recognizes that at times there are clear evils that must be fought resolutely, personified in Scripture by Amalek, the tribe who attacked weak stragglers among the Israelites as they left Egypt. Haman, a descendent of Amalek, attempted to murder the Jews of the Persian Empire, only to be foiled by Mordecai and Esther. Amalek must repeatedly be fought and defeated across the span of history. (Jews commonly identified Hitler as his seed.) But Jewish texts caution that, in most cases, political reality is not black and white. It demands a response that is both nuanced and sustained. That is one reason the rabbinic tradition generally counseled reform rather than revolution. Another is the fact that human nature is what it is. The sages urged the pursuit of justice in God's name, as the prophets had, but feared the suspension of social order and mob rule that are sometimes unleashed in the name of justice. Law is required to guide and restrain rulers and subjects (or citizens) alike.

※ ※ ※ ※ ※

It is striking that Pharaoh does not get a lot of attention in the Passover Haggadah, not much more, in fact, than Jacob's father-in-law Laban, who—we are told, rather mysteriously—"desired to uproot all" [of Jacob's family] in contrast to Pharaoh, "who decreed only against the males." Were the rabbis perhaps intentionally looking away from the disturbing fact that Pharaoh sought the genocidal elimination of the Children of Israel? Are Jews in our day doing something similar when they look away from the Holocaust and focus on issues of identity and assimilation—or on theology?! It is striking to me that antisemitism has received remarkably little attention in modern works of Jewish religious thought, my scholarly field of expertise. That has begun to change in recent years. The sharp rise in antisemitism in America and elsewhere, and its potent expression on American campuses during Israel's war with Hamas, have caused American Jews to take note of a phenomenon they had put on the back burner of concern. The subject is present in the Haggadah, but—at my seders at least—has rarely received sustained attention. I am sure that will no longer be the case.

Immediately after grace after meals, a participant at the seder is directed by the Haggadah to open the front door for the prophet Elijah, who according to Jewish tradition will herald the coming of redemption. Those present are asked to join in reciting a paragraph added to the Haggadah in the Middle Ages by Ashkenazi Jews who had experienced antisemitic persecution. "Pour out Thy wrath upon the nations that know Thee not, and upon the kingdoms that call not upon Thy name: for they have consumed Jacob and laid waste his habitations." Is revenge a prerequisite to redemption? Or is the point that redemption can never arrive if Amalek continues to prey upon the innocent? Some American Jews in recent decades have opted to omit this paragraph from their seder, or substitute one that calls upon God to *love* all nations that *do* "know Thee." One wonders if that custom will now be altered.

I believe that Jewish theologians must confront antisemitism for at least three reasons, all of which make the matter a religious as well as a political concern for contemporary Jews.

The first is that some Jews choose *not* to attend a Passover seder or participate in other Jewish events—religious, cultural, or ethnic—because they do not wish to be associated with a tradition and a people that have long been a particular target of hatred and still are today. Fackenheim observed pointedly in *God's Presence in History* that "at Auschwitz, Jews were murdered, not because they had disobeyed the God of history, but rather because their great-grandparents had obeyed Him… by raising Jewish children. Dare a Jew of today continue to… [expose] to the danger of a second Auschwitz himself, his children, and his children's children?" Antisemitism has not disappeared with Enlightenment or Zionism, as many Jews expected it would, but only taken on new/old forms, rising in America of late to levels of verbal threat and physical violence not seen in many decades. The 2013 survey of American Jews conducted by the Pew Research Foundation reported that 5% of its respondents had curtailed their participation in Jewish observance or events because of antisemitism. That number has since grown along with the spike in antisemitic and other hate crimes; antisemitic incidents have further increased during Israel's war with Hamas. The Holocaust for many Jews stands in the way of faith in the God of history. Antisemitism too can block the way to Jewish belief and practice.

The second reason for attention to antisemitism in a theological inquiry is that Jewish sources from the Bible onward have regarded hatred of Jews as bound up in hatred of Judaism and rebellion against God. It is not easy to demonstrate the truth or falsehood of that claim. One would have to disentangle the many factors at work in antisemitism as in other forms of prejudice—political, cultural, economic, and religious—and determine whether the set of factors at work in hatred of Jews is different in kind or degree from factors driving hatred of other groups. It does seem, however, that the relationship of kinship and resentment that both Christianity and Islam bear to Judaism is a major cause of hostility to Jews among those religious communities. What is more, members of the "chosen people" were until recently held responsible by official Catholic teaching for the crucifixion of Jesus, who of course took on human form as a Jew, and the holy Scripture of the "people of the book" forms part of Christian Scripture, despite the latter's claim to have superseded it. Jews are associated in the view of every church with conscience, covenant, and God; for their part, Muslims regard Jews not only as the people responsible for the State of Israel but as the faith community that according to the Koran rejected the prophet Muhammed. There is something unique, and theologically significant, in the animus directed against Jews, for all that antisemitism shares a great deal with other forms of bigotry. As one recent writer on the subject cogently observed, "By the very nature of our particularism, our refusal to give up on *our* God and give in to *their* beliefs, the Jews are a rebuke to any creed that seeks dominion over both our outer and inner lives."

I will never forget the priest who told me that the destiny of Jews is to be the "suffering servants of God," called at times to die in that service as Christ died on the cross. Some Jews agree with him, I know; for me his words, intended lovingly, are anathema. I make no theological claim when I recite the liturgical declaration that the six million murdered by Hitler died "in sanctification of God's name" regardless of their personal religiosity or the precise intentions of their murderers.

I follow Fackenheim in holding that Hitler wanted to destroy Judaism as well as Jews; the end of Jewry would be the end of Judaism. That is why those who were killed because they were Jews can be said to have died in the name of Judaism. They witnessed to the eternal worth of Judaism, a faith that is committed to the sanctification of God's name. Theology plays a crucial role in the persecution of Jews and must play a still greater role in making sense of the commitment for which, in part, Jews are reviled.

The third reason for theological investigation of antisemitism is that the persistence of Jew-hatred and other forms of prejudice renders commitment to the work of redemption both more urgent and more difficult. People who devote their lives to the causes of justice and compassion nourish hope of seeing history move forward because of their efforts. A person cannot reasonably expect to be thanked by every individual whom they have assisted. We know that history may not reward our efforts to change its course with tangible signs of progress. God likely will not do so either. One learns to be grateful for signs of redemption, however small, and to draw the encouragement from them that is necessary to continue. The work adds meaning to one's life. The people with whom you do the work provide an experience of "capital C Community" not readily available elsewhere. But the persistence of antisemitism after so many centuries; its refusal to disappear as a result of Enlightenment commitments to liberalism, reason, science; its refutation of Zionist claims that Jewish sovereignty would put an end to Gentile hatred of Jews; and its apparent disproof of the argument that, in this respect and others, "America is Different!"—all this discourages one from undertaking work for redemption. The work requires allies whose support for Jews, it now seems, cannot be counted on. If that is the case, the chances of success seem utterly hopeless.

One can leave the seder table boiling over with resentment at the many pharaohs who have hated and persecuted Jews over the centuries—the "they" who "have arisen in every generation to destroy us." One can feel discouraged at the need, after lo so many centuries, in so many parts of the world, to cry out "Let my people go!" But it is also possible to draw inspiration and purpose from the Passover narrative—as King, Heschel, Laurence Thomas, and so many others have done. With the help of that story, one can draw encouragement from the redemptive acts taking place right now, some of them nearby, including acts that we ourselves have performed. One recognizes this and leaves the table singing.

Miracle: Abiding in Astonishment

Martin Buber managed to combine sober appreciation for the depths of human depravity and the persistence of antisemitism—he fled Nazi Germany in the late 1930s for Palestine—with enduring belief in the possibility of redemptive work that builds just, "I-Thou" communities. Having arrived in Palestine, he agitated for a binational state; once Israel was established, he campaigned for greater cooperation between Arabs and Jews and lauded the kibbutz as a communal "experiment that has not failed." Buber has helped me more than any other modern Jewish thinker to understand what it might mean to speak of miracle in Jewish history while insisting that God is counting on human beings to write the next chapter of that history. I find two elements of his writings on the subject particularly important.

The first describes turning points in Israel's relation to God that Buber terms "theopolitical hours." Because "YHVH is present to Israel even with His most sublime and essential characteristic, His holiness," the people are "able to receive His influence, to follow His footsteps, and to place human activity at the disposal of His activity." This is what it means for a prophet to say that the nation of Israel is made holy by the Holy God. Isaiah speaks of God's holiness, Amos of God's righteousness, Hosea of God's loving-kindness. All testify and point to "the divine-human relationship" that for Buber is key to everything else.

Notice that Buber does not avow that God is more present at theopolitical hours than before or afterwards, or that God cares more about the people of Israel than about other nations. What changes in such an hour is the intensity of the people's faith that God is present:

right there with them at the time of greatest need. "Men trust the Lord of this kingdom, that he will protect the congregation . . . but at the same time they also trust in the inner strength of the congregation that ventures to realize righteousness in itself and towards its surroundings." The strategy may not work politically or militarily. "Keep still" as the enemy army approaches—the advice offered by Isaiah to Ahaz, the king of Judah—might or might not save them. Any political leader would be hard pressed to take such advice rather than mobilize an army for battle. But to Buber the course urged by the prophet "is holiness in regard to the political attitude of God and his people."

Buber was not a pacifist. When Gandhi proposed that the Jews fight Hitler with the non-violent means of resistance that he had practiced against British rule in India, Buber respectfully but forcefully told the Mahatma why that strategy would not work against the Nazis and should not be attempted. He did not advise Jews to "keep silent" and trust in God's saving power. I wish that Buber had shown more of the pragmatic realism that he displayed in his letter to Gandhi, and less of the idealism for which he lauded Isaiah, in his work for a binational state and, later, in his criticism of government policy. Reading the transcripts of Buber's debates with Ben-Gurion, I often find myself agreeing with the prime minister and not the philosopher. Nevertheless, Buber's theological insight into the perceived workings of God in history seems on target. We know what God demands of human beings and do not know when or how God acts to prod or punish. So Buber calls upon his readers—as the prophets called upon the people—to practice righteousness and loving-kindness to the maximum extent possible under the circumstances.

The teaching by Buber that is the most important to me, both theologically and personally, comes in a passage in *Moses: The Revelation and the Covenant*, in which Buber comments on the enduring significance of "the wonder on the Sea." The Book of Exodus, Buber explains, offers a different understanding of miracle than the usual one, which members of a scientific culture like ours with good reason cannot accept. A miracle, correctly understood, is "not something supernatural, or superhistorical, but an incident, an event which can be fully included in the objective scientific nexus of nature and history; the vital meaning of which, however, for the person to which it occurs, destroys the security of the whole nexus of knowledge for him." To believe in miracles is not to hold that nature has been suspended. The sun does not stand still; if the Reed Sea parts, as the Torah reports, it is because a "strong wind from the East" moves the waters. Perhaps a tidal wave occurs. "The real miracle means that in the astonishing experience of the event, the current system of cause and effect becomes, as it were, transparent and permits a glimpse of the sphere in which a sole power, not restricted by any other, is at work." One holds onto that experience ever after: "To live with the miracle means to recognize this power on every given occasion as the effecting one."

This makes a great deal of sense to me. It is how I read the Exodus narrative and apply the Passover story to contemporary experience. The people of Israel need a miracle to save them. The sea lies ahead; Pharaoh's army is approaching from behind. The wilderness is closing in. There is no chance of escape. Then the sea splits, the Israelites cross safely to the other side, and the pursuing army drowns, its chariot wheels caught in the mud. Some Israelites, reaching dry land, exclaim: "What a lucky break that a tidal wave came just when we needed it! Thank goodness we are saved!" Others see God's hand in the event and declare God their "strength and salvation." Sing to the Lord, they shout, for God has done valiantly. This was not an interpretation imposed upon a natural event after the fact, Buber explains, but an account of the event as they experienced it. And they do not let go of their sense of wonder the next day or the week after. "Abiding in the astonishment," they continue to bear witness to what took place and transmit that testimony to future generations.

I came to understand this teaching only after the most powerful religious experience of my life: watching my daughter, my firstborn, enter the world. I had reviewed a high school biology text in the months leading up to the baby's arrival to gain rudimentary understanding of the science of reproduction. My wife, Ace, and I faithfully attended a Lamaze class so that I could be helpful to her during labor. I was somewhat familiar, therefore, with the "current system of cause and effect" operating in the stages of fetal development, labor, and delivery. When my daughter emerged from the birth canal, and the nurses washed her off and handed her to me, I did two things immediately and without forethought. I danced around the room with her, singing the Supremes' "Baby, baby, I hear a symphony." And I said over and over, dozens of times, perhaps hundreds of times, uncontrollably, "Thank God, thank God."

The system of cause and effect had become "transparent" to me. The "sole power" stood revealed. I did not cease to believe in the laws of science. But you could not have convinced me at that moment that my wife and I had created a new life ourselves. One might say that it was an emotional moment, I was excited, my outburst should be explained in that spirit. Yes, I was excited, that is true, but my sense of miracle has not "dissipated upon reflection" in the decades since. I abide still in the astonishment of that moment. I "live with the miracle . . . recognize this power on every given occasion as the effecting one"—and witness to it gratefully.

* * * * * *

Buber's teachings open new possibilities of meaning in the Passover story. The Israelites who crossed the sea and breathed a sigh of relief at their amazing good fortune—the tidal wave arrived just in time!—did not need to find any greater significance in what had just happened. *Dayyenu*, they felt. "It was enough for us." *Dayyenu* meant something very different for the Israelites who experienced the moment as a redeeming act of God. They could not explain why God did this for them this time, after so many occasions when they and their ancestors had cried out in vain for salvation. (My wife and I could not explain why we had been blessed with a healthy child.) But there they (and we) were. The *dayyenu* that Israelites testifying to miracle sang at the sea, like the version we sing at our seder, lists a long series of events for which they were thankful. Each blessing flows to and from the others. Having received one blessing, a person of faith does not count on receiving more; they are thankful all over again when another blessing comes their way. Any one of the blessings we receive is more than enough reason for gratitude. If we are fortunate, there will be others, not just this one.

A person need not hold to any particular concept of God to feel this way. Some Jews, like my friend Liz, believe that God works immanently, from *inside* nature and history, and from inside the human beings created in God's image. Other Jews (such as myself) hold that God also works from the *outside*, transcendently, coming to assist us and the world from "some other place." What matters to me is that, regardless of our theological belief about God's role, one recognizes "theopolitical hours" in which work that advances redemption is particularly urgent and might be particularly effective. Whether God is immanent or transcendent, one can engage in the *relationship to God* and/or *partnership with God* that are central to the biblical writers, the rabbis, and Buber; no matter what one's theological stance, one can experience history as miracle and abide in the astonishment it creates. Sometimes "transcendent" notions of gift, instruction, or command from God seem to make the best sense of what we have learned from experience, tradition, and reason. At other moments, "immanent" images of unity with God or outflow from God seem more apt: birthing, merging, or a Star Trek-like "mind-meld" with a Force at work in, through and beyond us. We might feed the hungry and clothe the naked *as God does* or do so *along with God*; God might *inspire us* to do this work, and/or *do it through us*. The two conceptions can overlap, and the difference between them sometimes blur.

I come back to the lesson I find in the opening paragraph of the Haggadah and the story of Akiba's contest with his Roman executioner. Debate what it means that God redeemed our ancestors from Egypt, and us with them. Theology matters. But be sure to feed the hungry and clothe the naked in the meantime. When must we do these things? Now. Always. Thank God for the Passover story that is ours to tell and for the work of redemption that will be ours to do in the coming year and ever after.

Getting Ritual Right

The seder never fails to leave me with a sense of fulfillment; even holding it on Zoom did not take away the joy of the evening or its gravity.
There is something about sitting around a table set with symbols
unique to this occasion that lends special meaning to the moment.
You step out of normal time and into ritual time, fully aware that you
are doing so, and are somehow transported by prior agreement to a
different place. Something similar happens when the curtain goes
up in a theater, and you are not only *here* but also *there*. Participants
separated by miles and time zones at Zoom seders were not only *there*
but *here*. Ritual enchantment makes it so, year after year. "Next year
in Jerusalem," we chant at the conclusion of the evening—by which
I express not only my wish that redemption will come soon, but my
hope that friends and family will gather with me again next year to
think about redemption and resolve to assist its arrival.

A generation ago, it was common to hear people dismiss ritual as
"mere" ritual: behavior that was repetitive, thoughtless, and therefore
undignified. I thought of it that way as a teenager, until I realized that
ritual had a lot in common with the Bach inventions that I was playing with great satisfaction on the piano. The discipline of repetitious
practice was essential to the achievement. Getting the notes right
was non-negotiable, but it was not enough. I came to appreciate the
fact that ritual, like musical performance, involves emotion as well as
thought, body as well as brain. I needed that respite from the life of
the mind. At a Passover seder, one eats, drinks, and sings. Kids who
cannot sit still for long play a prominent role. Some Jews, following an old Sephardic custom, march around the room with packs on
their backs, re-enacting the Exodus rather than merely talking about
it. After dinner, adults as well as kids leave the table to hunt for the
afikomen. Singing tends to be loud or rowdy and includes rhymes on
which children can take the lead.

Theology takes a back seat, as it usually does in ritual. No one is
quizzed before sitting down at the table (or before leaving it) about

what they believe happened to the Israelites in Egypt long ago, or what part they believe God played, if any, in that and subsequent acts of redemption. One need not choose Heschel, Buber, Kaplan, or all or none of the above. The seder begins with ritual questions that are meant to stimulate multiple answers and further questioning. The sages who established the seder tradition believed that this is what the Torah wants Jews to do at Passover. How else could we tell our children that "this is what the Lord did for *me* when *I* went forth from Egypt?" We must own the story, as one would say today, to make it ours, in order to carry out the divine purpose that lies behind the Exodus story. God wants Children of Israel and everyone else on earth to perform acts of justice and compassion. This is the work of redemption.

As I have said more than once, serving God is not a simple matter, even leaving aside the difficulty of knowing the God Whom one hopes to serve. It is often hard to know what the right thing to do is in a particular situation. Sometimes it is difficult to do the right thing even when one knows what the right thing to do is. Hence the importance of ritual, which has this great advantage over other areas of life: When we put heart and mind to it, work at it, focus on it, there is a chance we might *get it right*. That was the satisfaction of the Bach inventions that I played on the piano as a teenager. If I mastered the technique through practice and became comfortable enough with the notes that I could "get inside them" with feeling, I had a chance to receive the gift of knowing that I had done the piece justice. I have had that sense after 25 hours of fasting, introspection, and prayer with my community on Yom Kippur. A taste of it comes with the wine of the *kiddush* on Friday evening if I have managed to concentrate on what I am doing for the 60 seconds it takes to recite the prayer without my mind wandering. (This too is not easy, I find, but it can be done.) I have rarely had the sense of getting parenting exactly right, or relationships with my wife and other people I love, or classroom teaching, or writing of any sort. Max Weber's warning that rational thinking rarely comes out even is not far from my awareness as I try to think and write clearly about what God expects from us. And theology is not the only area in my life that seems never to come out even.

But in ritual things sometimes do come out right. We can get them right. What a gift it is to complete something, to know it whole, to taste fulfillment! That experience encourages us to return to ritual again and again—and it equips us to venture forth from the ritual realm into the world outside and try to get things right there too.

The rabbis were forced to move Passover into the symbolic realm that it occupies today by the destruction of the Temple that previously had been the site where the holiday was observed. Going to Jerusalem was replaced by sitting at the seder table. Sacrifice of a lamb was replaced by talking about that sacrifice. "The Passover offering which our ancestors ate in Temple days, what was the reason for it?" An extremely powerful symbolic action—the sacrifice of an animal, which was then eaten at a meal shared with one's family and, as it smoked on the altar, was perhaps in their minds shared with God—gave way to another symbolic action, less powerful, perhaps, but still quite meaningful. One can only imagine what it was like to bring an animal to the altar and have it sacrificed there before one's eyes, or what it was like for the Israelites in Egypt to put blood on their doorposts so that the angel of death would "pass over" their homes and do its awful work elsewhere. At the Passover seders that we celebrated during the COVID-19 pandemic, that element of the story took on a new and powerful meaning. Many houses had not been spared. Reciting the traditional *shehecheyanu* prayer that thanks God, "Who has kept us alive, sustained us, and enabled us to reach this happy day," put us in mind of the hundreds of thousands of people who had lost their lives to the virus. Many of them had attended Passover seders the previous year and could not do so again.

Such awareness of the world where all is not right is always present in the ritual observance of Passover. Ritual points beyond itself. If it were "mere ritual," wives and husbands would not legitimately feel hurt when their spouses forget a birthday or anniversary, and we would not go to great trouble and expense to mark life cycle events with pomp and ceremony. Theology takes a back seat to ritual at Passover, but the quest for Meaning does not. Indeed, the seder would not mean as much to us as it does, if we thought it was just about the gefilte fish and the *afikomen*. The holiday is precious because it allows us to look unflinchingly at things from which we tend to look away on other nights—and, having seen them more clearly, to resolve to do work that we might otherwise have avoided. The prophets declared repeatedly that God has no need of, or desire for, animal sacrifices—good deeds are what we should offer—and the rabbis reasoned that if God had permitted the Temple to be destroyed, God must not require the sacrifices that had been offered there. Prophets and rabbis agreed that what God really cares about is the ethical action to which the Passover ritual and many other rituals point. Ethical actions, unlike priestly duties, can be performed by anyone, at any time—even if, unlike priestly duties, it is usually not possible to get them exactly right.

* * * * * * *

"Ended is the Passover seder," we recite at the conclusion of the ritual meal, "according to custom, statute, and law." The ritual was performed well, we declare, as only a ritual can be. Now it's time to do other and harder things, even if we do them imperfectly. The work of redemption awaits.

The most serious moment at a traditional seder comes just before or after the recital of the passage I just cited. It is often the most lighthearted moment of the evening as well. Participants are about to get up from the table but remain long enough to sing a cumulative song which, like songs at summer camp, gets faster and faster and more and more complicated as it proceeds: *Chad Gadya* "One Little Goat" ("that my father bought for two *zuzim*"). In successive verses, we merrily sing that a cat ate the goat, a dog bit the cat, a stick beat the dog, fire burned the stick, water quenched the fire, an ox drank the water, a slaughterer killed the ox, and the angel of death killed the slaughterer.

When my daughter was a teenager, I remember her asking at a seder why the Israelites could not have invited Egyptians into their homes that fateful night of the first Passover, and thereby outsmarted the angel of death. Did they try? (Had we done enough during the pandemic to foil the angel's work? Did we perhaps make his job easier by not doing all we could to stave off transmission of the virus and make sure that everyone had access to medical care?) What about all those Egyptians who were caught between Pharaoh's implacable, dictatorial will on one side and God's determination to redeem the Israelites from slavery on the other? I was studying in Jerusalem in 1976 when the news about the rescue of Israeli hostages at Entebbe was broadcast on the radio, so I experienced the national thanksgiving that followed firsthand. Ever since that day, the story of Pharaoh's army drowning in the Reed Sea brings to mind the Ugandan soldiers, some of them teenagers, who were killed by Israeli special forces because they were unlucky enough to be stationed that day at the airport guarding the terrorists who were holding the hostages.

So much unspeakable suffering spots the history of every nation! So much injustice! Redemption too has a terrible cost. We who are alive today and feasting at the seder are unwitting beneficiaries of all that has gone before. The goods of life are not distributed equitably—and neither is life itself.

How does one face up to a bitter truth like this? How do we bear the reminder—just as we are leaving the seder, having resolved to do our part to work for redemption in the coming year—that we live in a world sustained by the killing of one creature by another? We sing a silly song. Our bellies full, our spirits raised by wine and fellowship, we chant *Chad Gadya*, and by doing so announce our awareness, at some level of consciousness, that the whole sorry tale of history, punctuated by occasional redemptions large and small, will not fundamentally change until slaughterers stop killing oxen. That won't happen until the angel of death stops killing slaughterers, and for that to happen, the final verse of *Chad Gadya* must come true. "Then came the Holy One, blessed be He, and slew the angel of death."

That's when ultimate redemption from the world's evils will arrive, and what it will look like. Until then, we must do our best, and it will have to be enough.

Covenants of Mitzvah and Love

A Day in the Life

I began to draft this chapter in March 2021, midway through the week that led to Shabbat *Aharei Mot–Kedoshim*, named for the Torah portions that include the injunction to "love your neighbor as yourself." The news that day, and for many days afterward, was dominated by reaction to the guilty verdict in the trial of the white Minnesota police officer who had killed a Black man named George Floyd. *Aharei mot* means "after the death"; *Kedoshim* means "[be] holy." The pairing of these two portions of the Torah always reminds me of the existential situation in which Jews of this generation find ourselves. What should one say and do in the shadow of the Holocaust? If you try to explain how so many civilized human beings could have perpetrated murder of six million Jews and other innocent victims or stood by while it happened, you are stymied. Ask about the apparent passivity of God in the face of the mass killing of innocents, and—as we saw in the previous chapter of this book—you again come up short. A person cannot wait for such questions to be resolved before deciding upon the proper balance between idealism and cynicism or the terms of a personal relationship to God. Jews are forbidden to wait. The Torah's directive to love makes that clear. *"After the death"*—in response to overwhelming evil—we are commanded to *"Be holy."* Do good, however and wherever you can.

The headlines about the guilty verdict that day brought home for me the full import and difficulty of the Torah's command to love—an order mocked by the murder of innocents. "A rare rebuke of police violence in the U.S.," one headline called it. "With a Cry of 'We Matter,' Catharsis and Relief," read another. It was reported that the chance of a policeman being convicted of murder for a wrongful killing that takes place in the line of duty is something like one in 2,000. Week after week that spring, Americans heard about white police officers shooting Black people to death—killings that rarely resulted in charges against the officers involved. How can one stand up for holiness, or believe good works can be effective, in the face of such a pattern of injustice? The President of the United States, seeking to counter despair of improvement, called the verdict "a giant step forward in the march toward justice in America." The goal seems distant, and not one for which everyone wants to strive. Love of neighbor lies far beyond our reach.

Jews read *Aharei Mot* and *Kedoshim* that year amid other terrible news of death and injustice. The pandemic continued to claim victims in America and elsewhere. The nightly news as usual featured additional evidence of the evils of which human beings are capable: murders, molestations, robberies, etc. On the other hand—this too made news occasionally—the war in Ukraine had elicited an outpouring of generosity and kindness toward refugees and those wounded in bombings or battle. COVID-19 too had spurred good deeds too numerous to count on the part of "essential workers," caregivers, teachers, and everyone else. Promises made to God and human fellows were honored. Some neighbors, at least, were being compassionately and demonstrably loved. Thank goodness! I would otherwise be tempted to give up on the project of human transformation demanded by the Torah and would worry that God is tempted to give up as well. Every act of kindness makes me somewhat more hopeful.

Thinking about the matter as the rabbis often did, I imagine that God is aware of the news of the day and knows more than we do about the countless stories of kindness and cruelty that editors of the *New York Times* have not seen "fit to print." I can picture God reacting with grave concern when the latest data on suffering and injustice are brought before the heavenly throne. A merciful God cannot but grieve over the millions of deaths in the world due to the COVID-19 pandemic. I can barely take in a small fraction of the bad news of the day before turning for relief to the sports page or the crossword puzzle; at the height of the pandemic, I regularly lost sleep—a response widely shared among people I know. If the psalmist was correct, God "neither sleeps nor slumbers." Must God look without relief upon the near-infinite number of occasions—private and public, individual and collective, minor and major—on which human beings do the opposite of justice, compassion, or loving our neighbors as ourselves?

It is some comfort to me, though not to the victims, of course, that many of those who are guilty of wrongdoing did not know what the right thing to do would have been. We learned after the guilty verdict in the George Floyd murder that police officers in some cities do not receive adequate training in the use of the weapons they carry and get little or no instruction about what to do when called to a home where domestic violence is taking place. Other times, however, police officers, like the rest of us, know full well what the right thing to do is and fail to do it, or do the opposite. Either way, love of neighbor does not happen, blocked by the human condition in place since Cain killed Abel. I wonder sometimes why the Torah—which is resolutely realistic in its appraisal of that condition—nonetheless issued a command that is only rarely obeyed.

Skin Disease

The portions of the Torah that we read in synagogue immediately before *Aharei Mot* and *Kedoshim* prescribe rituals of purification to be performed on various occasions: after childbirth; upon the onset of contagious disease marked by swelling, scabbing, and discolorations of the skin; or in response to infestations of plague in clothing or in the walls of houses. Modern readers often scoff at these chapters. How primitive they seem, particularly when juxtaposed with the lofty teaching to love one's neighbor! How pathetic the priests who know exactly what sacrifices to offer, how to cut up rams or cattle into pieces, which parts can be eaten and which are smoked on the altar, and how to sprinkle the blood with the index finger on the right ear lobe or right big toe—everything except how to do what our physicians usually do routinely, and what the Levitical priests probably wanted to do but could not: prevent disease or cure it.

One cannot dismiss those chapters so easily in the wake of the COVID-19 pandemic. Vaccines against the disease are now available, doctors prescribe pills that mitigate the effects of the virus, and scientists have learned a great deal about the biology of this amazing microorganism—but the world remains vulnerable to the virus and anxious about successor viruses likely to plague us in coming years. Memories of the damage inflicted by this one continue to be vivid. It was not long ago that hundreds of millions around the world experienced the sort of quarantine that, according to the Torah's account, was to be imposed on Israelites who suffered from the contagious skin disease that scholars once thought was leprosy. (Its identification is now uncertain.) It is much easier today than it was only a few years ago to understand how moving it can be to hug friends and neighbors after a long separation or to sit in the same room with family, socialize with friends, or share a meal. Rituals have been developed to mark the renewed gathering of communities or to offer thanksgiving to the first responders and essential workers, whose personal sacrifices helped keep us alive. It is easy to see why Leviticus reminds its readers, in the chapters leading up to the command to love our neighbor, that we and our neighbors are mortal, vulnerable, and frail, and are essential to one another's well-being.

I find it instructive, as a contemporary member of the people known as the Children of Israel, to bear in mind the biblical character after whom Jews are named when thinking about love of neighbor and the terms of God's covenant with humanity. Jacob, who will be called Israel, one day, flees his parents' home in Be'er Sheva after stealing his brother Esau's birthright and blessing and sets out for his uncle's home in Haran. He stops for the night, falls asleep, and dreams of a ladder with angels going up and down. The Lord stands before Jacob

COVENANTS OF MITZVAH AND LOVE 101

and promises him numerous offspring, the blessing first bestowed upon his grandfather Abraham. God also promises to protect Jacob on his journey and bring him back to his homeland. Jacob awakes and recognizes what has just occurred. "Surely the Lord is present in this place, and I did not know it"—an experience with which many human beings can identify even today. God often comes upon us unaware. Jacob's initial response is to take the stone on which he had slept and make it an altar, and then he does exactly what many of us might do, or have done, during our lives: he offers God a deal. Remain with me and protect me, provide me with food and clothing, bring me back to my father's house as You have promised—"and of all that You give me, I will set aside a tithe for You." In other words: Do all this for me, and I will give back ten percent to You! Thus says the human being whom the Torah commands to love their neighbor.

We chuckle at Jacob's vow, but we also wince in recognition. How many of us have tried to bargain with God for the life or health of a loved one? How many of us give even ten percent of what we have earned to charity? I confess that I do not.

Life changes Jacob. When he sets off many years later on the journey home, he again meets angels (or messengers) of God on the way, recognizes them as "God's camp," and, fearful that Esau will seek revenge for the theft of birthright and blessing, sends messengers of his own ahead to greet his brother with gifts of appeasement. He divides his camp into two, thinking that if Esau attacks one, the other will be able to flee. Then after reminding God that He had ordered him to return home and promised to "deal bountifully" with him, Jacob makes a confession that is strikingly different in tone than anything that we have heard him say before.

"I am unworthy of all the kindness [literally, "too small for all the mercies"] that You have so steadfastly shown Your servant . . . Deliver me, I pray, from the hand of my brother, from the hand of Esau; else, I fear, he may come and strike me down, mothers and children alike."

The passage is one of the most beautiful I know in Scripture, and one of the most meaningful to me personally. It is true to the experience of humility in the face of blessing that cannot be earned. Jacob knows he is small under the canopy of the night sky. He is vulnerable and afraid in the face of a powerful brother whom he harmed years before. Jacob wants something from God; of course, he does. His prayer in that sense is less than pure. (Which of our prayers is not less than pure? Every utterance by a human being to the Everlasting God is similarly tainted by mortality.) Jacob wants to stay alive, and he wants to protect his wives and children. But he knows, too, that he has been blessed and that all that he has comes from God's grace.

I think that this is how Leviticus sees human beings: frail and mortal; given to selfishness and scheming; but capable too of rising to an occasion, showing great courage, and acting generously. This book of the Torah, more than others, asks its readers time and again—as in the sections dealing with skin disease—to confront the fact that we are bodies, subject to illness and death. It enjoins acts of sacrifice in which one brings an animal to the altar, places hands upon its head, hears its cries as it is slaughtered, feels the warm blood that streams forth, and smells the animal's death. Readers of the Torah know, as we stand there in imagination with ancient Israelites, that we too are mammals. Today the animal dies so that the person who brings the sacrifice can be ritually purified. Someday it will be that person who dies—and every person who *reads* about the sacrifice. Nature takes its course. The parade of generations continues.

The point of ritual sacrifice, offered on countless occasions of thanksgiving, atonement, confession, and daily or festival offerings, is not to make ancient Israelites—or readers of the text in any age— morbid. Leviticus is not seeking to chase away the joy we take in life. Rather, it wants to force us to confront the fact of death instead of repressing it—and to contain the threat that death poses to life's meaning by placing death safely inside a sacred order of significance and beauty. Leviticus time and again faces down the threat of death (some mystics and modern philosophers would say: the threat of non-being) through rituals involving blood, the life force par excellence. It ascribes these rituals of sacrifice to God, whose proper name, announced to Moses at the burning bush—YHWH—has Being at its core.

The chapter that calls upon us to love our neighbors as ourselves is followed by detailed regulations about permitted and prohibited sexual relations. Its authors knew from observation and experience that sex is the master passion, one of the principal ways in which human beings express love for—and do grievous harm to—one another. Sex is also the vehicle for creation of new life and, thus, humanity's most powerful weapon in the eternal battle against death. The Torah does not aim to fight sexual urges, but to direct them. It never condemns sex and never commands that sex, inside the framework of marriage, be limited to procreation. It seems to understand the meaning to life that sex can offer in that context, its role in the expression of love. But readers of the Torah are forcefully reminded that sex, wrongly used, has the proven ability to destroy marriages, wreck friendships, and tear communities apart. The point here, as it was with mortality, is not repression but awareness. Leviticus wants to contain sex within a sacred order of meaning and life-giving joy. It wants sex—like the rest of what makes us human, all the things we do in part to secure a measure of comfort in the face of death—to serve the cause of being holy.

The aim of the commandments said to flow directly from Israel's encounter with God at Sinai is the same. Justice must be pursued, and love extended to human beings not always well-suited to those tasks.

After Sinai

I do not know if the meeting at Sinai took place as described in Chapter 19 of the Book of Exodus, or if it took place at all. No one does. On this matter as all others, theology is rooted in uncertainties that it is powerless to resolve. Jewish sages, philosophers, and commentators, expounding on the ambiguities and evasions of the biblical account, offered multiple versions of the event at Sinai, thereby encouraging us to do the same. What mattered for them, and matters for me, is that Jews continue to try to live up to the responsibilities of the Covenant formed at Sinai, and that human beings continue to translate the ethical principles pronounced in the Ten Commandments into specifics relevant to our day. Together, we should seek to have (or at least be worthy of) the sort of encounter with God that the passage in Exodus strives mightily to imagine.

Is the voice (*kol*) of God that the Israelites hear as they stand at the foot of the mountain the same voice as the *kol* of thunder, the *kol* of the shofar? God explains to Moses before the event that its purpose is "so that the people may hear when I speak with you and trust in you ever after." Immediately afterward we learn that the people, "witnessing the thunder and lightning, the blare of the horn and the mountain smoking," retreated from the scene. "You speak to us, and we will obey," they say to Moses, "but let not God speak to us, lest we die." Jewish theologians now as ever are left to wonder what the people *did* hear. Did all of them hear the same words, if words were what they heard, in the same language? What exactly did Moses hear?

These questions have enormous personal significance to me. Whose words and which words will I hear when this portion of the Torah is chanted aloud in synagogue? Should I expect to hear words from God, in any form, on any occasion? Or will revelation—if that is what took place at Sinai—occur for me in some other manner? Rabbinic commentators have always disagreed on the matter, thereby opening broad space for diverse expectations of how God might enter a person's life and diverse interpretations of what obedience to the commandments entails.

Could it be, following Buber's helpful suggestion about what happened at the splitting of the sea, that some of the Israelites present at Sinai merely marveled at the amazing show of thunder and lightning they had just witnessed, while others came away convinced that they had experienced a revelation from God? It's not clear from the text what exactly was revealed to the second group, that is, what they actually saw or heard. Perhaps they witnessed a faraway Moses apparently listening to a divine voice that was inaudible to them.

The matter is of utmost importance for religious individuals who, like me, want to learn as much as we can from Scripture about God and God's will for us. How intimate a relationship can I hope to have with God? How much can I know for sure about what God wants from me in the realms of love and commandment? A lot is at stake—and the text seems to resist the quest for certainty. Here, as at the Seder table, the person who enlarges on the inherited account, makes it their own, ponders every detail, is "to be praised." Delving deep into the text, and joining the generations whose lives were ordered by its study and its commands, we have the satisfaction of walking a path on which Meaning has been found, and God encountered, for a very long time.

The rabbis had two general views about Moses's prophetic role. We might picture him and every prophet who comes after him as a stenographer who takes dictation from God word for word and transmits the record faithfully to the people and to us. This is the view of biblical literalists and fundamentalists. Or we might imagine Moses engaging God in a wordless meeting of minds in which the prophet intuits God's will and translates it into specifics of language and action. That is how Heschel understood matters. "As a report about revelation," he wrote trenchantly, "the Bible itself is a midrash." The Book of Exodus, in Heschel's view, does not and could not provide a historical account of the event that took place at Sinai. It offers an interpretation of what was done and said there.

That is my view as well. It is not important to me what percentage of the text in our hands, if any, was authored by Moses himself, and what comes to us from other authors writing from their experiences of standing in the presence of God. Nor do I think it matters overmuch if a portion of the people that became Israel experienced an event of revelation at Sinai, though I believe they probably did. The important point is that the Torah in our hands has inspired and directed Jewish lives for over two millennia. Thanks to Christianity, Islam, and the many cultures they influenced in turn, the Bible's account of the revelation at Sinai has inspired and directed a significant portion of humanity. To me personally, as I have attested more than once in this book, the Torah, is a "tree of life" to which I "hold fast" and which holds me. The way of mitzvah set forth at Sinai is the one on which I do my humble best to increase the measure of justice and compassion in the world. I hope that for me, as for the ancestors, the path will be graced by encounters with God.

* * * * * *

When a Jew reads the Torah week by week, as I do, the transition from grand ethical principles (e.g., "Thou shalt not murder") to specifics of law, ritual, or worship (e.g., oxen goring oxen; sacrifice; Sabbath observance) is nearly seamless. Over time it comes to seem both natural and inevitable. One moment, you are standing on your feet in synagogue, listening to recitation of the Ten Commandments, and the next moment—or the next week in synagogue—you are receiving instruction about what we today call civil law, criminal law, and torts. The Torah turns to those prescriptions without a moment's pause for reorienting attention or reflecting on the relation between theory and practice, principles and the application of principles. We are being taught by the Torah that human beings become serious about justice, compassion, and love only when ethical norms are translated into specific behavioral requirements. This is true of individual relationships and for the governance of societies and states.

We are taught another lesson "at Sinai" as well. Because human beings do not always reason our way to right action, and don't always do the right thing even when we know it is right, the Torah's demands must be formulated and enforced *as law*. The move from ethics to law, attacked by Christian theologians throughout the ages and, more recently, by Enlightenment critics of religion and of Judaism in particular, has been problematic for many modern Jews as well. Jewish law is no longer enforceable in any case, except in the State of Israel and in ultra-Orthodox communities in the Diaspora. This is a welcome development for Jews who believe that individual autonomy should not be infringed upon by religious statute. Mordecai Kaplan, who highly valued individual autonomy and recommended that the "commandments" be redefined as "folkways," asserted nonetheless that "the collective will" of a people such as the Jews necessarily "takes the form of law...Social life has as much need of a measure of involuntarism as physical life." The rabbis ruled long ago that in the Diaspora, where Jewish law lacks the power of enforcement, Jews should respect the law of the nation they inhabited. "The law of the state [to which a Jew belongs] is the law" (and must be obeyed). The sages shared the Torah's conviction that human beings need the guidance and constraint that only law can provide. Neither good intentions nor lofty principles are enough.

Aware that law may fall into disuse or disrepute if it remains unchanged despite changes in societal conditions and norms, the rabbis opened broad space for vigorous debate about how biblical law should be interpreted and applied. They encouraged the belief, which I share, that the covenantal partnership with God is reenacted—rather than disrupted—when the details of its application are reasonably, boldly, and lovingly reinterpreted. Change in the law is especially necessary during periods of rapid societal or technological transformation such as the present day. The "giving of Torah," Jewish tradition asserts, takes place again and again. The sages illustrated this point by radically reinterpreting the Torah's famous rule that punishment in particular cases was to be "life for life, eye for eye, tooth for tooth," as stated in the chapter that immediately follows the narrative of the revelation at Sinai. I was amazed at the rabbis' boldness when I first encountered their claim that the Torah's words, although utterly graphic and specific, are meant to convey financial compensation rather than corporal wounding. The Torah would not want to be taken literally in this passage, they reasoned. What good would it do for a person to take out the eye of the person who had taken out his or her eye? Vengeance might be satisfying for a moment, but it does not pay doctors' bills or compensate for income that has been lost, or might be lost in the future, because of the injury suffered. Justice would not be served by a literal reading of the text. Compassion would not be increased. Love of neighbor would not flourish. God's commandments are given to us to advance those objectives. God requires our partnership in the interpretive effort to accomplish this.

There is sometimes a frustrating gap between changed conditions or norms and a system of regulations that goes back more than two millennia. To those immediately affected—for example, women and LGBTQ individuals, two prominent subjects of recent changes in Jewish law—the rules of Leviticus have caused immense pain and suffering, and in many cases still do. But I think Kaplan erred when he translated mitzvah as "folkway" or "custom" in part because he believed that onerous and outdated halakhic regulations could not be changed. The problem to which he responded is real; refusal by Orthodox authorities to change certain laws has brought the entire halakhic system into disrepute. Like Kaplan, I have little patience for legal minutiae or the search for loopholes—he quaintly called these practices "pettifogging"—or the sort of legal acrobatics that have driven many people to flee religions that, like Judaism, seek to express devotion to God through faithful and detailed observance of law. The rabbis themselves did not escape these traps, as any student of the Talmud knows; there is always the danger that strict adherence to the letter of the law will outstrip attention to its spirit or to ethics. As one observant Jew wrote recently, presumably from personal experience, "There are, along the edifice of halakhic [legal] observance, quite a few cracks and crevices where you can go in and hide—for an extended period—from the light of the encounter with the Divine."

At their best, however, legal interpreters through the ages have demonstrated the relevance of the law to every aspect of daily life, personal and collective, thereby showing that every area of existence can become a vehicle for holiness: eating and drinking, doing business, building and governing communities, observing Shabbat and festivals, caring for bodies and souls.

To my mind this is a noble objective, for I seek wholeness. I don't want awareness of what is highest and holy kept far from what I do all day. I want as much of my behavior as possible to be as right as I can make it. I want to use my time on earth well, and to cleave to the Good—and to God—if I possibly can. Experience has confirmed for me the proven ability of law to keep a person on the right path by encouraging just and compassionate action and preventing, or at least discouraging, wrongdoing. Thankfully, I was taught at a young age not to see mitzvah as an all or nothing matter and learned over time to see the logic behind commandments that I had once found senseless or primitive. When one confronts ethical situations that are black or white, the Torah points out the difference so clearly that one cannot miss or avoid it and demands that one act accordingly. When one is dealing with shades of gray, as is often the case, the Torah assists navigation of that territory as well.

I need both sorts of guidance; I don't think I am alone in suffering from a certain obtuseness when it comes to accepting responsibility, correcting mistakes, and promptly going where my help is needed. My wife and kids will attest that I do not always hear what is being said to me or see what is right in front of my eyes. The Torah assists family, friends, and colleagues in cutting through my penchant for avoidance. Its guidance has saved me from a lot of mistakes. The constraints it places on me are a precious gift. Kaplan did not capture my relationship to mitzvah when he wrote that "the ancient authorities" exercised "a vote but not a veto" when it comes to contemporary Jewish observance. The tradition that goes back to Sinai has much more than a vote in how I live my life. Torah stands at the very center of my thought and practice. But it exercises far less than a veto, both because my obedience to the Torah's instruction is not coerced, and because my Jewish community plays an active role in interpreting the law and keeping it vital and up to date. I was privileged to take advantage of the openness to change that the rabbis built into Jewish law when, following a ruling by the law committee of Conservative Judaism, JTS under my leadership decided to accept LGBTQ individuals into its rabbinical and cantorial schools.

I want to highlight one more aspect of rabbinic teaching about mitzvah that I find especially meaningful: the fact that, according to the Torah, the commandments are given and received in a context of *relationship*. They are not impersonal decrees from a far-off tyrant, reaching us—as Kafka imagined in his nightmarish parable, *The Castle*—by means of nefarious intermediaries who may themselves have no contact with the "Count" in whose name they speak. Jewish tradition teaches that God communicates with human beings not only as master to servant, but as parent to child; not just as sovereign to subject, but as senior partner in an enterprise that requires the cooperation of free and intelligent human agents. I willingly accept the role of agent and junior partner. My experience confirms rabbinic teaching that God addresses human beings both from afar, indirectly, as it were in a *kol* of thunder, and up close, in a whisper of personal encounter, a wind, or the voice of a child. I follow divine commandments not only out of duty but out of love.

I struggle with the obvious paradoxes of this approach: God is far yet near; involved in history (and in the personal lives of human beings of all nations and creeds) but without control over history or human action. God is "in search of man," as Heschel put it, but hard to find. Even when encountered periodically by individuals and communities of faith, God remains hidden in cloud or fire or the mysteries of the ineffable, thereby leaving ample space for right or wrong human actions (or failures to act) and better or worse interpretations of God's will. We are partners to God in covenant, but remain free to choose our own paths in life. We can, and often do, disobey or wriggle out of the commands issued by conscience or Torah. But much of the time we do listen. We manage to love and be loved. Covenants are not only broken but kept, strengthened, and renewed.

God must have set things up this way, reasoned countless rabbis, philosophers, and mystics over the centuries. They held fast to both key tenets of every one of the paradoxes that I have described. I try to do the same, and sometimes succeed.

✷ ✷ ✷ ✷ ✷

The Torah demonstrates the relational character of mitzvah repeatedly and dramatically. Immediately following the establishment of the Covenant at Sinai, Moses, Aaron, two of Aaron's sons and 70 elders ascend partway up the mountain, where "they saw the God of Israel: under His feet there was the likeness of a pavement of sapphire, like the very sky for purity . . . they beheld God, and they ate and drank." Note that this remarkable text is careful to say that the human party to the meeting with God saw the *likeness* of a pavement under God's feet that was *like* the sky in its purity. Not more than that—but not less. God remains in hiding, even during this (and every other) so-called sighting. Nonetheless, it is a moment of great intimacy—and a still more intimate moment follows soon after, of a sort that the Torah believes has been granted to no human being before or since.

The Israelites—fearing that Moses has died on the mountain during an interview with God, and afraid that, lacking his direction, they are doomed to die in the wilderness—build and worship an idol, for which they are severely punished by Moses and God. Moses dutifully trudges up the mountain yet again to beg God's forgiveness on behalf of the people and secures a promise from God not to destroy them as punishment for their idolatry. He also receives a divine pledge to accompany the Israelites on their journey to the Promised Land even though they are "stiff-necked" and likely to sin grievously again. Moses then asks God's help in leading the people. This request too is granted—at which point he bursts out with a final plea, breathtaking in its audacity, that arrests us (and perhaps Moses himself, and even God) with its boldness. "Please show me Your glory!" or "Oh, let me behold your Presence!"

I imagine Moses exhausted from his repeated fasts and his two climbs up the mountain. He is drained as well by the relentless difficulties of dealing with his fractious people and his inscrutable God. The task had grown more arduous, rather than less, after the long struggle with Pharaoh ended at the Reed Sea. The roaring of the wind at the top of the mountain is so loud that at times it drowns out the roar inside Moses's head. The thunders without and within make it difficult for him to hear God's voice when it sounds or to decipher what God wants from him. Moses realizes that God has already granted him more than he had a right to expect. God has come down to the top of the mountain to meet him and has agreed to other meetings that will take place in tents erected for this purpose outside the camp. As if that were not enough, the stuff that is God and the stuff that is Moses seem to have come together, mind to mind, in a way that words cannot capture. Certainly, Moses does not understand it. The mystery of his relationship to God is wonderful, but it is hard—on some days, utterly impossible—to bear.

Moses tells God that to perform the task of leadership that God assigned to him, he needs to know what he has been doing right. "Pray let me know Your ways," he pleads, "that I may know You and continue in Your favor." Only when God replies favorably to that request does

Moses beg to see God's "glory" or Presence. He wants to be closer to this God Who always keeps a distance from him and everyone else. Moses craves firsthand, eyewitness knowledge of the sort that no human being has ever been granted.

God says no. Moses cannot have what he wants from God. No human being can.

That is how I read the passage until a few years ago, when a friend changed my picture of the scene at the top of the mountain by painting it on a series of four canvases. The colors and vectors of the paint altered my perception of the meeting between God and Moses, and in so doing transformed my sense of what a human being could hope to experience of God—what I could hope to experience. The distinction, blurring and apparent fusion of above and below on the canvas captured aspects of the biblical narrative that had previously escaped me. God says to Moses, "You cannot see My face, for no person can see Me and live." But, I now realized, God also utters a remarkable "yes" before saying that "no." God in fact promises Moses more than he could ask for or imagine. God not only will remain with the Israelites on their journey and (to some extent) forgive a transgression that Moses rightly feared was unforgiveable. In addition God will "make all My goodness pass before you," proclaiming (for the one and only time recorded in the Hebrew Bible) the name and attributes of the Lord. And God will shelter Moses "with My hand" in the cleft of a rock while "My Presence passes by" and then "take My hand away and you will see My back, but my Face must not be seen."

Moses cannot see God's face. The Lord's visage cannot be an object to Moses's gaze. The connection between them cannot be a thing that Moses controls or conjures. Religious people of every time and place need to know this. But Moses can and will be held by God: protected, forgiven, comforted, and loved. He can and will see where God has been, looking with an eye of discernment at the trace of the presence and action that God has left behind. We too can and do experience these things.

The passage is utterly crucial to the possibility and limits of human meetings with God. It is remarkable in other respects as well. The repeated use of anthropomorphic language as radical as any in the Torah, right after the Israelites were punished for their construction of an idol, is only one of the linguistic and theological puzzles that the reader confronts. What is the force of God's warning that no one can see God's face and live to tell about it? Does this mean that God has a face, literal or figurative and even Moses is not allowed to see it? Are human beings not permitted to look at God because we would be blinded by the light of God's countenance? Or is it the case that we *could* look without being killed or blinded but are prohibited from doing so because we are constitutionally incapable of seeing God's image *correctly*? Perhaps painted and sculpted images are forbidden because human beings inevitably would picture God incorrectly or inadequately—and this God wants to be known, within the limits of the possible, as God is and not as God is not.

The conundrums are many, and I treasure them, frustrated but grateful that they are irresolvable. Moses does not try. Neither does the Torah. Buber expressed the immense frustration that attends encounters with the Eternal Thou, complaining that revelation of the living God is often "nothing but a different form of hiding." That is not quite true, as we just learned. Although we cannot hope to experience more in an encounter with God than Moses did, we too can see where God has been—in nature, perhaps, or history, or the birth of a child, or the generosity of someone we have never met. We can envisage "likenesses" of God through color, metaphor, or music. Many of us have felt ourselves held by God, chastised, forgiven, comforted, loved. We can "abide in the astonishment" of such moments and hope that more will take place as we walk the path of mitzvah. And we have that path, which sets out more than enough good work for a lifetime.

Heschel's account of personal religious experience in *Man Is Not Alone* is particularly meaningful to me because I met the man, have read virtually all he has written, and admire him greatly for his learning, his piety, and his political activism, all of which were, at least in part, a response to personal encounter with God. Heschel's description of mystical experience bears a close resemblance to those that William James identified in *The Varieties of Religious Experience* as typical across religious traditions: light, awe, mystery, overwhelming power. But Heschel's account also resounds with strong echoes of the experiences of Moses and the Israelites at Sinai and of God's calling of the prophet Isaiah. It therefore concludes, as those reports do, with a summons to action. I quote the passage at length, albeit with ellipses.

> [One has] no power to spend on faith any more, no goal to strive for, no strength to seek a goal. But, then, a moment comes like a thunderbolt, in which a flash of the undisclosed rends our dark apathy asunder. It is full of overpowering brilliance. . . . The ineffable has shuddered itself into the soul. . . . We cannot think any more as if He were there and we here. He is both there and here. He is not *a being* but *being in and beyond all beings* . . .
>
> A tremor seizes our limbs; our nerves are struck, quiver like strings; our whole being bursts into shudders. But then a cry, wrested from our very core, fills the world around us, as if a mountain were about to place itself in front of us It is one word: GOD. . . . The word that means more than universe, more than eternity, holy, holy, holy; we cannot comprehend it. We only know that it means infinitely more than we are able to echo. Staggered, embarrassed, we stammer and say: He . . . whose question is more than our mind can answer; He, to whom our life can be the spelling of an answer.

My personal experiences of God's presence have never been as intense as those reported by Heschel, the mystics, and the Torah. They are much more the "still small voice" heard by the prophet Elijah than thunder or blinding light. I hold fast to them in fear and trembling nonetheless, talk about them haltingly if at all, and try to live in a way appropriate to the fact of God's being in my vicinity. I have described or alluded to several personal encounters with the divine in the letters to friends and in the rest of this book, and treasure reports of encounter with the divine by friends, family, and people I have never met personally, whether or not they are Jews, and whether they define themselves as "religious" or "spiritual." I suspect that Heschel's experience—or mine—would have been different if he or I had been raised a Catholic or a Buddhist, or been born in a different century, or been female. That is another reason to treat religious experiences with caution, even while holding on to them as gifts of grace. The rabbis theorized that God's summons to Israel at Sinai must have been transmitted in all languages, so that all the world could receive it directly. Even among Israelites, they asserted, the reception of God's speech varied from person to person so that everyone could understand it. A great deal is no doubt lost, though much can be gained, in the translation of religious experience from one biography and culture to another. No tradition can possibly hold the whole truth when it comes to the Creator of all.

There is nothing straightforward about divine revelation, according to the Torah, nothing at all. The saving grace for you and me is that each of us need not hear God's voice the same way. We need not agree in our imaginings of what could be seen behind the cloud if it were possible for a human being to do so. We just need to live side by side with one another in God's world, heeding the voice that tells us that God is just and compassionate and that we should be so as well. We stammer in every attempt to articulate the nature of divine encounter, but, as Heschel taught, "our life can be the spelling of an answer." How one responds to the presence of God in the world is the test of the truth or falsity of purported revelation. The test is hardly foolproof, but no better one is available.

Community

If most of the Torah described meetings between Moses and God at the top of a mountain rather than what happened among the Children of Israel down below, it would be hard for people who, like me, are not priests or prophets, not mystics or saints, to make the Torah a guidepost for life or to believe that they have a chance of making contact with God. Fortunately, that is not the case. The point of building the wilderness Tabernacle, and later the Temple in Jerusalem, was to provide a place in which, as God promises, "I will dwell among" the people of Israel—all of them. They did not need to reach the Promised Land to be assured of God's presence and concern, nor to be as holy as their priests or as exalted as their prophets; most of God's interactions with human beings, as reported in the Bible, do not take place at the top of a mountain but in local sanctuaries, the Jerusalem Temple or other accessible sites. This bodes well for you and me.

Contemporary Jews and Christians rarely experience the terror of God's overwhelming presence when we gather on a Sabbath morning in our houses of worship. The cloud of God's glory does not fill our sanctuaries. Most of us do not fall to our knees and shout in exultant praise, though some of course do. Nevertheless, the synagogue (or church, mosque, or temple) is, like the Tabernacle, a space of human construction where ordinary individuals are granted a heightened sense of holiness on a regular basis, and, on occasion, far more than that. It is not unusual for congregants to report experiences of God's presence that move them to tears or laughter. Prayers are offered—and sometimes, somehow, heard.

More than a year of worship on Zoom and livestream had the effect of increasing appreciation of what we miss by *not* walking into sacred places crowded with other congregants as well as with memories of especially joyful and mournful moment of our lives. Words and music are not the same when experienced alone at home. Prayer is not the same. One lacks the impact of swaying bodies and contrite or soaring spirits close at hand.

I have found over the years that familiar faces become bearers of meaning whether or not the people who bear those faces become friends. There is the person who used to sit in front of me during the long fast of Yom Kippur each year, and the one who was present at the bar- and bat-mitzvah ceremonies of my kids and at my daughter's wedding some 20 years later. A third person, whose last name I forget sometimes, helped make a minyan at my home for the shiva after my father died. The man who sat two rows behind me and several seats to the left once stood beside me at a soup kitchen where we fed homeless people. He has a beautiful voice and moved me almost to tears when he recited the Shema. I forgave him at that moment for being an inveterate gossip, the sort of person who corners you during services and won't let go. His wife sat beside me at the synagogue meetings when we debated designs for a new sanctuary and increased assessments of members to pay for it. She has repeatedly impressed me with her good sense and patience. Her singing is usually off-key. I try not to notice.

I take care not to idealize these people. God knows they have their share of faults: pettiness, ego, jealousies, microaggressions, and even cruelties. The spats among them can poison the atmosphere in the sanctuary or boardroom for the rest of us, sometimes for weeks. But I have also seen the members of my congregation rise higher than I ever expected they would, lifted by religious experiences at shul and by occasions of need when fellow congregants stood by them. I thought of such moments when I recently reread Melville's paean to humanity, and therefore to democracy, in *Moby Dick*.

> Men may seem as detestable as joint stock-companies and nations; knaves, fools, and murderers there may be… but man, in the ideal, is so noble and so sparkling, such a grand and glowing creature, that over any ignominious blemish in him all his fellows should run to throw their costliest robes…. But this august dignity I treat of …has no robed investiture. Thou shall see it shining in the arm that wields a pick or drives a spike; that democratic dignity which, on all hands, radiates without end from God Himself. The great God absolute! The center and circumference of all democracy! His omnipresence, our divine equality!

Much of the time, I admit, it is hard to credit Melville's opinion of humanity (the novel itself calls it into question repeatedly), just as it is difficult to take at face value the account of the Israelite community's response to Moses's call for contributions to build the Tabernacle. Everyone must give something, he tells them, but the nature and amount of the gift are voluntary. "And everyone who excelled in ability and everyone whose spirit moved him came, bringing to the Lord his offering for the work of the Tent of Meeting for all its service and for the sacred vestments. Men and women, all whose hearts moved them." The text exultantly describes the range of skills and materials brought to the task: a plenitude of textures, colors, scents, and precious stones. It exults as much, or more, in repetition of the word "all." Over and over the Torah testifies in these chapters to the congregation's devotion, at once unanimous and diverse. Each one comes alone, and all come together.

The historicity of the account is irrelevant—a good thing, since the reader is left to wonder where the Israelites got all those objects, and how they carried them through the wilderness. The point, once again, is not historical fact but the summoning of memory and aspiration. You and I have known people to behave with comparable generosity. We have perhaps done so ourselves and might do so again. We can appreciate the blessing of face-to-face Community characterized by longstanding mutual responsibility and commitment (as distinguished from casual associations or what the sociologists call "lifestyle enclaves"). If you have experienced this sort of Community, chances are you want more of it, whatever the shortcomings of its members, both for its own sake and as the setting where God can be felt to be among us. The benefits of Community to individual health, philanthropic giving and communal activism are well-documented.

I share two memories that help me to make sense of the Torah's account.

One: The congregation that my father attended on Shabbat in his old age, after my mother passed away, no longer met in the main sanctuary of the synagogue but in a small chapel in the school wing. The average age of the congregants was well over eighty, and the rabbi too was advanced in years. There was no cantor. Every week, in preparation for taking the Torah from the ark, two congregants would stand at the back of the room, as had been the custom in the far grander sanctuary. They solemnly marched forward as the congregation sang a traditional hymn, reaching the front in time to ceremoniously open the ark. The first time I saw them do this, I thought of the great cathedrals of Europe, where a Michelangelo or Raphael greets worshippers as they enter, and giant pillars raise all eyes to crossed arches that seem as high as the heavens. How pitiful was this chapel in northeast Philadelphia by comparison, how small the worshippers, I mused—until that thought was succeeded by another: that in God's eyes we are all tiny, however large or small the dimensions of the rooms in which we pray. All of us matter equally in the divine accounting. God's presence can be felt at Solomon's glorious Temple or in a portable wilderness structure that is assembled and disassembled repeatedly. Neither one can contain God. Human beings make these structures as beautiful as we can in hopes of bringing God close—that is, bringing ourselves closer to God.

Two: I flew from New York to the San Francisco Bay Area in the late afternoon during the week before the Sabbath of the Torah portion that describes the Israelites' contributions to the Tabernacle. I had a window seat, and the sky was cloudless virtually all the way across the country. I stared, and stared again, as frozen plains gave way to black-brown foothills and then to snowy mountain peaks, all this as the sun slowly went down, its setting lengthened by the journey west. Darkness eventually descended, but I continued to stare out the window. The scene had been magnificent beyond any words that I could find. I was not sure what to do in the face of its glory except to try and abide as long as possible in the wonder that I was feeling. I praised the Creator, thankful that I was there to witness the extraordinary occurrence of a sunset from the vantage of 35,000 feet.

Something like this grateful wonderment must have overwhelmed the Israelites who built the Tabernacle. They had stood at Sinai—a moment of indescribable awe for them and no small terror—and soon after they had had multiple reasons for fear. Now they had ample reason for gratitude. God would not only forgive their transgression but dwell among them throughout the journey through the wilder-

ness and beyond. The site of that indwelling would be a tabernacle
of their own construction, the product of their own gifts and skills.
God needed them to do this work and would need their help to build
a new sort of society in the Promised Land, obedient to the teachings
received at Sinai. This was surely an occasion for joy and generosity.

I want to be clearheaded in my thinking about the ways in which
human beings can experience God's presence and be faithful partners
to God in the world. It is important not to overestimate the capabili-
ties that people bring to that responsibility. The same week that I took
that flight to the West Coast, I happened to read a gripping account of
psychological research proving that a great deal of human thought is
much less rational than we like to believe. All sorts of biases, self-de-
ceptions, longings, and fears shape the way we see what is in front
of us. We filter out a lot of what we don't want to hear. We calculate
risk differently, depending on whether it is framed as possible gain or
possible loss; we exhibit a strong preference for the known, the status
quo, over what is unknown or strange.

Another recent study demonstrates that moral reasons are "the tail
wagged by the intuitive dog" rather than the actual causes of human
behavior. Human reason has been evolutionarily designed to seek
justifications for conduct, not truth. Rational human beings generally
interpret new evidence that comes our way to confirm what we already
think rather than to challenge existing beliefs, which is how Leviticus
views the human condition.

Indeed, the Torah represents an attempt to do what a leading cog-
nitive psychologist has called "a part of good science....to see what
everyone else can see but think what no one else had ever said"—just
the opposite of normal human behavior. We see God repeatedly trying to persuade humanity to see, think, and act differently than they
ever have in a sustained way before. The spectacle of the Israelites
fashioning the golden calf enables readers of the Torah to confront
the perennial tendency of human beings to worship idols of our own
making; story after story permits us to delve into the terrifying abyss
of the human propensity for self-destruction. Learning that God had
forgiven the Israelites for the sin of idol-worship encourages us to

summon hope, despite all we know about ourselves, that we too might prove worthy of God's presence, whatever we conceive that mystery to mean.

I doubt that we could undertake the work of constructing sacred spaces if we lacked such hope, much less that we could build just societies. Despairing in the face of the world's evil or our own impending death or the death of loved ones, we might lack courage to go on. By recounting in painstaking detail a construction project that joins divine direction to human creativity and initiative, one that results in a sacred space in which God is said to dwell, the Torah seeks to have us realize that sacred order *can* be ours if we work together to create it. The account of what a Community can accomplish is meant to guide us in the realm of ritual as well as in the domain of everyday life, where purity of heart and sincere devotion are much harder to attain.

You *can* be holy, the text assures us repeatedly. Individuals who are aware of their own inadequacy or paralyzed by their failures can never hear this too often. Your flaws and mine do not preclude nobility or achievement. Societies too have the potential to be holy, despite a record of cruelty and injustice that cannot be waived away. The recognition that God is present in the world, and in our lives, should spur us to strive for high achievement.

I have felt the power of a community engaged in common labors, moving to the rhythm of shared ritual practice, and committed to social or political action aimed at making the world more just and compassionate. Such a community can make a discernible impact on the larger society as well as on the lives of its own members. Communities serve as "plausibility structures" (a helpful term coined by sociologist Peter Berger): They render plausible, and perhaps compelling, claims and possibilities that would otherwise seem far-fetched. Communities of this sort become sources of obligation, responsibility, meaning, and mitzvah; vehicles for perceiving and responding to the will of God. They are even more important at moments of doubt or despair that God cares about what we do or that human beings merit God's attention. Seeing yourself or others do acts of justice or mercy can restore faith not just in humanity but in God. Heschel testified to this. "In carrying out a sacred deed we unseal the wells of faith. 'As for me, I shall behold Thy face in righteousness.'" The verse is usually read as referring to acts of righteousness performed by God; Heschel reads the psalm as referring to what *we* do, having been inspired and, perhaps, assisted by God. The "leap of action," the "ecstasy of deeds," can turn a community in the direction of the Holy One.

Fewer individuals in the modern world belong to Communities than in previous eras, and I fear that the assurance I have just described is harder to attain without such social ties. Some people, content with lifestyle enclaves—casual associations for limited purposes—have never experienced the blessings and allure of integral communities. Others—having suffered from the stifling conformity and intolerance of outsiders and dissent that have characterized many integral communities through the ages, and still do in some cases—want nothing more to do with them. If they step through the door, they are careful to leave options open for a quick escape. In my experience, Communities need not be narrowly exclusivist. In fact, they can serve as springboards to broad inclusivity. Concern for neighbors next door or down the block can radiate outward in wider and wider circles of responsibility and felt obligation, embracing other communities and neighborhoods, then an entire society or nation, and finally all of creation on God's earth.

* * * * * *

The communal gift of plausibility is particularly vital to minority religious groups such as Jews, which must struggle to convince members that their beliefs and their existence truly matter in the world. Why should one choose to identify or affiliate with a tiny percentage of the population, in defiance of a majority culture and its values? How can one defy the postmodern axiom that no values matter ultimately and that none is more significant than all, or any, of the others? Judaism once responded to challenges of this magnitude with a claim that God had chosen the Jews for unique obligations under the Covenant. Today, many Jews are inspired by the conviction that no other way of life offers more meaning, greater community, or a surer path to encounter with God. The fact that Jews and Judaism have survived and occasionally thrived for many centuries as a diaspora minority, despite frequent discrimination, oppression, and persecution, is itself cause for pride in being Jewish, and for belief that there must be something worth holding onto in Jewish practice, belief, and identity. The outsized achievement of Jews in America lends further "plausibility" to that claim; so does the renewed existence of a Jewish State in the Land of Israel after two millennia of diaspora, created in the shadow of the Holocaust. Each local Jewish community is part of a network that stretches across the generations and around the globe, a source of pride for many Jews and of hostility by antisemites.

These facts of contemporary Jewish life, which Soloveitchik called a "covenant of fate" binding Jews to one another and to God, are of major theological significance. The covenant at Sinai, according to the Torah's account, created a *people* as well as a *faith community*. The two are inseparable, even if, in the modern period, only a minority of Jews outside the State of Israel engages in rigorous religious observance. A larger number engage in selective observance and testify to some sort of belief in God, though we lack the qualitative evidence to speak with certainty about the nature of that belief or its salience in the lives of those who hold it. The point for me is that contemporary Jews, whatever their religious belief or practice, are impacted by the Sinai covenant. This includes Jews who have chosen to have nothing to do with the Jewish tradition or the Jewish community. All are embraced by the "covenant of fate," and a great many in both Israel and the diaspora choose to have some part in the "covenant of destiny:" doing good, spreading blessing, enhancing life.

How should a person of any religious faith, or none, act responsibly in the face of enormous blessing and imminent threat to life? There seems to be widespread recognition today that individuals, communities, and nations need to take decisive action to protect the planet from global warming, manage a worldwide refugee crisis, and preserve threatened resources—and widespread pessimism about the chances this will occur in time to stave off disaster. For Jews, the first step in obedience to this covenantal mitzvah is to build relationships, communities, and societies powered by love of neighbor and of God.

Loving Neighbors

With these building blocks of relationship and community in place, we can proceed (as the Torah commands) to think about what it might mean to love our neighbors (or fellow humans generally) "as ourselves." There are innumerable Jewish and Christian commentaries on the commandment (Leviticus 19:18), sustained discussions on the nature of love, and debates over whether, or how, love can be commanded. Freud famously pronounced the instruction to love the neighbor misguided (because not everyone deserves our love) and impossible to follow. He took the command as hyperbole that responds to the human propensity to do exactly the opposite. Rabbi Akiba, by contrast, called this mitzvah "a great principle of the Torah." Jesus named it, along with the command to love the Lord with heart, soul, and might, "the most important commandment." Modern Jewish thinkers and preachers, in my experience, have generally talked about love far less often than Christians, perhaps because they also talk much less about God. Their reticence is in keeping with the Bible's aversion to sentimentality and its preference for describing or commanding action rather than motivation or feeling.

I suspect that Jewish reluctance to talk about love might come from centuries of experience with people trying to convert us, by force or persuasion, in the name of love for us or love for God. There is, too, the sad experience of being hurt by friends and family members who say they love us, and perhaps do, but bring us more pain than pleasure. One grows wary of such love and suspicious of its proclamation. And—back to Freud—are all or most of our neighbors near or far really deserving of our love? It's hard enough to *like* many of them much of the time.

Let's stipulate immediately that the Torah recognizes that there is more than one sort of love but considers the various kinds of love to all be closely related. The love that Jacob feels for Rachel is a different sort than the love Leviticus commands us to extend to the neighbor or the stranger. Elsewhere in the Bible, there is the love of close friends, evident in the charged relationship of David and Jonathan. Michal, the daughter of Saul and sister of Jonathan, loves David as well. We are told that all of Israel loves him too. Significantly, the word "love" is *not* used to describe God's mysterious attachment to David, a bond maintained throughout David's life despite his many flaws and crimes. God is said to love the people of Israel. The rabbis, who spoke frequently about that love, daringly interpreted the erotic desire between man and woman that overflows in the Song of Songs, a desire heightened by fantasy and longing, as an allegory for God's love of the people Israel. They attached great importance to the fact that the Torah uses the same word in the commandment to "love your neighbor" as in the commandment to "love YHWH your God with all your heart, all your soul, and all your might" (Deut. 6:5).

Some kabbalists saw the two loves as one: in loving friends and neighbors, we love God and are united with them in a love that is literally divine. Even a straightforward reading of the Torah suggests that each of its various injunctions and paeans to love is related to all the others; at the very least, each influences our thinking about the others. Every instance of love among human beings helps to shape the way we imagine and experience love for and by God. All take place against the background of sober recognition of human foibles and the power of evil inclinations, aspects of the human condition that are especially evident in affairs of the heart. I doubt the Bible could have held millions of readers in its sway for so many centuries and in so many cultures—I know it could not have held me—were its teachings about love less complex or less profound.

It is striking that the Torah asserts no monopoly of insight into love. Indeed, in these chapters of Leviticus more than in others in the Torah, the text seems to address all human beings rather than Israelites alone, thereby inviting all its readers to bring their diverse experiences of love, and reflections upon love, to bear on its interpretation. Biblical scholar Richard Elliot Friedman has demonstrated conclusively that the category of the neighbor includes members of any national group who come into our proximity and not only literal neighbors or members of our own ethnic or religious community. The Torah articulates experiences of love that are universal and personal as much as they are particular and collective. It holds out the possibility for exalted human relationships with every society or culture.

I find it helpful to read Leviticus' command to love in dialogue with the wonderful passage in Plato's *Symposium* in which the goddess Diotima defines love as "the desire to have the good for oneself always." Plato begins with desire: higher and lower, conscious and unconscious. He surely got that right. Note, too, his insistence—also very much in accord with Leviticus—that human beings, at our best, desire not only the people we love but the *good* that we hope to attain through them. We aim to be better than we are. We want our close friends and our partners in life, who know us as we are and love us nonetheless, to help us realize that aspiration. And we want this love to be *forever*. The meaning of that wish varies from person to person and culture to culture. Modern adults, religious or not, want at the very least to walk in a way that is larger than themselves and perhaps everlasting. We want to be connected to, and serve, the very essence of things; to live life with a capital *L*. I want, in addition, to love those I hold close with love that comes to us from the Source of all things and of all life.

However, there is one salient difference between Diotima's definition of love and the understanding of love that one finds in Leviticus. The focus in the latter is not on desire but on *action*. The first half of the verse that commands love of the neighbor forbids taking vengeance or bearing a grudge. Earlier verses in the chapter, enlarging on the general command to "be holy, for I, the Lord your God, am holy," pertain both to ritual obligations of sacrifice and to ethical duties toward the poor, the stranger, and members of one's community or society. We then read: "You shall not insult the deaf, or place a stumbling block before the blind. . . . Judge your kinsmen fairly. Do not deal basely with your countrymen." Immediately following the command to love the neighbor, without any pause whatever, the Torah commands that cattle not be allowed to mate with animals of a different species, fields not be sown with two kinds of seed, and garments made from a mixture of two kinds of material not be worn. These rules—unaccompanied by explanation—are followed by laws concerning forbidden sexual practices and a variety of ethical matters, before returning to love of the stranger and honesty in business dealings. "You shall faithfully observe all My laws and all My rules. I am the Lord."

Jewish commentators have long debated the purpose of these ordinances. The point for me is the Torah's conviction that love is a matter of *behavior*, of action impelled by emotion and empathy, and not of feeling alone. Love does not dwell inside individuals but *between* and *among* them. The syntax of the Hebrew directs love *toward* rather than *at* the neighbor. As always, the Torah focuses on the objective realm that people share and the communities or societies they build together. (This is one answer to the question of how love can be commanded.) Friedman notes that in the known literature of the Ancient Near East, the command to "love the stranger" occurs 52 times—all of them in Leviticus and other priestly passages of the Torah.

To love strangers or neighbors is to treat them in the way that we would want to be treated. This can be done only if we look into ourselves and exercise empathy and sympathy toward others. Israelites can do so, "for you were strangers in the Land of Egypt." Empathy and sympathy—based on understanding that the stranger is like us in fundamental ways—add the subjective component that informs or drives the objective behavior that the text calls loving.

We first learn to love in this way at home, if we are blessed with loving parents, grandparents, or siblings, and we continue to practice love-in-action throughout our lives. As one recent book on marriage states, connecting internal emotion to external behavior, "vulnerability [is] what love is all about . . . yielding control, revealing weakness, embracing imperfection, and opening ourselves up to the possibility of loss."

My experience, echoing what Liz reported in her letter to me, is that marriage and parenting increase the fervor with which one loves. More seems to be at stake. My wife has taught me more about love than anyone else ever did or could, and thankfully offers that instruction daily. Kids are a close second in this respect. One fervently hopes that children will store the love one gives them and share it with others; that they will be good to a degree their parents have never attained; that life will be good to them; and that suffering will not come their way too often. The desire for "always" takes on new meaning when children join parents, friends, and spouses in the congregation of those we love—and quickly overtake all others in their ability to arouse passion, concern, and fear. I remember the terror that seized my wife and me when our daughter was tested for (and thankfully escaped) serious illness. And I will never forget my strong emotional response to Steven Spielberg's movie *Hook*, in which Robin Williams, as a latter-day Peter Pan, rescues his children from the pirates in Neverland. Lest we think the story simply a fairy tale, one of the Lost Boys on the ship is killed in a life-like battle. I cried all the way home from the theater.

Somehow everything matters more with kids at home, including the communities of which one is a member. Relationships are more fraught. Love is fiercer and more prone to jealousy. We give more as parents than we ever thought we had or could. We also hold back in surprising ways. Our anger may grow stronger, commensurate with how much we fear to lose or damage. Sex takes on new urgency when one hopes it will result in children or it has done so in the recent past. Wrapped in each other's arms or inside each other's bodies, lovers powerfully experience what it means to create and sustain life with a person who is otherwise distinct and perhaps very different. Having had children, and so bearing responsibility for a new generation, we love friends, partners, and parents (as well as siblings, grandparents, and other family members) differently than we did before. Life takes on added immediacy and texture.

We would not be the people we are, and Leviticus would not speak to us half as powerfully about love, if our behavior was flawless or we were not plagued by insecurity and self-deception, subject to desires that sometimes impel us to do good and at other moments to do the opposite of good. But here we are, sometimes causing pain to others and especially to those we love, and at other times doing all we can to ease pain, risking all to protect those we love as well as the fact of love itself. Love may not last. It may be betrayed. Friendships grow or lessen in intensity over time as friends move in and out of sync with one another. Marriages feel the multiple strains of shrinking areas of shared interest; tensions born of care for parents and children; burdens, distortions, and scars left from previous relationships; deficiencies of character; and the inevitable loss of passion to routine and time. Our love for spouses and parents rarely lacks deep ambivalence, and love for children, too, is rarely pure, that is, unmixed with fear and anger. Only occasionally do we attain that ideal state, freed for a moment of the baggage of mixed experiences with love from childhood, adolescence, and adult relationships. Occasionally, amid blessed normality, love may enable us to find real peace.

All these features of love for neighbors and friends, as we shall see in the following section of this essay, inevitably inform believers' notions of love for God. At this point I want to note the parallels—and tensions—between the command in the Holiness Code of Leviticus to love our neighbors as ourselves and the injunctions and laws presented in the Covenant Code of Exodus. The more that behavior moves outward from the inner circles of family and neighbor to wider circles of community, society, state, and world, the greater the emphasis on objective action and the less on inner feeling. Love gives way to justice, compassion, and respect for human dignity. The Covenant Code legislation seeks to govern everyday life in real-world communities and societies. Leviticus, as one might expect from the lexicon of love and holiness, is both more aspirational and more interested in the emotional content of human relationships. The former orders bonds that are more stable and less intense than the latter. In Buber's terms, "I-It" prevails over "I-Thou," and thankfully so, for if it were otherwise, institutions would collapse and predictability vanish.

Together, the two sections of the Torah teach that interaction with fellow human beings is not a zero-sum game: if I win, you lose, and vice versa. Conflict and competition among individuals and societies can be managed through good intentions and proper restraints. Both covenant and love are capable of overcoming barriers created by difference; indeed both are sometimes made stronger by that difference.

Like holiness, love thrives inside a well-defined covenantal order of permissions and restrictions. It must be practiced over and over, and even then we may not get it right. We keep trying; as we go through life, there are rituals to be observed, sanctuaries and institutions to be built and maintained, struggles to be fought for good, and communities to be tended carefully. The creation of a just and compassionate society depends on baby steps and giant steps alike. One wants to do right by family and friends and to leave the world better than we found it. Both goals, for a religious person, are part and parcel of what it means to love and serve the Lord our God.

Loving God

As difficult as it is to secure agreement on what it means to love our neighbors, it is infinitely more difficult to know what it could mean for a human being to "love the Lord your God," let alone to do so "with all your heart, all your soul, and all your might" (Deut. 6:5). A theologian who is humble about giving voice to the Unsayable must be especially cautious about joining the verb "love" to the object "God" in a sentence that has a human being, or a group of human beings, as its subject. We learn about loving God from reflection on the complicated experience of loving neighbors, friends, and family, and we must be alert to differences between the two.

I am reminded of the Hasidic story in which a man assures his friend that he loves him, but when asked "What do I need?" confesses that he does not know. "How can you love me if you don't know what I need?" asks the friend. Heschel was convinced that Moses and the other biblical prophets, in addition to intuiting God's will, had "sympathy for the divine pathos." In other words, they felt God's pain at the suffering of God's children and God's "need" for human assistance in easing that suffering. It is a daring claim. If a prophet cannot presume to know God as God is and is unable to behold God's glory, what could it mean to have more than an inkling of God's pathos? But if a prophet—or anyone else—does not know God's "need" for humanity, how shall they follow the command—

and the inestimable blessing—to love God?

Not being a prophet, I'm reassured by the fact that two of the greatest rabbinic sages interpreted that command to mean something that human beings *can* understand and achieve. Akiba believed that he fulfilled the command to love God with all his heart, soul, and might when, as we have seen, he gave his life for the teaching of God's Torah. Ishmael believed that he fulfilled the command to love God by loving his neighbor as himself. Rabbi Meir taught that sages showed love for God by studying God's Torah day and night for its own sake. This too makes intuitive sense. You want to understand and fulfill the wishes of those whom you love and who love you. One abides in that love by walking on the path that it marks out, loving with the supply of love that originates with God. Feminist theologian Catherine Keller expressed it this way: "The difference made" in one's world because of the love received from another "*is* the return [for love]—not to the giver as such but to the world the giver loves . . . Actualizing the radiance, we too radiate . . . not giving *back*. But giving *forth*."

Akiba's willingness to die for God, to teach God's Torah even at the price of his life, is analogous to the readiness of otherwise unheroic parents to run into a burning building to save their children or to trade places with them in the operating room. We often express love for our friends by caring for their children, giving generously to causes they hold dear, or teaching lessons they have taught us. There is no way to think about the unknown other than to reason from what we know to what we do not know. That is doubly true with respect to God, whom we yearn to know well but never will. Simile and metaphor are everywhere in the vocabulary of faith, and nowhere satisfactory. God is God, and we are human. We have no choice but to think about God in terms of human relationships, including those that go badly or in which the longing of one partner is not reciprocated by the other. No one is easy to live with all the time. We ourselves are not always easy to be around. I understand from experience the rabbis' plea that we not give up on bringing God near, even after repeated frustration of our desire for intimacy with God. A literary scholar of the rabbinic corpus has noted that of all the characters who appear in those texts, God is the most difficult to pin down. The experience with God reported by the rabbis was rarely easy.

At times humanity's vexed relationship to God, as described in Jewish texts, seems to resemble an arranged marriage. God had selected Abraham's descendants as partners to the Covenant and is not eager to start over with another clan. Neither party is entirely happy with the other but over time they grow accustomed to the alliance. Inevitably, there are ups and downs in the relationship; divorce, however, is unthinkable. The rabbis liked to imagine that the two parties to the Sinai marriage contract called Torah chose one another freely. God tried out other options, but every nation except Israel declined to accept the terms set forth. The Children of Israel could have declined God's offer but said yes even before hearing the details of the agreement. Both God and Israel needed partners; neither wanted to be alone in the world.

This set of metaphors too speaks powerfully to me. Indeed, the variety of marital arrangements today—including serial monogamy, same-sex or nonbinary relationships, and long-term partnerships that are never sanctified or legalized with a religious or civil union—may expand theological reflection about the variety of human relations with the divine. Love for friends and lovers waxes and wanes, and so too does relationship with God. My understanding of love for my wife has evolved over decades, and the love itself has changed shape; so too has my thinking about God's nature as person or force for good, ground of goodness, doer of good, Holy One, or Creator of Worlds. Every love is characterized by alternating distance and proximity. One party hides when the other seeks—I've done my share of both—or both hide simultaneously, or seek where the other is not to be found. Wonder of wonders, they might meet for a moment or join for a lifetime and together create a new life or a new world.

I'm trying here to follow the Torah's encouragement, in God's name, to perform the seemingly impossible exercise of empathy with God. Perhaps Moses had to strike down the Egyptian taskmaster whom he saw beating an Israelite slave to prepare himself for a process of liberation in which many people—Israelites as well as Egyptians—would die at the hands of God as well as at his own command. The Israelites take the bones of Joseph with them when they leave Egypt as Joseph had requested before he died, thereby experiencing what it means to fulfill a promise made long ago, at the very moment that God fulfills the promise of deliverance made to Abraham. Only because you and I have the experience of love, multiple experiences of love, can we hope to grasp what it might mean to love God or to be loved by God.

Franz Rosenzweig—who placed the commands to love God and love the neighbor together at the very center of the careful literary architecture of his magnum opus, *The Star of Redemption*—helped my understanding of that mystery greatly by explaining how love of God or human partners can be commanded. Only one person can *command* my love: the Lover who loves me, and cries out, in the passion of that love, "Love me!" This is what God does, according to Rosenzweig. God loves humanity first by *creating* it and the world, and renewing creation daily. (Rosenzweig was not interested in the attempt to reconcile scientific accounts of the Big Bang with the opening chapters of Genesis, and never clarifies the specifics of what he means by creation.) God's love continues in the *revelation* to human beings that we have been created in God's image. There is point and purpose to human existence! We are not the accidental consequence of molecular interactions that might just as easily—indeed, far more easily—never have occurred. We can do good, and life can be good. We therefore have good reason to hope that someday, in ways unimaginable and unthinkable to us, God will *redeem* humanity and the world.

I believe—as I move past the age of seventy, savoring friendships that have lasted half a century, a marriage of forty-plus years, relations with children in their thirties, and now two grandchildren—that whenever you and I love, we love because of love ultimately planted in us by God. It is hard to state such a truth more precisely (Rosenzweig tried in *The Star*), and utterly impossible to prove its veracity. I think about it this way. If those who raised us had not showered us with love, it would be difficult for us to give love to others. The same is true for each generation that draws on love stored up from childhood experiences; ultimately, as the Torah speculates, love shown by primal ancestors had its source in love bestowed by God. Love could not have made its way to us if God's love were not ever-present in the world, in our communities, and in our families. Because we do love, however imperfectly, we can be confident God's love is present, like the central seam of the *tallit* in which I drape myself when I pray. If that seam frays, the *tallit* falls apart; the fact that the *tallit* holds together bears witness to the integrity of the seam.

Love is the connective tissue linking us to God—and via God, to one another. One can imagine it as a sort of umbilical cord that has nourished humanity from the infancy of the race and continues to do so ever after. We experience the gift of that love repeatedly. It is very much present, not at all past. "Blessed are You, Who gives the Torah." "Blessed are you, Who loves Israel." These praises and many others are offered in present tense.

Several years ago, I began to translate the Hebrew particle *et* in the command to "love the Lord your God" (*ve'ahavta et Adonai elohekha*) not as the necessary preface to a direct object but in the other sense in which the word is used throughout the Torah (and in an adjacent chapter of Deuteronomy). *Et* also can mean "with." "Love *with* the Lord your God."

The seven blessings traditionally recited under a Jewish wedding canopy resound with that connection, making God a part of the ceremony as we celebrate a love of which God has been an integral part. All that exists, we declare, has been created by God to circulate God's *kavod* (glory, presence, honor, dignity, weightiness) among ourselves and then back to God. Human beings are fashioned in God's own image, enabling us to be loving, creative partners for good. Zion—a symbol for the community to which bride and groom belong—rejoices at their happiness. "May God grant joy to these loving companions" (*re'im*: literally, "neighbors," the word used in Lev. 19:18) and "perfect joy stored since the Garden of Eden. Praised are You, YHWH our God, who created joy and gladness, bride and groom, love and harmony." At that moment under the wedding canopy, family and friends fervently share the couple's desire to have the good for themselves always. Each wants only to cleave to this partner, as God promised the first couple would do; inchoately, perhaps, one wants to cleave to the Source of enveloping love as well. Hasidism pronounced this cleaving (*devekut*) one of the greatest of human virtues.

I think we love *with* God whenever we love, and never more than when we love our children. Because we love with God, we can do so, at our best, with *all* our heart (meaning: with emotion as well as intelligence), *all* our soul (however one understands this spiritual faculty and life force), and *all* our might (ability, energy, will). This is what the Torah commands us to teach our children morning and evening—not only by drilling them in recitation of the words but by demonstrating what is it to love. Immediately before these verses in the Torah, we encounter the declaration that the rabbis made the credo of Jewish faith, recited by observant Jews morning and evening and, if one can, at the moment of death. Of all the attributes the Torah could have chosen to characterize God in this "Hear O Israel!" passage, the one selected and urged upon us is that God is One. *Ehad.* Unique. This form of address is supremely personal, even colloquial. "Listen, Israelite! God is One." I suggest, as the mystics did centuries ago, that God's oneness makes possible the "all-ness" of our love— heart, mind, soul, and might—and the ability of human beings to love with all our *assembled* hearts and minds: all our *diversely faithful* souls, all our *collective* might, all our wisdom and knowledge, all our experience, all our arts and sciences, and all that we can learn from hummingbirds and blades of grass.

These loves are made possible by God's oneness. We can love our neighbors as we love ourselves because God loves them and us. We can give all of ourselves to a few people whom we love with special intensity and constancy and still have enough for the others we love, because the supply available is not finite. We can love human fellows and the world and still have love for God, Who (the Torah assures us and experience may confirm) wants to be loved in that way. The prayer book we use in my synagogue on the High Holidays contains a poem that in part reads: "My God/open windows within me/to let the world enter/calmly and peacefully . . . the world that I love/cry over/and love again and again."

That prayer sits side by side in my consciousness with a far more prosaic memory. A younger me half a century ago, fearing commitment and self-disclosure, combines prayer, hope, and resolve as I drive home from a date that did not go very well and pay grateful homage to the Beatles. "Hey, Jew," they call to me. Take the sad song of the world and your own loneliness and make it better. Don't hang back; let the world—and this woman you like a lot—under your skin. Then you'll begin to make it better. There are moments when the older (and perhaps wiser) me wants to direct the same song, the same plea, to God. Please come closer, I urge. Don't hang back. Help us all to make things better!

Creatures who are created in God's image cannot help but imagine God in our own image sometimes, ever aware of how inadequate those images are, and humbled by the inadequacy of our love. Nevertheless: we do love. Grounded in love and grateful for life and one another, human beings exercise care for others and ourselves every day. We also demonstrate concern for the many people and things we do *not* love—whether because we do not know them, or do not care for them as much as we care for others, or disagree profoundly with what they say or do, especially what they say or do in the name of God. All this love and respect are ultimately made possible by love from God, I believe. This is one way that God is close by, as the Torah puts it: "not in the heavens or across the sea" but as near as "our mouth and heart." Under our skin. And this is the major way that human beings express love for God and obey the command to love God, heart soul and might.

* * * * * *

I want to share one final thought on the matter of loving God, prompted by the fact that the command to do so is often paired in the Torah with the command to be "in awe of God." For good reason the term *yir'ah* is often translate as "fear." There cannot *not* be an element of fear in the relation of a frail and imperfect mortal to the everlasting God, Sovereign of the universe, Creator of heaven and earth, and Judge of the truth of all that is, including us. The word "awe" nonetheless seems to me a more accurate description of the complex set of emotions and behaviors that human beings exhibit and experience, or should exhibit and experience, in God's presence. The word "reverence" captures some of what is needed, as long as the word does not connote standing at a deferential emotional distance. The meaning of *yir'ah* is clarified when one meets people, religious or not, in whom *yir'ah* is utterly lacking: individuals convinced that they don't need God's love or anyone else's, or that God loves them just as they are and does not want them to change. Their God does not hold them accountable or responsible for anything. Buber said of these people that "[h]e who begins with the love of God without having previously experienced the fear of God, loves an idol which he himself has made, a god whom it is easy enough to love. He does not love the real God who is, to begin with, dreadful [that is, Who elicits dread] and incomprehensible."

That judgment of the matter seems right to me. There is a balance to be struck, which, like anything worthwhile, requires sustained effort and schooling through experience. Armed with an enduring sense of God's love, awed by God's majesty, humbled and empowered by God's grace, and blessed with the love of family and friends, a person can do a lot of good.

Mitzvah

Whenever I taught American college students what Buber and Heschel wrote about the good that should come of relationship to the Eternal Thou or the "God [Who is] in search of man," I was asked why these thinkers needed to talk about God so much when what they really cared about was ethics. Couldn't one be a good person without believing in God or believing that, in doing good, one was obeying the will of God? Indeed, some students added—not knowing that their question had been raised by the rabbis in the Talmud and articulated forcefully by Moses Maimonides and Immanuel Kant—wasn't it more ethical to do something because it was right and *not* because the Creator who might judge you after death told you to do it?

Yes, I'd reply, one could certainly be ethical without being religious; but no, Buber and Heschel did not *decide* to bring God into their thinking about ethics. Rather they responded to God's overwhelming presence in their lives. The existence of the divine call was not in doubt for them, so the question they faced was how to answer God's summons appropriately. Buber would have agreed with Heschel's avowal that a person can only stammer in response to an encounter with God. No words are adequate. Only our *lives* can begin to be "the spelling of an answer."

Most of us have not been graced by dramatic encounters with an overwhelming presence of God. Nor have we received an unimpeachable divine call to action. I-Thou relationships with human beings do not often serve as a "portal" to an encounter with the Eternal Thou. My students, like many others, have at most experienced occasional "signals of transcendence:" a fleeting vision on a particularly starry night of oneness with the universe; a not-to-be forgotten glimpse, in the midst of a forest of redwoods, of unity with all of nature; or a sudden piercing of the veil of mystery at the sound of a random passage in a Beethoven sonata or at the sight of a stroke of yellow in a painting by Van Gogh. The students perhaps detected God's work in acts of kindness, creativity, or courage that they had witnessed; or when, performing such acts, they discerned divinity in themselves. Usually they labeled these experiences (and therefore referred to themselves) as "spiritual, but not religious." The concept of God did not fit easily in their vocabulary.

I was relieved to find that the concept of *mitzvah* was much more accessible to them, and I have since learned that this is the case for many contemporary American Jews of all ages. Mitzvah enjoys especially widespread understanding when the word is pronounced with a short "i," and the stress is placed on the first syllable, a borrowing from Yiddish that has made its way into the lexicon of many non-Jewish Americans. (The Hebrew pronunciation places the accent on the second syllable and pronounces the first with a hard "e".)

American Jews (and many non-Jews too) understand mitzvah to be a good deed, the sort of generous act that you know you should do more often, like giving charity, visiting the sick or comforting a mourner. People whom we call good perform a lot of mitzvahs.

There are the sort of actions enumerated in the blessings that, according to Jewish tradition, are to be recited each morning. A crucial element in all of these blessings—part of the rabbis' aim in having us say them daily—is that they greet us where we are (in this case, waking up from sleep) and endow that moment, in that place, with ultimate meaning. In many cases, significance is bestowed on physical actions that are performed as a matter of course, without thinking. Having been awakened by the sound of a rooster, literally or figuratively, one blesses God for giving a rooster the wisdom to distinguish day from night. Opening our eyes, we thank God for giving sight to the blind. Putting on clothes, we thank God for clothing the naked. Stretching, we bless God for releasing those who are bound and raising those who are bowed down, and so forth.

The point of reciting these blessings each morning is twofold. First, they instruct us to be thankful: that is, to regard aspects of everyday existence that we might otherwise take for granted as blessings given to us by God. In this way we learn, as my father did when he awoke from a coma as a teenager, to see God's presence where we might not have noticed it. "There is God in this place," Jacob said upon awakening from his dream, "and I did not know." Now we do know (a matter of faith, of course, and not of cognition or proof). We cannot rationally explain the matter and cannot empirically see the divine glory, but we recognize that God is, in some sense and in some way, present in our world, and we feel a need to act accordingly.

Second, we are taught to see ourselves and everyone else as a potential partner in creating the world as God would like it to be. The rabbis understood the commandment to "be holy, for the Lord your God is holy" this way: As God clothes the naked, so you should; as God frees those who are oppressed, so you should. The core of their theology—and mine—is that God clothes the naked at least in part by *our doing so.* God strengthens people with courage by means of other people whom they see acting courageously. God "brings forth bread from the earth"—the words in Judaism's prescribed blessing before meals—by means of sustained and varied human effort.

I am not saying that God acts *only* by means of human beings or that we act *only* with potency supplied by God. We cannot know the truth of the matter in either case. Not infrequently, however, we see ourselves or people we know performing feats of courage or kindness of which we or they would otherwise not have been capable, and we attribute the added capacity to divine assistance. At other moments, we see extraordinary altruism and self-sacrifice on the part of people who do *not* believe in God; some of them may resent the notion that any force other than their own was involved. I have no wish to convince them of the opposite view. Thankfulness is a virtue, whether or not God plays a role; whatever one's belief or lack of belief, the hungry need to be fed and the oppressed set free. God's part in helping the poor and the oppressed is not demonstrable in any case. I too do not witness it; rather, I witness *to* it.

Belief in a dual covenant that joins us to God as well as fellow human beings is fundamental to my view of the world. It is a core truth without which Jewish commitment would lose its driving force and *raison d'être*. Covenant is the key to the structure of the Torah, the central message of the prophets, and the guiding principle of the rabbis. Living up to the demands and possibilities of covenant—walking the way of mitzvah—is a task that fills my life with meaning, from the time I wake up in the morning to the moment I put my head on the pillow at night.

I have learned from study as well as experience that the word "mitzvah" means far more than "good deed" or "commandment" (the most common translations). Even in the Torah, the term also connotes obligation, responsibility, instruction, and duty performed out of love. Not all individual mitzvot are distinctive to Judaism, but the constellation of mitzvot and the set of meanings they carry *do* distinguish Jews from other communities. I am especially enamored of a Hasidic etymology that derives the word "mitzvah" from *be-tsavta* (together). Mitzvot are actions that we perform together with Jewish or human neighbors and—indirectly, inexplicably, and never demonstrably—with God. Some Jewish authorities throughout the centuries have insisted that there is only one valid source of authority for the mitzvot—God's will—and only one legitimate reason for performing mitzvot—obedience to God's will. Thankfully, others (and most notably, Maimonides) have disagreed, citing reasons for the commandments that include inculcating or expressing fundamental principles of faith; schooling Jews in right conduct; keeping the inclination to evil in check; ordering communities, societies, and states; enforcing the rule of just law; and eliciting compassion and love.

The latter approach is convincing and necessary for the project of covenant in our time. God needs human partners who use their intelligence and exercise initiative; human beings now, more than ever, want to know that there are good reasons for doing what we do. The German-Jewish philosopher Hermann Cohen wrote at the start of the twentieth century that ethical commandments are the heart of Judaism and make it the quintessential "religion of reason." Emmanuel Levinas, an influential French Jewish philosopher who wrote in the shadow of the Holocaust, held that ethical behavior not only is the primary commandment that governs human life but is the purpose of religion, indeed the meaning of God. Heschel, who wrote in the same period, awarded great weight to other types of mitzvot as well, believing that the Torah and God encompass more than ethics alone. The three thinkers agreed that Judaism is inconceivable without the covenant and its mitzvot. You and I are here to make the world more just and compassionate.

* * * * * *

In the spirit of inquiry into what Jewish tradition calls the reasons for the mitzvot—and curious about what contemporary Jews regard as the source of authority for their own performance of mitzvot—I asked hundreds of American and Canadian Jews those questions during my tenure as Chancellor of JTS. I arranged for frank discussion of the topic among thousands more. Not surprisingly, the reasons for performance, non-performance, or active avoidance of mitzvot varied enormously. Contemporary Jews recognize more than one source of authority for mitzvah. Some cited the Torah, revelation at Sinai, or rabbinic law codes compiled through the centuries. Others said they respond to demands of conscience, perform duties owed to parents, or obey the authority of tradition. I will not soon forget an all-night study session on the holiday of Shavuot when a prominent member of my congregation, a man who loved to fish, said he would not eat the "creepy, crawling things at the bottom of the ocean" that are prohibited by the dietary laws of the Torah. Why? "Because they are inherently disgusting," he said.

An older woman to whom my family was close said she learns what is right and wrong—which mitzvot to follow and which can be ignored—by listening to her conscience. "No God in the picture?" I asked. "No," she replied without hesitation. No God at all. Innumerable contemporary Jews strive to live up to a high ethical standard without reference to the language of mitzvah. They believe the term only makes sense if there is a divine commander, which, for them, there is not.

The source of authority for mitzvot is not singular or straightforward and probably never has been. Jewish commentaries and law codes aplenty testify to that fact. So does the behavior of contemporary Jews. I think back to the decision that some of my parents' friends made in June 1967 to take out second mortgages on their homes so that they could send money to Israel at its time of need. They were not particularly religious people. I do not know whether they believed in God and doubt that, if they did, they acted in obedience to a divine commandment. I do know that they felt responsible to stand with the Jewish community and the Jewish people, and my guess is that part of what motivated them and many other Jews to support Israel in this way—22 years after the end of the Holocaust—was the commitment captured in the slogan, "Never again!" The same resolve motivated many Jews to play active roles in the campaign soon after to free Soviet Jewry. Jewish history and felt obligation to community have long served as powerful drivers of mitzvah and continue to do so today. I suspect that these motives were operative when Jews in the Diaspora as well as in Israel responded to the Hamas attack in October 2023 with an outpouring of generosity and support. The sense of mitzvah, for many Jews, does not depend on the existence or revelation of a divine commander.

Theologian Irving Greenberg touched a nerve among Jews when he declared, around the time of the Soviet Jewry movement, that even if God had reneged on the Sinai covenant by allowing so many Jews to be murdered in the Holocaust, Jews should continue to observe the terms of the partnership. I don't know about the God side of that claim, but Greenberg's point about the human side makes a great deal of sense to me. The mitzvot remain in force, Holocaust or no Holocaust. A rabbi cited in the Talmud said it best when he quoted God as declaring, "If they abandon Me, let them at least continue to observe My mitzvot."

I imagine that rabbi walking by the ruins of the Temple in Jerusalem, despairing of the Messiah arriving any time soon and perhaps—like me and many other Jews of our day—feeling God's absence far more keenly than God's presence. At moments of darkest depression, he may have doubted that God was in the universe at all and wondered if there was a reason to get up in the morning, let alone to study Torah or do good deeds. But he did get up each day, recited the dawn blessings prescribed by *halakhah*, and—in accord with that same law—performed the mitzvot of clothing the naked and raising up those who are oppressed. He recognized that because he did these things, his time that day was well spent. If he did them every day, he would die knowing that his life had been worthwhile.

One would probably find broad agreement among secular as well as religious Americans, Jews and non-Jews alike, that service to others is the key to a worthwhile life. Resistance to seeing this pattern for living well as a divine command is likewise widespread. Nonbelievers of course reject the notion of obligation to a Higher Power, but believers sometimes practice evasion when God seeks their help. Adam and Eve were the first in a long line of human beings to duck the "Where are you?" question from their Creator. Most of us occasionally hide from friends or family members whose presence or need summons us to responsibility. In "My Fair Lady," Eliza Doolittle's father sings,

"The Lord above made man to help his neighbor, but with a little bit of luck, when he comes around you won't be home."

I thought about that line after my wife and I had our first child and I realized at about the same time that I had to care for my aging parents instead of relying on them to care for me. I didn't particularly want to get up in the middle of the night to see why our daughter was crying (*"You go this time. No, you go. It's your turn. Okay."*), nor did I relish flying across the country when my parents needed my help (or, as often occurred, when they protested that they would be fine, don't come, no need for me to worry about them.) I did both not only out of duty but with motivation that was one part obligation with an equal part love. Liz articulated this sense of mitzvah eloquently in her letter to me. As a co-creator of new life, I found myself accepting greater responsibility to the parents who had given me life. Whatever the reason, the mitzvah to honor them—the fifth of the Ten Commandments—took on new meaning. I came to regard my relation to the Creator of all life—senior Partner to the Covenant—differently as well.

Some people seem never to be there when you need them. Journalist Michael Pollan reports that he found widespread agreement among contemporary Americans that *the self* is what matters most and is the measure of what is most important in the world. The sentiment is common among "sovereign selves" who take the notion of autonomy to an extreme that would have been anathema to Kant. "No one can tell me what I should do as far as Jewish observance goes," several dozen American Jews insisted in the late 1990s during interviews for *The Jew Within*. No one had the right to dictate the rights and wrongs of ritual or ethical practice: not their parents or their rabbi or their spouse. They would do what gave them pleasure or meaning at the moment (as long as it did not directly harm others), and if not, not. A prospective mitzvah had to pass muster before that high bar or they would not engage in it. What is more, I learned, they not only believed strongly that it was their *right* to make such decisions, and not just a fact of life in a free society, but that it would have been *wrong* of them *not* to choose in this way. It would be wrong to defer to community, custom, family tradition, or religious prescription.

Sovereign selves who exhibit this degree of opposition to authority—some would call it narcissism—stand at one end of a spectrum on which we find, at the opposite end, people who try to love their neighbors as themselves. Fulfillment of that mitzvah, as we have seen, requires stepping out of oneself enough to feel unreserved empathy or sympathy for others. Treat the stranger well because you have been a stranger, the Torah commands. You know what it is like. Leviticus— the book of the Torah in which we are commanded to love our neighbors—asserts that the earth is God's, not ours. We are all temporary residents in God's territory, here only for a short time. God loves strangers, and so, therefore, should we. Our lives are on loan from God, and so are the lives of all the children—ours and God's—for whom we care. The same is true of the time at our disposal. None of these belongs entirely to us to do with as we please.

For some individuals, this conviction carries import that is utterly concrete. I recently heard a rabbinical student who is a recovering alcoholic express the belief that "the ego and God cannot coexist." The aim for an addict in recovery, he declared, is not self-actualization, or any other ambition of the modern self, but survival. "There is no cure, only one reprieve and then another." The student was expounding upon Leviticus, which teaches that human beings cannot earn the right to exist on earth. We are not owed anything by God or by life. Gratitude for life drives one to perform good deeds—indeed, for a recovering alcoholic, that attitude makes life possible. Twelve-step programs demonstrate to their participants that one cannot make it alone. A supportive group of loving neighbors is required, along with a loving Higher Power.

* * * * * *

Honest advocates of mitzvah and community are duty bound to acknowledge that sovereign selves are given good reasons for protecting autonomy and options at all costs by vocal religious authorities who value obedience and conformity far more than individual creativity or human dignity. All too many religious communities place more emphasis on keeping people out than bringing people in. This drives some individuals to be suspicious of all authority and to keep a safe distance from any community; stepping into such a community on a trial basis, they may retreat at the first sign that individual freedom is being curtailed and individual opinion is not valued. I have never been subject to repressive religious authorities, in part because I have been privileged with gender, skin color, education, and relative affluence, all of which afford a measure of security against discrimination and unwanted intrusion. (My parents, and the schools they chose for me, also deserve a lot of the credit.). These advantages no doubt account, at least in part, for my attraction to the balance of communal direction and individual initiative that the covenant describes and requires. Reason and experience have persuaded me that the Torah is wise to see the building of the wilderness tabernacle as one that Israelites build *together*.

Ideally, that will be true of all the communal structures in which we live together today. Construction of a good society—a task that must be repeated as humanity in all its varieties of situation and purpose proceeds through history—relies upon coordination of the diverse skills, knowledge, and gifts of all members of the community. This takes leaders who not only know the territory (Moses called on the expertise of his father-in-law for that guidance) but know how to marshal the initiative and commitment of the group's diverse members to serve the collective good. The success of democracies such as America seems to depend upon the conviction on the part of the great majority of their citizens that the trade-off between individual freedom and communal good is worthwhile.

The students to whom I taught the notion of mitzvah would inevitably ask at a certain point where they should begin to practice this life if they should decide to do so. What was most important? What would do the most good? I would emphasize that observance of the commandments has never been an all-or-nothing proposition. One should not be scared away from mitzvah by fear of not living up to its high standard. Most of the 613 mitzvot enumerated in traditional law codes are not observable by most Jews today in any case. The sages would never say this, but some mitzvot are more pressing than others, depending on context and circumstances. When I met Heschel in 1971, he asked me where I was from and, upon hearing the answer, solemnly declared that "the number one religious issue of our time is not the number of kosher butchers in Philadelphia. It is to end the war in Vietnam."

Several years earlier, responding to Israelis who emphasized the sacredness of the Land of Israel above all other Jewish values, Heschel wrote pointedly that "our imperishable homeland is in God's time. We enter God's time through the gate of sacred deeds [mitzvot]. . . . The great sacred deed for us today is to build the land of Israel." To me, that remains a mitzvah for Jews today, as Israelis and Palestinians seek a way forward after the devastation that took place in the fall of 2023. Performance of mitzvot in Israel is not restricted, as it often is in diaspora, to the private sphere of home, school, and synagogue. Jewish sovereignty and majority status make possible new scope for fulfilling the covenant and loving neighbors, including non-Jewish neighbors. The challenge is to bring healthcare policy in line with the guidelines of Torah, as well as educational policy, foreign policy, and the conduct of war—while at the same time respecting the human and civil rights of Palestinians and other minorities and democratically enacting the conviction that every human being bears the divine image. The state is theologically significant for another reason as well. With half of the world's Jews now residing within its borders, Israel helps to guarantee the survival of the Jewish people, without which there is no future for Judaism.

What is the "number one religious issue of our time"? In my view, as I indicated earlier, the answer is unquestionably proper stewardship of the planet so that it remains inhabitable for humanity and other living creatures. My fear, as I contemplate the terrifying prospect of failure to undertake that effort, is not divine encroachment on human freedom but the inability or unwillingness of human beings to assume the responsibility laid on Adam and Eve in the Garden of Eden to "tend and preserve" the Earth that we have been given. Human hands are not tied by God or fate. The problem is that, despite being free and having immense scientific knowledge at our disposal, we do not always know what to do and cannot bring ourselves, our governments, and one another to do the right thing once we figure out what it is. It was not clear during the COVID-19 pandemic how to balance reasonable desires to preserve jobs, protect livelihoods, and keep schools open, with the need to avoid or minimize the devastation wrought by the transmission of the virus through horrific rates of sickness, hospitalization, and death. If humanity should somehow secure agreement on what should be done to mitigate the effects of climate change, one cannot be sure that we would marshal the will to do it. Current prospects are not good.

"The day is short and the work [is] great," the rabbis taught. That has never been truer than it is today. Were the situation not so urgent, one might draw comfort from the fact that fidelity to covenant is never a straightforward matter. It is never clear how a society, community, family, or individual should prioritize the various mitzvot that we are called upon to perform. Energy and resources are always limited and triage always required. The Torah rarely dictates specifics of law or government policy (which in our day must be determined democratically in any case). However, the Torah always offers guidance that cannot be ignored by Jews faithful to the covenant, and points the way for anyone, of any faith or people, who is determined to obey the command to choose blessing, choose good, and choose life. That guidance is sorely needed right now.

Of one thing I am certain as I consider humanity's current prospects: puppets on a string are the very opposite of what God wants or needs from human beings. The poet Denise Levertov expressed my experience of the matter well:

> Something is very gently,
> invisibly, silently,
>   pulling at me—a thread
> or net of threads
> ... Not fear
> but a stirring

of wonder makes me
catch my breath when I feel
the tug of it when I thought
it had loosened itself
  and gone.

* * * * * *

When will the love and mitzvot of many centuries finally result in a world that is just and compassionate? Will redemption ever come or, at least, greater clarity on how to cope in the meantime? Consider the difficult ending to the well-known talmudic story in which Moses and God are together at the top of Mount Sinai. Moses asks why God is not ready to give him the Torah. God replies that there still is work to be done on the little curlicues or crowns that adorn the letters in the scroll (rendered as "jots and tittles" by the King James Bible). Someday, God tells Moses, a learned rabbi named Akiba would develop reams of interpretations based on those bits of calligraphy. Moses asks God if he can be transported through time to see Rabbi Akiba at work. God agrees, and Moses finds himself in Akiba's academy. The sage is teaching his students Torah, and Moses is dismayed that he does not understand a word Akiba is saying! The prophet is comforted when Akiba tells the students that Moses is the source of everything he is teaching them.

The rabbis write tongue in cheek, of course, and we smile at the story because we recognize its truth. Were Moses to visit our academies, accompanied perhaps by Akiba, and joined by sages and teachers from as recently as a generation or two ago, the group would be surprised to find women studying to be rabbis, halakhic decisions concerning artificial intelligence and genome editing, and legal reasoning that draws on conceptual developments not available to earlier interpreters. We, the teachers in these academies, would say, sincerely and correctly, that we learned the Torah that we teach by drawing out implications inherent in the original text. Some of our readings might be more convincing than others; some derive more directly from precedent and others less so. This was no less true of rabbinic readings two millennia ago. Like the rabbis of old, we cite multiple sources, legal and non-legal; and as the authors of later sections of the Five Books of Moses that relied on earlier sources, we are selective in our citations. One passage in the Torah or the Talmud trumps another that we find less relevant or convincing. We adopt one teaching from Maimonides or the Baal Shem Tov, but not every teaching by these or other thinkers. Only in this way does the Torah live as a guide to life rather than as a historical or literary artifact.

But the story of Moses in Akiba's academy does not end where I just left it. Having asked to be shown Akiba at work, and having seen him teaching Torah, Moses asks to be shown Akiba's reward—and sees him being executed by the Romans. "This is Torah, and this is its reward!" Moses exclaims to God in protest. "Be silent," God replies firmly. "This is the way that I have determined it."

The rabbis who told this story knew that Akiba had in fact been executed in a cruel manner by the Romans. His execution was historical fact and not a midrash. They also believed, as Akiba did, that such a thing could not happen in the world unless God allowed it to happen. God had surrendered the world to idolatrous human beings who often did terrible things to one another: the very opposite of the justice and compassion God had intended. It made no sense. God had likewise given the interpretation of Torah over to human beings, who would sometimes get Torah right and sometimes get it terribly wrong. The final reading of Scripture would come only if and when history as we know it ends. Then, maybe, we will know what it's all supposed to mean: what the texts mean, what our lives mean, what history means, and why it makes sense to perform mitzvot, despite—or because of—the failure of the world to reward good deeds. Until then, we have no way to know.

A related midrash has God tell the people of Israel, "My Torah is in your hands, and the End is in Mine." This too is a part of the deal called Covenant. "We need one another. If you need me to bring the End, I need you to observe my Torah. . . . Just as I cannot forget the End. . . . You cannot forget the Torah."

I take great comfort from the fact that nothing is over yet. Ours is not the End-Time. The universe itself has not reached its final form. Human beings might yet change dramatically for the better. God may one day relate differently to the world: hide less, perhaps, and speak more clearly. So long as that has not happened, we must go on doing the best we can, bringing all we can and all we are, heart and mind and soul and might, to the reading, teaching, and living of Torah.

These are the terms of the covenant that God made with us, as matters look from our side. Such are the terms of the covenants that we make, at our best, with one another. As to how things look from God's side, we can only speculate, be silent, offer thanks each day— and get to work.

Turning, Together

Yom Kippur in Israel, 1975 and 1976

I first experienced Yom Kippur as an adult around the same time that I learned I was going to die one day.

The relation between the two is surely not coincidental. I arrived in Jerusalem for graduate studies at Hebrew University in 1975, two years after the Yom Kippur when sirens pierced the uncanny quiet of the day to summon soldiers to battles from which, in all too many cases, they did not return. Everyone I met that fall had either fought in the war or spent the month of October 1973 worrying about loved ones at the front. My closest Israeli friend had been in Sinai; another friend had been seriously wounded in a tank battle on the Golan Heights. The family who informally adopted me during my years of graduate work had lost their only son in the 1967 war and had spent this war worrying that Israel would lose all that seemed to have been achieved at great cost six years earlier. Walking the streets of Jewish neighborhoods just before sunset as the holiday approached, I couldn't tell how much of the eerie calm I encountered everywhere was due to the unique holiness of Yom Kippur and how much arose from anxiety, even trauma, at the recall of the suffering that the holiday had brought in 1973.

Life and liturgy were uniquely and painfully fused to a degree that I had never experienced. The day was different for everyone, not just for me. On Yom Kippur morning, on *every* Yom Kippur morning or afternoon all over the world, every congregation recites *Yizkor*, a prayer service in which Jews remember—and ask God to remember—family members and friends who have passed away over the years. Congregants recite *Kaddish*, the prayer reserved on other occasions for mourners or those observing the anniversary of the death of a loved one. This Yom Kippur, I knew, Israelis would be saying *Kaddish* to mark the yahrzeit of fathers, brothers, or sons who had died that day in 1973 or soon after. They would join others in praising and petitioning God over and over, in the course of the day, as the God of life: "Remember us to life, O Sovereign, who delights in life, and write us in the book of life for your sake, God of life." The book of life that had been written and sealed on Yom Kippur in 1973 did not include those they now were mourning.

The streets, bearing witness to that loss, overflowed with people walking quietly and with obvious purpose. Men wore prayer shawls to *Kol Nidre* services, in keeping with the custom for the holiday. Almost everyone was dressed in white. Unending streams headed to synagogue—most to pray, but others (I soon learned) to gather on the steps outside. In the morning, the near-total silence on the streets was accentuated by the rising sun, which seemed to reflect off the white of worshippers' garb as it does off winter snow. It occurred to me that I had gone to synagogue on Yom Kippur for most of my life by car, almost always with my parents. This year, on foot in Jerusalem, I was alone among the thousands in motion on the street. Yom Kippur had, as it were, come to me this time, surrounding me with meaning that I did not choose and that I would have had to make great effort to escape.

There was no escape. The announcement of that existential fact of facts came to me early one autumn evening around the holiday season in 1975 or 1976. The exact date is not clear in my mind, but I remember exactly where I was: walking on Rachel Imeinu Street in the German Colony of Jerusalem, a neighborhood I often stayed in or visited. Emek Refa'im, the commercial center of the area, was several blocks behind me. I was approaching the corner of Kovshei Katamon. There was a bus stop nearby on my left. I recall no tug on my sleeve, no voice at my ear, and certainly no apparition of the angel of death; just a sudden and powerful awareness that I never had before despite years of reading books in which the subject of death featured prominently. The study of religion required frequent immersion in literature about the meaning of life and the meaning, or lack of meaning, of death. But nonetheless a new awareness came to me forcibly that evening: I, myself was going to die one day.

My parents were both alive at that point and in decent health, so I had no special reason to fear on that score. I have no siblings. Death had long stalked my childhood and teenage years for reasons I will come to in a moment, but the shapes of those imaginings did not form in my brain that evening either. I remember thinking how ridiculous it was for me to have assumed until that moment that I would be the first exception in the history of humanity to the rule that every living thing must die sooner or later—and how impossible it was to accept the fact that I too was subject to the rule. I screamed "No!" at the top of my lungs and quickly looked around to see if anyone had seen or heard me. No one had. Thankfully, the street was deserted. Shutters on nearby apartments were closed. I was alone and walked faster, in a sweat, shaking my head at the knowledge I now carried.

Life has never been the same. The study of religion at once took on added urgency. Faith in God now had a new dimension and new complexity. I had more to be grateful for, more to fear, more to be angry about. I appreciated Yom Kippur as never before.

"We Have Sinned Before You"

I shall retrace my path through the Yom Kippur liturgy in some detail in this chapter. A great deal of the meaning that I find in Jewish tradition and the truths that I hold dear as a religious human being comes to the forefront of consciousness on the Day of Atonement. So does much of what I find problematic in Jewish theology of former eras and widely-held notions of what it means for a human being to stand before God. I love this holiday even though I find several of its major themes off-putting, misguided, or utterly wrong. Significant numbers of the Jews who come to services on Yom Kippur, I know, have similar issues with the liturgy, and feel a degree of alienation from it far greater than mine. I hope my reflections will help Jewish readers find greater meaning in the day commonly referred to as the holiest in the Jewish calendar and assist every reader's projects of return and renewal throughout the year.

For me, the meaning of the day is announced at the very beginning of the *Kol Nidre* service, even before the chanting of the prayer that gives that service its name. "By the authority of the court on high and by the authority of this court below, with divine consent and with the consent of this congregation, we grant permission to pray with those who have transgressed." This declaration, made by Jews at no other point in the year, seems by equal measure audacious and absurd. It merits close theological scrutiny.

The rabbis who invented the Yom Kippur liturgy many centuries ago asserted God-given authority to introduce far-reaching changes in Jewish belief and practice, none more dramatic than the transformation of the observance of Yom Kippur. They had to accommodate to the reality that animal sacrifices could no longer be offered in atonement for sin because the Jerusalem Temple had been destroyed. To adapt, they seized on the fact that Chapter 16 of Leviticus commands "affliction of souls" on the Day of Atonement along with sacrificial offerings. Prayer, fasting, and the resolve to turn and return to God would substitute for animal slaughter at the altar. The "court [or academy] on high" was a fiction of the rabbis' imagination, and even the "court below" did not exist as such in most Jewish settlements over the centuries. But due to that phrase in Chapter 16 of Leviticus and several others, divine consent could be claimed for the Jews' good faith effort to ask God's forgiveness through fasting and prayer. This is still the way Jews like me observe Yom Kippur today.

That's the audacious element in the opening declaration of the evening. But—the absurd part—why must permission be requested and received to pray with sinners? This seems to make little sense. Is there anyone else with whom a Jew (or anyone else!) *can* possibly pray on Yom Kippur or any other day? Every single row of the synagogue is occupied by individuals who belong to the category of "transgressor." (Scholars emphasize that the word usually translated as "sin" connotes "missing the mark" far more than "doing evil."). All of us are included in that category by virtue of our humanity.

Of course, that is the point: on Yom Kippur there is no hiding from the fact that one is a sinner, and no need to hide from it because without exception everyone in the room proclaims this truth at the outset of the holiday. Chances are good that the people with whom you are seated in synagogue are among those you have hurt most grievously over the past year, intentionally or by accident, and among those are some who have hurt you. There is special satisfaction in proclaiming, aloud and together, that you are part of a "congregation of sinners." You have barely taken your seat and are already making the first of many collective confessions of sin. You may have walked into the room as an individual but as soon as you are there, you find yourself speaking repeatedly and naturally in the plural.

The sages believed that a Jew should want to be part of such a collective because the Torah has assured us, in words recited immediately *after* the chanting of *Kol Nidre*, that "The entire congregation of the people of Israel shall be forgiven, as well as the stranger who dwells among them, for all have erred." Contemporary Jews are encouraged to read this verse from the Torah as a divine promise that our prayers for forgiveness are not in vain. God has promised to take the wrongdoing of the Children of Israel in every generation, including ours, as *shegagah*: unintentional sin, mere error—and therefore will not hold our wrongdoing entirely against us or exact a full measure of punishment. "I have forgiven, as you have asked." The Torah reports that God said those words to Moses after one of many sins by the stiff-necked Children of Israel in the wilderness. We have every reason to be confident that God will forgive our sins as well despite our stubbornness, wanderings, and repeated transgression. The verse has special resonance for me: my father liked to quote it whenever I asked his forgiveness after blowing up at him in anger. I hear his voice and see his smiling face each time the verse is recited at *Kol Nidre*.

Despite that welcome reassurance, I often approach Yom Kippur

depressed at humanity's slim prospects of attaining or deserving forgiveness from God. What are the chances that the world's billions will
change their behavior substantially enough in the coming year to be
worthy of divine pardon? I have failed at true repentance so many
times! This seems to be true of everyone I know. It is likely the case
with all humanity. That's why it is so important to hear God's promise
of forgiveness emerging from our own lips at the outset of the holiday, lest we give up on the collective work of teshuvah even before
the work has begun. It is not beyond the realm of possibility, I tell
myself, that this year I will finally manage to turn away from habitual
shortcomings and turn toward loved ones, in the direction of God.
Perhaps others, many others, will too. And if not this year, then the
next. It is important to know as well that, repentant or not, all of us are
promised the opportunity, for as long as we live, to stand before God.

The Yom Kippur liturgy, like the preponderance of Jewish thought
on the subject, insists that a person cannot ask for or expect forgiveness from God until they have requested and received it from the
human beings whom they have injured. Maimonides's codification
of the laws of *teshuvah* dwells on this point at length, explaining what
one needs to say, and what to do if one's overtures of repentance are
rejected. Martin Buber, recognizing that one cannot always ask for
or receive forgiveness from the people whom we have hurt, taught
that "the wounds of the order-of-being can be healed at infinitely
many other places than those at which they were inflicted." At several
points in my life that wisdom saved me from despondency. I knew I
could not repair the harm I had done, but I could do good elsewhere.
This gives one hope for the world, so much of which seems beyond
repair—never more than now, as the clock ticking toward catastrophic
global warming approaches midnight. Do the good that one can do,
wherever one can do it. If enough of us do the same, the world may
turn. The balance sheet of sin and virtue may change.

Yom Kippur directs our attention to obligations and responsibilities
close to home rather than allowing us to focus on what *other* people—
or humanity as a whole—need to do. It wants attention trained on
the people affected by what we do or fail to do. This is what we might

call the horizontal axis of teshuvah: repair of relationships with family, friends, and co-workers. I have adopted the widespread custom of speaking to friends and family members one by one, pushing myself to ask forgiveness even when the ask does not come easily, and reminding myself to extend forgiveness in return. I find that a cleansing of sorts occurs in this process: a sloughing off of burdens that I have carried for too long and an opening of possibility, a freeing of energy. I acquire a measure of the hope that always seems to attach to new beginnings. To some extent at least, at specific points of relationship or character, one can and does start over. The horizontal work is hard and sometimes proves impossible, but it is a prerequisite to the vertical axis of relationship with God. That is harder still.

A lot in this holiday is hard, I find. Although I sway gratefully to familiar melodies and rhythms, appreciate the psychological acuity of its liturgy, and feel immensely grateful for the opportunity the day affords for self-improvement and the righting of relationships that have gone awry, I realize anew each year as the *Kol Nidre* service gets underway that key aspects of the liturgy are not only alien to me but, if taken literally, profoundly wrong. Immediately after the chanting of the *Kol Nidre* prayer, for example, the congregation sings a traditional hymn—beloved by many—that compares human beings to "clay in the hands of the potter, who thickens or thins it at will," and "stone in the hands of the mason, who preserves or breaks it at will." One encounters similar images and notions throughout the Yom Kippur liturgy. Thankfully, paeans to passivity are countered by passages that teach exactly the opposite. Time and again, Jews are called upon to take responsibility for the world and are reminded that with all our imperfections, human beings are fully capable of doing so. We are not mere clay to be molded at God's will. Our actions are not "negligible," as another beloved hymn proclaims; our power to do good or evil is considerable. As Maimonides asserted in his influential codification of the Laws of Repentance, the Torah would not have commanded us to "choose goodness" and to repent for sin, were these decisions beyond our ability. Leaving the welfare of the world entirely to God is not an option.

The liturgy abounds in contrasting notions of this sort. Images of helplessness are countered by calls to activity; God writes in the book of life, and we are empowered to "choose life." I have learned to take each problematic element in the liturgy of the day—and there are many—as a summons to attention and an occasion for reflection. It takes work on my part to overcome the gap between my personal convictions and some of the prayers on the page, as it takes work to accomplish the turning that Yom Kippur demands of me. I do not always succeed in either effort, but I take comfort in the fact that the rabbis who constructed this liturgy hundreds of years ago—sinners like me and everyone else—daringly reinterpreted the Yom Kippur observance that they had inherited from Temple times. I am following in the rabbis' footsteps when I reinterpret their words, lest the holiday so crucial to my relation to Judaism and to my relation to God disrupt both of those relations. The path I chart through the liturgy of Yom Kippur, the meaning that I find there, and the theological choices that I make along the way, mark the Jewish path that I walk every day throughout the year.

* * * * * *

The image of the day that most calls for reinterpretation, in my view, strikes me as profound and problematic in equal measure. I refer to the picture of God consulting a ledger of individual sins and good deeds over the past year, and on that basis deciding which names to write in the book of life for another 12 months. The verdict of life or death, we chant repeatedly, is "written on Rosh Hashanah and sealed on Yom Kippur." A medieval hymn known as *Unetaneh Tokef*, which I will discuss at length later in this chapter, asserts that God is "judge and prosecutor, expert, and witness" all in one. I do not find this image comforting. I do not believe that God decrees death and life. The notion gives me no impetus to confess my sins or obey God's commandments.

One knows on some level, of course, that the book of life is every bit as much a metaphor as clay in the hands of the potter. God does not write in any book or seal it. I understand, too, that the liturgy invites us to ponder the significance of this image and others like it; we are not asked to subscribe to them as belief, accept them as dogma, or affirm them as creed. What is more, I must concede that the purpose these images serve is worthwhile. The rabbis were probably not wrong to assume that most of us need a strong incentive to mend our ways. Longstanding habits are hard to break. It may have been wise on the part of the sages to try to *scare* us into repentance on a day when we are weakened by fasting and frequent standing during the service. Even sincere atonement may not be enough to sway God's decision on our future, the liturgy advises—and how many of us can hope to achieve that sort of repentance?! The warning of punishment by God in this world or the next sends a tremor down the spine, no matter what the mind thinks of the matter. In my congregation we use a prayer book that translates the reminder that sins, great and small, take place "before God," to say that these transgressions are actually committed *against* God. That raises the stakes of sin higher still, and—if the message is effective—considerably increases fear of divine punishment.

I prefer the literal meaning of the words: we stand *before* God when we sin, as we do when we seek and offer forgiveness, or when we perform good deeds. God is present in our world and calls us to responsibility. The notion of God keeping careful account of our sins and decreeing suitable punishment reminds me of Santa Claus "keeping a list and checking it twice." Jewish teachings that urge us to serve God out of love rather than fear are far more meaningful to me. I appreciate the solemn beauty of the poetry and accompanying music in which the image of God writing in the book of life is couched, and I hear something other than threat of punishment in the refrain. To me it provides assurance that we are noticed by God and that ultimate reality is bound up with God. Yom Kippur inspires confidence that human beings and our world matter greatly and that both can be better than they are. God, rather than mortal powers, holds the key to humanity's future; God, and not fate or sheer accident, is in charge. Due to this divine involvement in the world, your life and mine bear Meaning. The good that we do is needed.

"Remember us to life, O God Who delights in life. Write us in the book of life." The melodic line, chanted in three-quarter tempo, carries one forward, like a river, into more and still more life, filled with the resolve to be better than we have been in the past. A great deal of Judaism moves me in this way despite explicit or implicit theological claims that run counter to my experience and my convictions.

Esau McCaulley's recent book, *Reading While Black*, offers further insight into the nature of the assurance conveyed by the image of God writing in the book of life. For African Americans, McCaulley writes, it has been important during many centuries of insecure existence and frequent persecution to know that "they have a place in the kingdom of God." Particularly in circumstances of oppression and poverty, believers may doubt that "we are God's children." The congregation of worshippers needs to be reminded again and again that no earthly ruler, country, or group has a "say in determining [their] value." This view is welcome news in any century or circumstance, including our own, and is especially relevant to Jews, a small community of faith that believes its teachings are important to all humanity. It is a great comfort to know that the God Whom one addresses in prayer is the author of the only book that ultimately matters. One is motivated to *teshuvah* and good deeds by the belief that future chapters of the book will be shaped significantly by what human beings do with the days of life that are granted to us.

Yes, we are sinners, but we are sinners *before* God, Who needs us to turn and do good.

※※※※※※

That "we," more than anything else, is what binds me to Yom Kippur observance: the reminder that in sin, as in all else, I am not a *solitary being* untethered in the world. I do not exist free of all ties to others except those I undertake voluntarily for the limited period and purpose for which I undertake them. The very opposite is true: I am bound in relation, partnership, and covenant, both to other human beings and to God. Saul Bellow's protagonist in *Humboldt's Gift* offers a devastating critique of "the single self, independently conscious, proud of its detachment and its absolute immunity, its stability and its power to remain unaffected by anything whatsoever." Like it or not, Yom Kippur teaches (and I often do not like it), each of us is part of a larger whole, and of more than one such whole. Some of the people to whom I am indissolubly connected stand around me at Yom Kippur services: members of my family or my community. Others, I know, could be found at similar services around the world and across the generations: members of the Jewish people and non-Jews who have cast their lot with them. Still others belong to the outermost of the concentric circles to which I am linked: the assembly of all human beings, all of whom are created in God's image.

Yom Kippur reminds us of these connections repeatedly over the course of 25 hours that begin with *Kol Nidre* and end the following evening with the *Ne'ilah* prayers. The liturgy urges us to believe that being part of, and responsible to, larger wholes is a positive thing rather than an infringement on individual freedom (which it is, at times) or a burden of unlimited obligation (though that obligation is substantial). During COVID-19 lockdown, all of us received a renewed sense of the debt owed to others. Essential workers were exempted from restrictions imposed on everyone else. Their service was publicly celebrated. I find Yom Kippur's view of the "we" to which every "I" is bound persuasive, despite inborn resistance to the claims that various groups make on my allegiance. My theological doubts about the prayer book do not extend to the avowal that significant meaning is added to my life through membership in communities of mutual responsibility and care.

The most effective persuasion of that mutual dependence has come to me from experience. Pope Francis impressed several hundred religious leaders with the power of community across religious, racial, and national boundaries when he came to New York a few years ago and gathered us in the depths of the 9/11 Memorial at Ground Zero. Many came dressed at his request in the religious garb distinctive to their traditions. This made it all the more moving to join together in prayers for healing, remembrance, and reconciliation. Near that same site, just over a century before, Walt Whitman captured in "Crossing Brooklyn Ferry" something of what I felt keenly in the presence of the Pope and sense with renewed force every year at Yom Kippur. It is the feeling of the "impalpable sustenance of me from all things at all hours of the day;" the fact of being part of a "simple, compact, well-joined scheme," connected not only to the people with whom I share a room, a community, or a period of history, but to human beings who came before me and will come after me. I am not a mystic, far from it. But there are instances when the cross-generational bond of which Whitman spoke seems a plain and simple truth to me. We are not isolated selves moving alone through time and space. Something connects us. "It avails not, time nor place—distance avails not. I am with you, you men and women of a generation, or ever so many generations hence." This recognition is a source of strength to me in the face of implacable death and the sight of unrelieved suffering and wrongdoing.

The Yom Kippur liturgy takes pains to stress the close relation of the congregation to God, but it is the close relation that each of us bears to *other mortals*, including people whom we do not like or do not know, that is most striking and meaningful to me in the prescribed confessions of sin repeated throughout the day. Every verse is couched in the plural. "We have sinned, we have been unfaithful, we have stolen what is not ours, we have slandered." The so-called "longer confessional" speaks of "the sin that we have committed before you willingly or unwillingly . . . the sin that we have committed before you in hardening of our hearts . . . by stubbornness . . . and by betraying of trust."

You ask yourself at every point in these comprehensive, alphabetical listings of transgression, "Am I actually guilty of that sin?" If the answer is yes, you take comfort from the fact that you are not the only one who is guilty. If not, you recognize that you are part of a community or society in which others have done each of these things, and people have suffered because of it. You too perhaps have paid a price for the sins of others, directly or indirectly, just as others have paid for the sins *you* have committed. And you have likely benefited to some degree from the wrongdoing of others, perhaps taking for granted the resultant privileges or possessions.

Whitman understood that the confession of shared transgression can increase the sense of solidarity with fellow mortals. Despite the pain we have suffered at the hands of others or inflicted on them, and the guilt we bear toward those we love, we are sometimes brought closer to one another, even across the distance of generations, by the fact that we all have sinned.

> It is not upon you alone that dark patches fall,
> The dark threw its patches down upon me also.
> Nor is it you alone who know what it is to be evil,
> I am he who knew what it was to be evil,
> I too knitted the old knot in contrariety,
> Blabb'd, blush'd, resented, lied, stole, grudg'd . . .

The poet's words are uncannily similar to Yom Kippur confessionals. Put the poem in plural rather than singular voice ("We too knitted the old knot"), imagine a congregation chanting the words and swaying together to the promise of God's forgiveness (usually in the rhythm of a waltz)—and you will grasp one reason why I love Yom Kippur dearly despite the fasting, the constant standing-up and sitting-down again, the endless (and for me unnecessary) reminders about mortality, and an underlying theology (God doling out life or death) that I feel compelled to reject. The negatives are outweighed by the repeated assurance that as Jews no one stands alone before God or anywhere else on this day or any other. We sin with others, atone with them, do good with them, and become better people with their assistance.

This is not just good news for me, an only child who thrives on connection and community, but an absolute prerequisite of *teshuvah*. A solitary individual attempting repentance would have little chance of success. A single community or society, acting alone, likewise would likely prove unable to modify its moral direction and change course. Together, we can turn.

God of Life, Judge on High

Two other major features of the Day of Atonement give me pause, both central to Judaism as a whole. The first—a ritual reminder of mortality—is one that I have not needed since the awakening to death on Rachel Imeinu Street. The second—God's dual role as Source of Life and Judge on High in this world and the next—makes it more difficult to approach God in prayer, given real fear that I will not prove worthy of another year of life. Believing and not believing as I do, my prayer to God is that I will be deserving of more time to do good.

Is my unceasing awareness of my own mortality exceptional? Students of the subject seem to agree that contemporary Americans generally do a good job of avoiding the knowledge that they will die. We've all met people who will not visit friends and relatives in the hospital lest they be reminded of what awaits them someday; we know people who laugh nervously or make bad jokes when the subject of death comes up in conversation and, if they read obituaries, do so with equanimity born of repression. Charlie Citrine, the narrator of *Humboldt's Gift*, hides from the title character one day because "I knew that Humboldt would soon die . . . he had death all over him. I didn't approach him. I felt it was impossible. I was, as they say, 'in great shape' . . . so how could I talk to Humboldt? It was too much." If philosopher Ernest Becker is right, denial of death motivates a host of daily behaviors by great numbers of ordinary people in the modern West, things large and small that we tell ourselves we do for all sorts of other reasons.

The sages who formulated Yom Kippur liturgy and ritual, like the Jewish thinkers who added to the day's meaning over the centuries, no doubt brought personal experience—and perhaps fear of death— to their theological reflection. Franz Rosenzweig began his magnum opus of Jewish philosophy with the declaration that "[a]ll cognition of the All originates in death, in the fear of death . . . Let man creep like a worm into the folds of the naked earth before the fast-approaching volleys of a blind death from which there is no appeal."

He reportedly wrote those words from the Balkan front during World War I. Maimonides, author of some of the most important teachings about *teshuvah*, mourning, and the afterlife in the Jewish canon, lost a brother at sea and was never the same afterward.

I had no sibling to lose because the two brothers who were born to my parents after me both came into the world prematurely and died after several days of life. I remember the second death keenly; I was about seven or eight. Someone called me in from playing outside, and I found my father on the phone at his desk, getting the news from the hospital. I have a similarly vivid memory, from around the same age, of the death of my grandfather, with whom I shared a bedroom, and another of the death by gunshot wound a few years later of a next-door neighbor not much older than I. Although my family lost no close relatives to the Nazis, it was clear to me long before the Holocaust entered the general consciousness of Jews and Christians in America that I was a survivor of sorts and as such had special obligations and responsibilities.

I knew, too, that my dad thanked God every morning for another day of life, and I understood why he did so. He was struck down as a teenager by the encephalitis epidemic that gripped America in the 1920s, sank into a coma that lasted weeks, and was not expected to live. When he awoke, he and his mother made a vow of thanksgiving to God. He kept that promise of faith. Neither of my parents was punctilious in their religious observance (though our food was kosher, and they went to synagogue every week; my father after his retirement went nearly every day), but they both were pious in the old-fashioned sense of gratitude to God for being alive. I am heir to that gratitude for life, as much as to the awareness that life is fleeting and not ours to hold onto for long.

That is why I nod in recognition, rather than recoil in shock, at the many prompts to awareness of mortality in the Yom Kippur liturgy. I suspect that the rabbis hammer away at resistance to awareness that death awaits us in full confidence that the Jews they addressed could stand up to the pounding. They seem to have believed that *memento mori* would make us stronger, more appreciative of the time we have left, and more likely to turn from sin, which is of course the point on Yom Kippur. I am grateful for their confidence in flawed human beings such as I and grateful too that the liturgy holds out the possibility that death is not the end. I return to that hope—dare I call it a promise?—later in this chapter.

* * * * * *

Before doing so, I want to reflect further on the liturgy's assurance that the God before Whom we sin is both God of life, Who delights in life, and judge on high, Who metes out punishment that in some cases includes death. How shall we make sense of this?

I have suggested that the author(s) of the Book of Lamentations perhaps felt compelled to attribute the terrible sufferings of their nation to God, rather than to fix blame on the adversaries who were the immediate cause of their pain, because they could not hope for a better fate if God were not the reigning power Who determines the course of history. The people of Israel would always be a small nation at the mercy of great powers such as Egypt, Assyria, and Rome. Only the Lord of heaven could protect them from lords of the earth. Moreover, Israelite individuals perhaps had experienced salvation in their personal lives. Recovery from illness and escape from danger were causes for thanksgiving to God and for continued reliance upon God. And life was often good! There was much reason for gratitude inside the framework of sacred rituals and texts. Blessing was evident and sometimes abundant. Israelites (and, centuries later, Jews) could praise God with a full heart despite suffering and periodic persecution. Besides, what else could they be? What else could they do but obey God's commandment?

I suspect that similar reasons impel or reinforce the belief—pervasive in liturgy and still held by many Jews—that God is "up there" keeping track of *individual* transgressions and imposing judgment in this world and the next. Jewish theology has held that divine providence is individual and not just collective; what was true for the Children of Israel in ancient times, we are taught, remains the case for every one of us in every age, including our own. Deuteronomy offers the most explicit statement of this view of things, and the rabbis included one particularly unequivocal paragraph from that book of the Torah in the twice-daily recitation of the Shema. That passage promises explicitly in God's name that obedience to God's commandments will lead to "rain in due season" and that disobedience (i.e., sin) will lead to drought. Maimonides did not believe that this was true in any literal sense, and neither do I. The *Guide for the Perplexed* daringly compares the promise of rain in return for obedience to a parent's promise of sweets to a child as a reward for good behavior. It was a divine "ruse," he wrote, designed to get ancient Israelites to do the right thing, even if for the wrong reason. The right thing is to serve God out of love and to do good because it is good. Not believing that the Torah was divinely revealed to Moses, I do not have to account for the promise of rain. But I stand with Maimonides and many other Jewish teachers over the past 2,000 years in believing that we cannot expect reward for good deeds or punishment for bad ones, certainly not in this world; I cannot speak about the next. The image of God writing in the book is a metaphor meant to direct us to a life in which we are worthy of divine favor. God is the Source of that life and our Guide in living it.

The rabbis hinted at this approach when they truncated the passage from the Torah describing God's attributes to omit the words that promise retribution. "The Lord, the Lord, merciful and gracious, long-suffering, abundant in loving-kindness, extending kindness to thousands, forgiving iniquity, transgression, and sin, but Who will by no means clear the guilty: punishing the iniquity of the parents on the children, and on the children's children to the third and fourth generations." Jews recite these words with special fervor before the open ark on Yom Kippur, taking care to leave out the part about "not clearing the guilty" and the punishment of third and fourth generations. The sages wanted it that way—a daring departure from the text and intent of Scripture, apparently ordered to bring Jews like me closer to Torah and to God.

Ironically, the part of the declaration omitted is the one that history repeatedly has proven to be true. Children suffer for the sins of their parents all the time. What is hard to believe is that, as the prophet Ezekiel promised, the person who is just "shall surely live" whereas the person who commits abomination and wickedness "shall not live . . . he shall surely die." One wants this to be true, wishes it were the case (except when we ourselves are guilty of sin), and—at certain difficult points in life—*needs* it to be true, lest we lose reason to carry on with life. But one cannot depend on being rewarded for virtue. The frequent suffering of innocents is undeniable. Confronting these facts of life, it is sometimes difficult to marshal the courage required to fight against injustice and turn ourselves toward the practice of virtue and good. Why not live for the moment, *carpe diem*, and take one's chances with what will happen on the Day of Judgment—if there is such a day or a judge on high like the One to whom Jews pray on Yom Kippur?

In my experience, people rarely believe—no matter what their theology preaches—that friends and family who suffer serious illness or death at a relatively young age deserve that fate. (Think of Rabbi Akiba's dispute on this matter with his Roman executioner.) We reject the notion put forth by Job's "comforters" that death and disease are visited upon loved ones as punishment for sin, even as we fondly attribute to God instances of personal salvation that we have experienced, heard about, or witnessed. Some events *do* seem truly miraculous: a cardiologist happens to be nearby when a friend is stricken with a heart attack, or a tree falls on the kids' bedroom one minute after the children have left the room to go to breakfast. Many of us owe our lives to drugs, surgeries, or political upheavals that not long ago were beyond imagining. Most of us can cite examples of individuals who successfully recovered from illness in a manner so exceptional that only miracle seems an adequate explanation.

God's role in those outcomes can never be established, of course, but it seems undeniable that some of those who suffer would be unable to bear their suffering if they lacked firm belief that God was the source of their strength. Survival itself seems to them proof of God's awareness of their plight. Nothing else and no one else could have "sustained [them] and enabled [them] to reach this day." I sometimes tremble at the thought that, lacking fear of divine punishment, some people do not or will not muster the good that is within them and overcome the evil urges that seem to drive so much of history and family life. Perhaps it is true, as Nietzsche famously warned, that if [belief in] God is dead, all things are possible; then again, real fear of divine judgment was in place in most parts of the world during many centuries of widespread atrocity and remains in place today with no appreciable rise in love or virtue. Is the world's moral ledger worse now than before? Perhaps—but things might be better. It seems impossible to do an accurate accounting of the gain or loss traceable to belief or non-belief in God's punishment of sin. Hundreds of millions of acts of justice and kindness are performed in the world every day, with or without hope for divine reward or fear of divine punishment. A great deal of good is encouraged by experiences of Community and Meaning such as those that inspire me at Yom Kippur.

This is how I make sense of the avowal by the liturgy that God is both source of life and judge on high. I wonder if my ancestors, too, had difficulties with the prayers that perplex me. Perhaps, like me, they donned the symbolic equivalent of stereo headphones that enabled them to hear in one ear the words written on the page and, in the other ear, the interpretations they had learned to give those words over the years. If life is good to me and if God is good, I will return about 12 months from now, headphones in place, and sway to Yom Kippur's music once again.

Averting the Evil of the Decree

The consummate statement of the theology of divine judgment that I find so troubling is a medieval hymn chanted by the prayer leader at the midpoint of the Yom Kippur service: *Unetaneh Tokef.* "The great shofar will be sounded, and the still small voice will be heard. Angels will be alarmed, seized with fear and trembling, for the Day of Judgment is at hand." God is about to determine the fate of every creature. "On Rosh Hashanah it is written, and on the fast of the Day of Atonement it is sealed." Who will live and who will die. Who will have a long life, and who will have a short life. Who will perish by fire and who by water; who will be raised up and who will be brought low.

I know many people take this prayer quite literally and derive great reassurance from its message that everything is in God's hands. Despite society's evils, nature's cruelties, and all there is to fear in life, one can rest confident that God is the author of every person's destiny. However, I have also known the prayer to cause mental anguish and religious distress. One Yom Kippur I sat several rows behind a friend afflicted with a terrible and terminal cancer that had attacked her months after her daughter had been killed in an automobile accident. Did she find comfort in the belief that these events came at the hands of God? Knowing her, I doubt that the prayer brought her solace. More likely, she trembled at the notion that God makes all decisions of life and death and does so as "Judge and Prosecutor, Expert and Witness, completing the indictment, bringing the case, and enumerating the counts." That would mean, if it were true, that both she and her daughter had been found guilty of crimes that carried the death penalty. The thought is as intolerable to me as I assume it was to her.

Would Jewish tradition have wanted my friend to entertain this thought, even for a moment? Would you and I have wanted her to believe during her final weeks of life—in any manner or to any extent—that the automobile accident and the cancer were divine verdicts and therefore for the best? We would not. Justice and compassion both demand that we reject this explanation of events. Jews who share this conviction with me, but treasure the prayer nonetheless, separate its first section—which declares God a righteous judge, and thereby undergirds the call of conscience and the rule of law—from its second part: a rhythmic litany that asks, "Who shall live, and who shall die?" The prayer can be read as a reminder of how frail and uncertain is our grasp on life. We stand during the cantor's recital of this hauntingly beautiful prayer—whatever theology we embrace—the way we stand at a funeral: knowing that the privilege of hearing and saying words about life and death will come to an end one day.

The *Unetaneh Tokef* is redeemed for me by the verse on which the hymn pivots: "But turning, prayer, and acts of righteousness can avert the evil of the decree." The Hebrew for the threefold sequence of trans-formation is alliterative: *teshuvah, tefillah, tzedakah*. Some interpreters translate the final words of the verse to say that these three actions not only mitigate the severity of the decree but avert or cancel the de-cree in its entirety. Only the former translation seems credible to me. Much of the suffering in the world cannot be eliminated or avoided by repentance, prayer, and righteous action. Either way, however, that transformative triad places us at the crux of what Yom Kippur and Judaism are about. I want to dwell on the meanings that I have found in each of the three instruments of repair, one by one, and reflect on the notions of God and God's will that they entail.

Teshuvah: The focus here—necessarily so—is on the *self*. The pro-cess of change begins with those who pray for it. I must do better than in the past; be more caring, generous, courageous, and loving; be less judgmental, obtuse, insensitive, and closed-minded. That is clear—for I am not good enough as I am. I am not a particularly bad person; looking about, I see others who are, and do, far worse. If I cannot turn myself around, and others do not turn either, what chance is there that more justice rather than less will be performed in the coming year, or that more acts of loving kindness will take place? How will the cycle of hatred, violence, and indifference ever be broken? If there is no hope for these personal turnings, it will be hard for me or anyone to maintain hope for our nation or the world. And if I cannot change where change is needed, what right do I have to demand that my community, my society, or the world do so?

I suspect that experiences from childhood and adolescence—and not only lessons learned from marriage, parenting, friendships, and books—have shaped my notion of the limits and methodology of *teshuvah*. I remember hearing my piano teacher say on numerous occasions, as he sat beside me at the keyboard, that it was okay to make mistakes as long as I did not repeat them. He believed that im-provement was possible—if it wasn't, his teaching was in vain—and he persuaded his students to believe it too. Every recital furnished evidence of progress. Practice did not make perfect, but it did make our playing better. This was precious knowledge, carried forward into harder and harder musical compositions, and carried away from the piano bench into life.

My parents gave varied instruction in *teshuvah* in the ways they disciplined me, the examples they set and in their differing approaches to doing crossword puzzles. My mother—a competent pianist—used a pencil for crosswords. She always pressed lightly and erased with care. Act prudently, she taught me, and you are likely to have less for which to be forgiven. My mother was generous in offering forgiveness. Our conversations about my faults and transgressions were usually quiet affairs held in the kitchen to the accompaniment of milk and tollhouse cookies. My father—a first-rate and passionate pianist—usually punished me more loudly and severely. He did crossword puzzles in ink, crossing out mistakes as needed and writing over them with darker strokes of the pen. (I, too, do puzzles this way.) He taught me that one cannot be overly cautious in life. Boldness is required and would be impossible if there were no chance to repent for mistakes and wrongdoing and start over. He too was generous with forgiveness. I learned at home that whether using pencil or pen, proceeding through life prudently or boldly, it was necessary to try to be better than I had been. *Teshuvah* would not come easily, but it was possible. You must know that sin can be forgiven—erased or written over—by those whom you have hurt, by God, and by yourself. Lacking that hope, there is little that can be accomplished.

I learned another important lesson about Yom Kippur from a Stanford student who explained to me that he preferred the quarter system to semesters because quarters offered more chances to start over. One could study new material, develop new skills, make new friends. I feel that way about Yom Kippur. One must not waste chances to begin again. Friends who have spent years in therapy testify that significant change is difficult but not impossible, a conviction confirmed by friends such as Adam who have devoted their professional careers to providing therapy to others. My own experience with *teshuvah* leads me to agree with that assessment. Change comes with difficulty, but it comes. The years can make one more comfortable with challenge and so with change. Age can increase resistance to change or bring a measure of wisdom. The same holds true for pain.

Given these elements of what seems the human condition, it does not make a lot of sense to me to complain about God's turning away from humanity, or to wait passively for God's renewed turning toward us. We should double down on *teshuvah* without regard for whether God will reward or assist our efforts. The biblical prophets were right to declare that as long as we have not done our part, individually and collectively, it is sheer arrogance to call God to account for the mercies not bestowed from heaven and the prayers left unanswered. It is striking that a plea to God to help in our turning that is often repeated in Jewish liturgy—"Turn us unto You, O Lord, and we shall return! Renew our days as of old!"—is couched, like the confession of sin on Yom Kippur, in the plural. A person who belongs to a community that encourages and rewards turning is much more likely to undertake *teshuvah* despite the risk of rejection, ridicule, and shame that sometimes results from requests for forgiveness or confession of wrongdoing. A nation or culture that values the restoration of respectful relationships and rewards kindness is more likely to opt for truth and reconciliation among families, communities, and ethnic or racial groups. Collective turning on any level encourages the belief that the world is not doomed to destruction but can be renewed. God may turn if many of us do so together. The severity of the decree may be altered. This result cannot be expected from my or your turning alone.

To me, God's hiding is a given. God does not make it easy for anyone to have faith or remain faithful; to turn ourselves or trust God to do the same. I try to keep this in mind when I recite the prayer that calls on God to turn. My plea is fervent. "No more 'hiding of the divine countenance,' please, O Lord! Come back to us, please come close, help us come closer to You! Now more than ever, Your earth and ours seems to be living on borrowed time. Turning from both sides, Yours and ours, is imperative and urgent."

* * * * * *

Tefillah: The focus here is not the self but the relation between individuals—alone or gathered in communities—and God. Regardless of how God is understood, imagined, or addressed, we approach the Source of Being by means of prayer offered together with other human beings on behalf of all of us. The hymn sung by Jews upon entering the synagogue in the morning gives praise and thanks to the congregation before moving to praise and thanksgiving to God; indeed, the point of transition from one to the other is blurred. "How goodly are your dwellings, people of Jacob, your sanctuaries, O Israel . . . I come to your house in the bounty of your kindness, and bow in awe of You in Your holy sanctuary." My longing for assurance of God's presence and care is sometimes as intense as my craving for life itself. That assurance comes more readily in the company of others who seek—and sometimes find—it alongside me.

I seek God in full awareness that, as the *Unetaneh Tokef* reminds us, a human being is "a broken shard, withering grass, a shriveled flower, a passing shadow." These words are utterly and sadly true. I desperately hope—and, at some moments, manage to trust—that I stand nonetheless in relation to "You [Who] are the Sovereign, living God, ever-present." I love life and love the God who gives life. The direct and indirect encounters with God to which I can personally testify reached their peak when I thrilled to see my daughter enter the realm of the living (an experience described in the first chapter of this essay). I thanked God repeatedly and uncontrollably as I danced my newborn child around the room. My son's birth three years later was no less an occasion for thankfulness, although it came more suddenly; the umbilical cord was wrapped around his neck, making a quick delivery imperative. My wife and I were so grateful when he emerged from the womb alive that we forgot to ask the nurses if our child was a boy or a girl. My prayers to God ever after, and still today, express recognition and gratitude (the two words are one in Hebrew) that life is on loan to me and the rest of my family for another day. That is particularly the case when I pray on Yom Kippur.

Not having a way to know much *about* God, and knowing God a bit from episodic contact and intense longing, I do not expect that I ever will understand how prayer works. I cannot reliably say that a particular prayer of mine, or of my community, has been answered or heard, let alone how or why. I can testify only to the belief that some of my prayers over the years have been answered. I do so testify; I believe this. At fleeting moments, I have strongly sensed God's presence in the world that we share. I wish that those moments had not been fleeting, but they have come, and some have been vivid, including instances of prayerful encounters. When the wording of a prayer gets in the way of such encounter and offers welcome or unwelcome distraction, I remind myself that the language of the liturgy abounds in metaphors that emerge from the thought-worlds of psalmists, sages, and medieval poets and not from the experience or imagination of a 21st-century American Jew. It is remarkable that the words on the page capture my intent, experience, and longing as often as they do. I am occasionally taken by surprise when this happens. My mind's wandering is arrested. Some verses, on some days, seem to know me better than I know myself.

Keenly aware of images and concepts that block my way to heartfelt prayer, I understand feminist objections to liturgy that employs exclusively male pronouns to address and speak about God, Whom we believe has no body and so no gender. I am also persuaded by the argument that theology is not only shaped by political and social realities—in this case, male privilege—but plays a part in shaping them. The pursuit of justice—and not only theological accuracy—demands revision of a liturgy that alienates many worshippers even as it draws attention to its own inability to find words adequate to the task and privilege of addressing the Holy One. There is no easy answer to this problem. I do not want to sacrifice the form of personal address that has enabled many generations of Jews to approach God; nor do I want to dispense with language that has borne me aloft since childhood. Alternation between male and female pronouns and (in Hebrew) the accompanying verbs seems to me preferable to impersonal or wholly new formulations; as I noted earlier, I am hopeful that our culture's experimentation with non-gendered personal pronouns will prove an important resource for liturgical innovation. I want to continue talking to God; I need to keep doing this; I can't do it without summoning as much presence as I can in second-person address to an Eternal Thou Whose presence I crave.

A conversation between an "I" and a "Thou" is one important metaphor for what takes place during *tefillah*, but it is far from the only one; indeed, "prayer" is often not a useful or adequate translation for the diverse set of actions that are said to help "mitigate the severity of the decree." Petition, too, is only one form of tefillah. The act that we call prayer can take the form of meditation, avowal, praise, encounter, thanksgiving, confession, or greeting. I yearn, I seek, I think, I cry out, I dream. On some days, I literally burst into song with love or gratitude; on other days, I brood at a distance and occasionally hold back tears. I sometimes whisper a prayer, not sure that I want it to be heard, but at other moments I want to shout across the room or down the hall to my Creator, Who seems at that instant to be within shouting distance—but no closer. Following hours spent online, prayer can seem like dispatching a message into cyberspace or writing an email message and clicking "Send." Then again, I sometimes picture myself cupping words of prayer carefully in my hands and then releasing them, like Noah's dove, in the direction of heaven. Sometimes I sense God hovering near me, attentive to the words I form and to the inchoate desire for which I can form no words.

There are moments when I feel totally unworthy of God's attention. The liturgy for daily morning prayer contains a meditation that begins, "Master of all worlds... What are we? What is our life? Our goodness...What shall we say in your presence?" I find myself saying, "I don't know exactly Who You are or whether You are listening to me right now. How can it be that words emerging from my mouth, some of them conceived in my brain, all of them bursting forth from my heart, can be heard by You—Who, to the best of my understanding, have no ears to hear with, and Who may not be entirely separate from me in any case? Mine is but one voice among the voices of billions of Your creatures. I am one droplet in the ocean of Your bounty. Why should You pay attention to Me? Are my thanks not gratuitous in Your eyes? Does my praise add anything to Your glory?" To which the liturgy responds: "But we are Your people, partners to Your covenant." The rabbis who wrote these words intended them to apply only to Jews. To me, they speak for and to anyone who presents themselves before God.

Lest we not engage in *tefillah* because we know so little about the God Whom we are trying to address, the siddur includes the "Hymn of Glory" written by a Jewish mystic approximately a thousand years ago. The author's determination to pray, despite lack of adequate knowledge of the God Whom he addresses, speaks to me directly. "I will sing sweet songs and weave together melodies because my soul longs for You . . . I will tell of Your glory although I have not seen You; I will liken You and name You without having known You . . . The prophets [too] imagined You, not as You are, but measured You according to Your deeds. They envisioned You in old age and vigorous prime, with hair that is grown white or still youthful." The poet multiplies examples of such anthropomorphic images from prophets and psalms. His hymn concludes as it began. "May You find my words sweet and pleasing for my soul is longing for You."

I love this hymn. It captures my situation when I prepare to address God, or when I engage in reflection *about* God. I pray—and think or write—because I feel an imperative to do so that is born of need, love, and hope. Love in particular needs to declare itself—to the beloved first of all but also to the world.

There is so much that I do not know about myself or about the people whom I love most—and yet I love them. I think it really is them that I love and not just the act of loving or the state of being in love. What they and I do not know about one another is of course dwarfed in scale by what none of us knows about God. And yet the analogy helps me to pray, as it has helped human pray-ers of every faith tradition for many centuries.

I don't want to leave the subject of *tefillah* without mention of one other passage that is particularly precious to me because it offers both caution and permission to anyone attempting to stand before God or think about God. We are asked to imagine angels as they pray and, thereby, encouraged to emulate the angels' purer pursuit of the hiding God. "All of them beloved, all of them clearheaded, all of them powerful."

How much better we would be at prayer and so much else in life if we had the love we need (or think we need), did not feel compelled to grasp and scheme for it, could share it freely, and were not driven to seek it in all the wrong ways!

Imagine if our thoughts and feelings were not distorted by hunger for what we do not have! Suppose our minds were free to work and play undisturbed by lust or hatred.

Picture what it might be like to be *gibborim* in the rabbinic definition of that term: not powerful over others but in control of our evil urges; strong enough not to lash out in combinations of anger, weakness, fear, and greed.

The angels, being angels, are not brought low by those all-too-human urges, so they can easily and contentedly "give one another permission to sanctify their Creator, together." What do the angels pray for? They do not eat, drink, or love. They need not fear death. Do they too wish for greater access to God's elusive presence? We who are flesh and blood have that and many other things to pray for. The point of the passage about the angels is that we *can* and *should do so.* A congregation of souls who are not as beloved, clearheaded, or in control of base urges as we wish to be can nonetheless proclaim God's holiness and God's oneness together.

It always is the case that some of us are unable to pray for one reason or another. This is true for some people for their entire adult lives. The *Unetaneh Tokef* names three ways of mitigating the evils of the world, not just one. For those who cannot pray, opportunities for *teshuvah* and *tzedakah* are at hand. *Teshuvah* in any degree, at any point of repair, improves our relationships with the people we love but continue to hurt. *Tzedakah* of any sort makes the world that much more just and compassionate. You and I can do these things despite all that prevents us from fully becoming the people we ideally would like to be and all that gets in the way of prayer. Resolved to work at *teshuvah* and engaged in *tzedakah,* we fulfill the promise of the Day of Atonement even in the absence of prayer.

* * * * * *

Tzedakah: The call to justice directs attention *away from the self* and *outward toward the world* that each of us shares with other human beings and that faith teaches we share with God. "Justice, justice, you shall pursue," the Torah commands. Calls to justice are pervasive in much of the Hebrew Bible. At least until the Messiah comes, justice can only be sought and increased but never fully achieved. The pursuit of justice is halting and imperfect because the human beings who undertake it are only human: that is to say, flawed. But the command to seek justice proves that Yom Kippur language of human abasement and inadequacy should not be taken literally. Human beings are God's partners in Covenant; not equal partners—God is God, and we are not—but partners nonetheless. All the talents and abilities that we can possibly bring to the task are required for the job assigned to us.

The passage about averting "the evil of the decree" is recited on Yom Kippur shortly after the chanting of Isaiah's declaration that the fast that God wants has nothing to do with "starving [our] bodies [and] bowing the head like a bulrush . . . This is the fast I desire: unlock the fetters of wickedness and untie the cord of the yoke to let the oppressed go free . . . share your bread with the hungry and take the wretched poor into your home." This is remarkable; during the fast, we are told in God's name that fasting cannot be the point of the day. The aim, now as always, is justice, and obedience to that command requires all the wisdom, knowledge, courage, and creativity that we can muster. Jews are not permitted to forget this for even one moment. The ultimate purpose of Yom Kippur observance is not our repentance, but the good that, having repented and been forgiven, we undertake in the world. We can undertake that work, and therefore we must.

Isaiah's insistence that God wants justice and not sacrifice accords with my friend Karen's choice of politics over theology; the Yom

Kippur liturgy as a whole drives home the message that *both* are required. The two tasks are inseparable. Racism is a form of idolatry, Heschel taught; the behavior of bullies and tyrants has the effect of eroding the faith that God cares about justice or cares about us. The threat has seemed especially acute in America lately. Hate crimes are surging. Verbal and physical acts of hostility are markedly on the rise. Antisemitism has increased substantially. The percentage of Americans who give charity is declining. Civil debate in the public square or the classroom is more and more the exception to the rule. Social media promote dissing and doxing. A prominent pundit not given to alarmism noted recently that the nation seems to be undergoing a "long-term loss of solidarity." That verdict is confirmed in the authoritative survey of American attitudes and behavior published in 2020 by political scientist Robert Putnam. His claim, backed up by a wealth of statistical evidence, is that the nation has undergone a profound "cultural shift from 'we' to 'I'" in the past half century. "The arc of the twentieth century," Putnam concludes, has bent decisively toward individualism. God's credibility has suffered from these developments.

These trends demonstrate the wisdom of the Talmud's insistence that *tzedakah* should be understood not only as charity—acts of kindness that human beings perform for one another out of the goodness of their hearts—but as justice: obligations that human beings *owe* one another by virtue of shared membership in a neighborhood, city, country, or world and that they can be compelled by law to fulfill. I have been touched and assisted at many points in my life by acts of kindness, but I know that, in ways beyond number, I enjoy protections and benefits every day that are guaranteed by law. Jews who are knowledgeable about their people's history or their family story understand the need for law and justice to protect minorities and "strangers" from mob violence. Only force of law prevents the bigots, haters, and antisemites from making life miserable and trust in God more difficult for Jews and other vulnerable minorities. Only determined acts of justice on our part can avert that evil.

Excursus: Reason, Tradition, and Experience

I want to step back at this point, as Jews are encouraged to do during the Day of Atonement, and reflect upon the concepts that figure crucially to the way I think about *teshuvah, tefillah,* and *tzedakah.* As I have noted previously, it long has been my practice to triangulate among three related, but distinct, sources of authority when weighing notions of God and relation to God. My beliefs and commitments rest upon a conjunction of *reason, Jewish tradition, and experience.* I never proceed without consideration of all three, nor do I allow any one of the three to declare either of the other two illegitimate or superfluous.

Reason includes logic, scientific knowledge, rational argument, and the finest thought of contemporary secular culture. *Jewish tradition* comprises the many and diverse voices found in Scripture, legal and non-legal rabbinic literature, and medieval and modern philosophy and mysticism. It also includes lessons taught by liturgy, rituals, and observance of the Sabbath and festivals, all of which are based directly or indirectly upon the Torah and its claim to express or contain the word of God. (I consult and learn from other religious traditions such as Christianity but do not regard those sources as authoritative in the same way.) *Experience* includes lessons derived from my own life and the lives of people I know; from the historical events I have studied and lived through; and from the imagined experience conveyed in music, poetry, drama, fiction, and visual arts.

Every one of the three is essential to my reflection. None automatically trumps the others, although I give benefit of the doubt to Jewish tradition whenever possible. My thinking often derives from experiences and proceeds with the assistance of reason and tradition. Each of the three has salient weak points and blind spots. I cannot endorse "religion" or "faith"—or even "Judaism"—in general, any more than I can affirm the truth of "philosophy" or "experience" (which philosophy? what experience?). So many disparate voices claim to speak in the name of God and Torah! God and the devil are both in the details, as the sayings go. Faith maintained in good faith does not lend itself to the sort of over-simplification to which every religious tradition is subject. Nor can faith be disentangled from the biographies and existential situations of the individuals who hold and transmit it—this despite the tendency of theologians to indulge in system building and the formulation of dogma and creeds.

When people approach me after lectures and begin, as they often do, by making it clear that they do not believe in God, I ask in reply—not to be clever, but just to understand them—"Which God is it that you don't believe in?" (Spinoza's God? Rabbi Akiba's? Heschel's? Kaplan's?) I want to get a sense of their personal background, their acquaintance with or ignorance of Jewish tradition, and their thought process in matters of religion, identity, and love. "Yes" and "no" tell us little where belief in God is concerned. Survey questionnaires are of limited usefulness. Belief is usually not the only thing that matters in terms of a person's faith and may not be the one that matters most.

It is hard to know which of the three sources of authority takes logical or chronological precedence over the other two when considering a particular question of religious truth. Do I, for example, place special value on the importance of kindness because *Jewish tradition* praises Abraham's hospitality to the angels who appear at his tent one day (a story that I first read as a child) and highlights Ruth's kindness to her mother-in-law Naomi (a narrative chanted on the holiday of Shavuot)? Do I value compassion so highly because it is one of the two divine attributes stressed in God's proclamation to Moses on Mount Sinai, the other being justice? (This passage in the Torah has etched a profound mark on me.)

Or am I drawn to these sections of the Bible more than to others, and to the preeminent importance of this virtue, because I (who have a notoriously poor memory) retain the memory of kindnesses done for me decades ago? Here is one such *experience*: I am in fifth grade. My classmates and I are having a swimming lesson from a man who believes that the best way to teach children to swim is to have them dive into deep water while holding their breath, thereby learning that they will not drown. I do not agree with this pedagogy and refuse to jump. My classroom teacher, a former nun, consoles me at the side of the pool afterward as I weep. I will never forget her kindness.

Do I stress the importance of compassion because it, along with justice, is central to every work of ethics and theology that I know? Maimonides's *Guide for the Perplexed*—appealing to *reason* as well as to Scripture for authority—makes compassion essential to the very definition of Judaism. Rousseau is one of a long series of philosophers who have believed it an essential part of human nature and/or a virtue necessary for proper functioning of society. Evolutionary theory seems to have modified the Darwinian account of struggle for survival among species to include evidence of altruistic behavior within them. I would be surprised if new knowledge about humanity's place on Earth or in the universe dislodges the importance given to the virtues of justice and compassion.

The same is true of the human quest for God. Given more presence of mind at the time, I might have said to the teenager who asked me, "What is true?" that at this point in my life, guided by the triad of tradition, experience, and reason, the reality of God is axiomatic for me. Whether God is essentially more like person or force, I do not know, although I suspect that God is infinitely more than either. (The concept of energy as simultaneously both wave and particle is helpful here.) Unlike some contemporary theologians, I am comfortable using the word "God" without fear of identifying the Holy One with a bearded king on a heavenly throne. The Bible does not picture God this way, nor do most rabbinic sages and subsequent teachers of Judaism. I can address God in prayer, in the ways I described above, because I believe that personhood is among God's infinite attributes. How could one say definitively that it is not? No one who addresses God, seeks encounter with God, feels inspired by God, or believes they have come near to God, can possibly have an accurate conception of the God whom they are addressing, encountering, approaching, or serving. Like my friend Adam, I am aware that I sit at my desk on a little planet whirling around a star that is one of billions or trillions in the known universe. How much can I hope to know about the Creator? But I also believe that those who seek and address God are not deceived in their conviction that they have had contact with a Reality not contained within the bounds of common sense or the domains of the microscope and telescope.

It is also axiomatic for me that God in some sense cares about human beings and our world. I am not as certain as Heschel was that the prophets of the Hebrew Bible had a correct understanding of divine concern (or that one can ascribe common understanding to those prophets, a highly diverse group, as Heschel did). The prophets were human beings, after all, however inspired or graced with divine encounter. But I stake my life on the conviction that God exercises concern for humanity, however episodically and unpredictably. It must be the case that the Aristotelian notion of God as "Unmoved Mover" is wide of the mark. Human beings need to know that justice and mercy are among God's attributes, which is why these two are announced by God to Moses, according to the Torah's report. We must be confident that when we perform acts of justice and mercy, we stand with God and so can legitimately say, in these cases, that God is on our side—because we are on God's side.

Unlike the Greek gods who often derive pleasure from being gods, the God of the Bible and of the rabbis derives pleasure only when human beings do God's will. God's frustration with humanity is often apparent, and—according to the Torah and the prophets—is expressed sometimes as anger. God's desire to be known and God's search for partners and allies have led Jewish authors from the Bible onwards to imagine that being God is cause for profound loneliness. God might have wished at times to be the Unmoved Mover that Aristotle described but, to the best of Jewish knowledge, God is not. Justice and compassion require God's involvement in the world, in a manner that surpasses human understanding.

I write this and similar sentences hesitantly. Caution must be the rule when attempting to describe the hiding and unknowable God. Maimonides taught a profound lesson when he instructed theologians and believers to proceed negatively when talking about God. We can say what God *is not* but not what God *is,* and we need to recognize when we should say nothing at all. I do not hold with the prerequisites that Maimonides stipulated for meaningful theological speech (higher mathematics, physics, and metaphysics) and I reject the primacy that he assigned to our rational faculties in knowing God and in determining a person's chances for a share in life in the world to come. But I understand his point. I too am uncomfortable with religious convictions that venture too far beyond what Immanuel Kant called "the limits of reason alone," although I believe that faith must transcend those limits more than Kant allowed in order to remain faithful to experience and tradition. Unlike Kant, I do not believe that every human being, if they reason correctly, will arrive at the same conclusions, let alone at mine. Experience, tradition, and reason are too various to permit such unanimity among theological worldviews. I would hate to see the richness of human faith hollowed out in a vain search for religious consensus.

I try, as Heschel put it, to tell this to my mind as well as I can. Then, no matter how well or how poorly I perform that effort, I return to the important business of mitigating the severity of evil decrees.

The Living God, God of Life

The Torah, like the Yom Kippur liturgy, is relentless in confronting its readers with the fact of death. From the first protagonists of the human story, Adam and Eve, to the Torah's last and greatest hero, Moses, every human being in the book goes the way of all flesh, and does so without a promise of life beyond the grave. No amount of repentance, prayer, and righteousness can alter this decree. Its effects are especially vivid in the chapters from the book of Numbers that are read in synagogue during the summer months that lead up to Yom Kippur. Korach leads a rebellion that challenges the authority of his cousin Moses right after God sentences almost the entire generation of the Exodus to death in the wilderness as punishment for their lack of faith in God's promise to lead them into the Promised Land. Even after the earth opens to swallow Korach, and fire from the Lord consumes the 250 rebels who followed his lead, the Israelites refuse to submit to the authority of Moses and Aaron, instead blaming them for "bringing death to the Lord's people." When God appears in a cloud and threatens once again to destroy the people, Moses instructs Aaron how to stop the plague that causes 14,700 Israelites to perish. At this point, God fecklessly conceives yet another demonstration of Aaron's authority: his staff alone, among the many lined up for the test, will sprout overnight. The Israelites, in response to this feat, testify not to faith but to their abject terror of death. "Lo, we perish. We are lost, all of us lost. Everyone who . . . ventures near the Lord's Tabernacle must die. Alas, we are doomed to perish."

They are not wrong: every adult among them except for Joshua and Caleb (who brought back a faithful report from the spies' expedition) will die in the wilderness. Their children will die at some point as well, of course, albeit in the land of Canaan. At times God seems uneasy with this reality, finding it necessary to explain that Aaron will die "because the two of you disobeyed my command about the waters of Meribah," where Moses struck the rock instead of ordering it to gush forth water at God's command. Later God tells Moses that he "will be gathered to your kin, as your brother Aaron was" because "you disobeyed My command to uphold My sanctity in their sight by means of the water." God seems to be casting about for an excuse to do what must be done. (Moses is 120 years old!) The excuse that God finds is not terribly convincing. When the time for Moses to die finally arrives after numerous warnings that it is near, God not only shows Moses the land he will not enter from the summit of a mountain across the Jordan, but buries him there—another act of special kindness. Moses dies with his eyes undimmed and his vigor unabated but without miraculous ascent to heaven or a promise of eternity. The Children of Israel mourn him for 30 days. He is a great prophet, but he is mortal.

The Torah extends one consolation to the reader: it teaches that our stories, like that of Moses, need not end with our deaths. The portion in Genesis called *Chayyei Sarah*—"life of Sarah"—describes the death and burial of the matriarch and of her husband Abraham. No euphemism is involved: Sarah's story continues in the story of her son Isaac, as his story—told in the next portion of the Torah, *Toldot* (literally, "generations")—chiefly concerns the vexed relationship between his twin sons, Jacob and Esau. We read soon after about "the *toldot* of Jacob," which begin with these words: "Joseph was seventeen years old." The Book of Exodus moves from the narrative of a clan to the history of a people, meaning that the story of every child of Israel henceforth can continue in this way: from parent to child, teacher to student, generation to generation. Those who join their personal stories to that of their people and its covenant walk a path that is eternal. (Other religious traditions extend similar promises, to similar effect.)

This understanding is what enables every congregation of Jews to declare in good faith, quoting the words of the psalmist, "And we will bless the Lord, from this time forth and for evermore, Hallelujah." Each person who says this identifies with a group that, by virtue of the Covenant, will exist "evermore." Sometimes this guarantee seems so convincing to me, the order of things to which it attests so right and true, that even for me its promise of eternity is sufficient. I have felt that way most acutely at boundary moments where life and death touch. The memory of those moments, refreshed by annual chanting of the prayer to be inscribed in the book of life, is vivid as I write.

There was the day, soon after my wife and I brought our newborn daughter home from the hospital, when I sat with her in a rocking chair, listened to the breath of her sleep, sang a lullaby I cannot recall, and said—aloud, if memory serves—"It's okay. My death will be okay." Not good, but okay.

There was the visit I made one fall day to the graves of my parents, just before the Sabbath on which *Chayyei Sarah* was to be read in synagogue. I could not help thinking back to the times when I had come to the cemetery with my father (whose original name was Abraham). We would stare at the double monument that on one side bore my mother's name and on the other side was blank, waiting for his name. A copse of trees separated the cemetery, crowded with deceased American Jews, from the Gentile neighborhood that surrounded it. The biblical Abraham's relation to his Canaanite neighbors was very different, I reflected. America was home for my family and me in a way that the Land of Israel never was for the patriarch, even with Sarah buried in its soil. My mother lay in the soil of suburban Philadelphia, and my dad was at peace with the reality that he would soon join her. I tried to be so as well and at that moment almost succeeded.

Acceptance comes at other moments too, due to experiences that are widely shared: when flowers poke out of a lawn or field that had recently been covered by snow; when, turning a corner on a mountain road, I encounter fall foliage so spectacular that I cannot take in the scene; or when a person half my age pursues commitments to which I have been dedicated for decades, and does so in a way that I could not have imagined and know to be wise. One savors life with special satisfaction in such moments, and gains glimpses of eternity. I have felt this after praying all day with my community on Yom Kippur, blessed to be part of such a congregation, and blessed—as the liturgy assures us—with God's company as well. Buoyed by tradition, community, and the sense of God's presence, one can be more determined than ever to do good with the years remaining. Reason assents to the conviction that life is good and death will be okay.

※ ※ ※ ※ ※ ※

The Bible and the rabbis left behind no dogma on the afterlife, no creedal affirmation of what to expect after death, but they did offer numerous teachings that bolster confidence in a world to come. Virtually all the sages—and nearly all the philosophers, mystics, and commentators who followed them over two millennia, well into the modern period—affirmed that something awaits worthy human beings on the other side of the grave. It might be spiritual immortality or resurrection of the body, or—for the truly wicked—*gehinom*, a fiery hell. Maimonides was particularly vehement in rejecting popular notions of heavenly reward and infernal punishment. Just as a blind man cannot experience color, he insisted, "bodies cannot attain spiritual delights" or correctly imagine them. The best we can do is to picture beings who, entirely freed of bodies, know only spiritual delights. "We will be like them after death." His is but one view among many. But I remind myself during Yom Kippur, when confrontation with mortality is the order of the day, that the great majority of Jewish thinkers believed that life somehow continues after death in a world to come. Forgiveness is granted to all who repent. Virtue somehow is rewarded or proves to be its own reward.

I take comfort as well from the fact that the sages, despite their confidence in life eternal, felt the fear of death as keenly as I do and gave vivid expression to that fear. Recognizing that there is no escaping the end, they were not averse to trying to delay it as long as possible. Consider the brief Talmudic tale of Rabbi Chiyya, who knows that the angel of death cannot seize him if he engages in the performance of God's commandments. He studies Torah day and night until one day the angel of death, disguised as a poor beggar, knocks at his front door. If Chiyya fails to interrupt his study to give the beggar alms, he sins. If he does interrupt his study, he sins. No human being can avoid sin, any more than any of us can defeat the angel of death. One way or another, sooner or later, the angel will prevail.

Still more moving to me is the long, drawn-out rabbinic tale of Moses's multiple attempts to persuade God not to take his life. As if he had read Kubler-Ross, Moses at first practices denial (drawing a small circle and announcing that he will not move until the decree is annulled), then shows anger, and then tries to bargain (let me remain alive in the form of a beast, he pleads, or maybe a bird). God is irritated but patient. "Such must be the way of the world," God explains to him. Each successive generation will put forward its own interpreters of Scripture and have its own chance to serve God. Moses eventually reaches the stage of acceptance, but when he does, God cannot find an angel willing to carry away his soul. God comes down from heaven to do the job. When Moses's soul refuses to leave his body, God kisses him and takes the soul, as the Torah reports. Moses dies "by the mouth of the Lord."

Accept the decree when your time comes, the sages seem to advise; know that this is the way of the world and try to be prepared. "Repent one day before your death," urges a sage in Pirkei Avot, meaning of course that one should repent *every* day. If you are afraid, remember that Moses was once in your company. You will soon be in his. Know too that life is good despite the fact of death. Spend the time you have doing good. If God is with you, there is no cause for fear.

That, I think, is the most important lesson offered by Jewish tradition about death, a lesson made more forceful than it otherwise would have been by God's mysterious personal name, revealed to Moses at the burning bush. God's name contains the word for *being* in a form that seems to indicate perpetual future tense. "I will be what I will be," God says, and soon after, God instructs Moses to tell the people that "'I Will Be' sent me to you." God's being will continue, perhaps in opposition to, and through the overcoming of, the opposite: non-being. Perhaps God also promises to be *present* for the Israelites—to be there for them in Egypt, as God had promised to their ancestors. Biblical names generally give insight into the nature or character of the individuals who bear them. God is God of life. God *is* in a way that no other existing being can be.

The Jewish philosopher Michael Wyschogrod argued persuasively in *The Body of Faith* (1983) that Jewish faith in the living God stands or falls on the conviction that somehow, in a manner that surpasses human understanding, Being rather than Nothingness is the ultimate truth of things. God, as it were, encompasses non-being rather than being limited, surrounded, or overpowered by it. One cannot *know* this, of course. Reason may well lead to the opposite conclusion. The triumph of Being is a matter of faith to which a person witnesses in the good they do and in the hopes they nourish. Only because God's Being is a more ultimate reality than Nothingness can you or I reasonably hope that the way we walk in life has a connection to eternity and that, walking that way, so do we. I'd put it this way: the Being of God outreaches non-being and reaches out to us, thereby enabling us to muster what the Protestant theologian Paul Tillich famously called "Courage to Be." What we most want to be true might *be* true despite our wanting it so badly. The love of God, "as strong as death," may extend even beyond death.

"Blessed are You, Lord our God, for giving us the Torah and [thereby] planting eternal life in our midst. Blessed are You Who gives the Torah." I have said these words hundreds of times, standing beside the open Torah in the synagogue. On good days I believe them in the sense that Wyschogrod expounds.

The rabbis would say that God *wants* us to think this way. They prescribed blessings to be recited every morning to thank God for creating human bodies designed for the sustaining of life. We are invited to declare that the soul, breathed into each of us by God, will "one day in the future be taken from me and, in a more distant future, returned to me." Saying these words upon awakening is meant to encourage us to regard sleep as a sort of death and waking as a return to life. Oblivion comes upon us unaware with sleep; we lose control and consciousness, lack agency entirely, and do not know whether five minutes or five hours have elapsed before we awake. Think of death that way, the rabbis urge. Imagine God, "who neither sleeps nor slumbers," as a loved one who watches over you as you sleep and will wake you as promised when the appointed time comes.

* * * * * *

Max Weber—apparently speaking from personal experience and not only as a sociologist of modern Western rationality—argued in his essay "Science as a Vocation" that lack of confidence in what the rabbis called the world to come had undermined the ability of modern men and women to "meet the demands of the day" in this world. Approvingly citing a view that he attributed to Leo Tolstoy, Weber suggested that the "process of disenchantment" had resulted in a widespread conviction that "death has no meaning . . . because the individual life of civilized man, placed into an infinite 'progress,' according to its own imminent meaning should never come to an end." The biblical Abraham could die "old and sated with life" because he knew all there was to know about what mattered. We, on the other hand, know how much more we know about the workings of nature, the course of history, and the forces that drive the self than ancestors who lived long ago. We know, too, that our descendants will know a great deal more than we do about these matters. Unlike the ancestors, we lack confidence that death is not the end of us. "And because death is meaningless, civilized life as such is meaningless."

Weber was surely wrong about Abraham, whose incomprehension
and protest at God's doings are manifest in the biblical account. Evidence from many religious traditions refutes Matthew Arnold's claim
that before the modern period, the "sea of faith" was "at the full," sup-
pressing all doubt and disbelief. Elegies to faith are common among
non-believers who are not unhappy that belief is no longer a live possibility for them. Abraham did not understand very much about the
God with whom he interacted. Nor did Moses, the greatest of the
prophets, and nor did Maimonides, widely considered the greatest
of Jewish philosophers. Weber's blanket pronouncement about death
and life is likewise unreliable as a characterization of belief in the modern West. For millions of thoughtful individuals, secular or religious,
the fact that death comes as interruption rather than completion has
not rendered death, let alone life, "meaningless." Reason, tradition,
and experience offer testimony that contradicts Weber's claim.

I suspect, however, that Weber did not miss the mark in two respects. The death of a loved one in our modern secular culture renders
many a person of faith uneasy, planting fear and doubt that no amount
of prayer can resolve completely. And it does seem that faithful individuals, like everyone else, face the prospect of death differently than
most human beings—members of religious societies and cultures—
did for the past several millennia. Weber is asking, in so many words,
whether the gains of science and the advances made in the modern
age in so many respects were worth the price paid in loss of ultimate
meaning. We know so much more about everything, due to science,
history, and other disciplines, he asserts; but in our "disenchanted
world" we cannot establish the value or meaning of anything we know.
Weber concluded "Science as a Vocation" with Isaiah's call to "return,
come" but, unlike the prophet, could not instruct us how to return
or where to come, on whose authority and with what hope. In the
absence of "prophets and saviors," he believed, no ultimate meaning
or truth is available. Isaiah of course believed that the opposite was
true, as does the liturgy of Yom Kippur.

Tolstoy, whatever his personal view on the matter, labored mightily
in his masterful story, "The Death of Ivan Ilych," to dispel the fear of

death and to foster confidence in the meaning of life. After last-minute repentance for the wrong he has done and the good he has failed to do during a thoroughly conventional existence, Ivan passes from this world. The mourners who gather afterward are likewise paragons of convention. We do not know if they are shaken by the fact of Ivan's passing, but thanks to Tolstoy's narrative omniscience we do know what happened to Ivan in the final moments of his life. "And suddenly it grew clear to him that what had been oppressing him and would not leave him was all dropping away at once from two sides, from ten sides, and from all sides . . . Where are you, pain? . . . And death . . . where is it? . . . There was no fear, because there was no death. In place of death, there was light."

Ivan Ilych's death poses the Yom Kippur question of questions: How do you want to live, fully aware on this day (more than at most other moments of your life) that you are mortal? God is present in the world and expects your partnership in the work of redemption. Are you perhaps too afraid of God, or death, or the opinion of others, to do what must be done? Will you turn on people, turn and run from them, or will you turn yourself in repentance? How do you want to be when death interrupts your life? You'd better act now to make things right.

Tragically, I think, fear of death often gets in the way of making the turning required to lessen the fear of death. Saul Bellow's protagonist, Charlie Citrine, comes to the realization midway through *Humboldt's Gift* that "life was a hell of a lot more bounteous than I had ever realized. It rushed over us with more than our senses and our judgment could take in." Perhaps it was true that "after the greatest, most passionate vividness and tender glory, oblivion is all we have to expect, the big blank of death." Suppose, however, "that this brilliant, this dazzling shattering delicious painful thing (I was referring to life) when it concluded, concluded only what we knew." What then? "To assume, however queerly, the immortality of the soul, to be free from the weight of death that everybody carries upon the heart, presents, like the relief from any obsession . . . a terrific opportunity . . . The first result is a surplus, an overflow to be good with."

That is exactly the relief that Yom Kippur seeks to provide, equivalent to the joy that ancient Israelites felt, according to the sages, when the high priest emerged alive from his annual one-on-one encounter with God in the Holy of Holies of the Temple on Yom Kippur, an event recalled in the holiday liturgy. The high priest reportedly emerged from the rite confident that he had secured the promise of another year of life for the people of Israel. Contemporary Jewish worshippers may experience relief at having another chance to right the wrongs they have committed, or at least to start with a clean slate. What a lightness one feels, free of the burden of failure and guilt one had been carrying and, therefore, able to concentrate on the good that needs doing. What a joy it is to feel confident, even for a moment, that God is present in this world, and may be nearer still in the next! Empowered, unafraid, one can resolve with fresh determination "to unlock fetters of wickedness and untie the cords of the yoke to let the oppressed go free." At that instant a person who calls on God can believe, as Isaiah promised, that "Adonai will answer."

It takes a settled mind to do good, a strong dose of courage and a measure of at-homeness in the world. It takes help from God to give one's all to the cause—heart, soul and might—and readiness, when the final interruption comes, to gracefully return your life to God.

Bringing the Kingdom

My reflections in this book are couched almost exclusively in terms of Jewish rituals and texts. This is the way I have thought about God and experienced relationship to God from childhood onward. Long before I began the study of religion in college, God had become a part of my life through prayer in synagogue and holiday observances at home. Bible stories and accounts of Jewish history were reinforced by my mother's lighting of Sabbath candles and my father's recital of the priestly blessing. I have proceeded further into life for seven decades with the help of Passover and Yom Kippur, the Torah, and the sages. I have reached further into rituals and texts with each successive year or stage of life. I don't believe that I could have learned what I have learned any other way.

I cannot be sure of that, however. Even as a teenager, I realized that the Torah and the rabbis offered one set of answers to questions that were universal. There were other answers, perhaps no less valid, that might have led me to do good and encounter God, had I been raised in a different home or culture. The Bible seems addressed to all human beings and not just to Jews; the rabbis believed that when redemption comes, it will transform the entirety of creation. Many of the mitzvot that the Torah prescribes and the rabbis explicate—certainly the love of neighbor and of God—obligate everyone. Almost all the themes highlighted in the Yom Kippur liturgy are of universal concern: confession and forgiveness, atonement and mortality.

So, although I have made the decision to spend most of my days inside the framework of a single tradition and community, I am fully aware that I would have acted, thought, and related to God differently had I been born into a different faith. I can't really imagine what I would have been like as a Christian or a Buddhist (or as a woman, or a person alive in a different century). I've tried, however. We all do, to some extent. This is the pleasure provided by history, anthropology and the arts. Unlike most believers of previous eras (and perhaps unlike many contemporary adherents of the world's religions), I have also engaged in serious scholarly study of other faiths and, as a result, have a strong sense that I have missed something in *not* experiencing another religion from the inside. There are insights and wisdom unavailable to me that I might have treasured; things I might have known, but never will know. A colleague in the field of religious studies has perceptively called this awareness "spiritual regret." I feel that regret keenly.

More immediately and palpably than these considerations, there is the fact of love and friendship that cross religious boundaries. One sometimes finds cause for love in the differences that love happily bridges or overcomes. If Judaism were concerned with Jews alone, it would be untrue to my experience of love as well as to my study of religion. That seems especially true on Yom Kippur when the person I am stands face to face most honestly with the person I would like to be.

This is why I am grateful for the *Aleinu* prayer, recited at the conclusion of Jewish prayer services every day of the year but invested with added significance when said on the High Holidays. When *Aleinu* is chanted on Rosh Hashanah and Yom Kippur, worshippers are invited to do more than the usual bending of the knee before the "King of kings of kings, the Blessed Holy One." Many prostrate themselves head to toe. Muslim worshippers do this daily, but for Jews it is rare—a sign that the process of *teshuvah* has reached a climactic moment. The name of the prayer, best translated colloquially as "it's on us," conveys its principal message. Bringing God's kingdom to the earth is *aleinu*, "on us." Not on you or me alone and certainly not on some anonymous "them." It is "on us." Just as confession of sin is made in the plural, and forgiveness of wrongdoing is awarded collectively, so too is the assumption of responsibility for the work that follows turning. And just as no person stands before God alone, Jews do not stand before God as the sole community of faith. No human group does.

Thank goodness this is so: the world's 16 million Jews, acting without allies, could not possibly bring redemption much closer to realization. Nor could a billion Catholics, Muslims, or Hindus. The burden of responsibility, *Aleinu* maintains, falls on all who recognize the authority of God, thank God for the gift of life, and yearn for more and closer contact with God. *Aleinu* is a collective pledge to take responsibility for moving the world closer to the day when everyone on earth will believe—and act in accordance with the belief—that "this is our God, none else . . . the true sovereign, there is no other." The prayer concludes with the vision of the prophet Zechariah: a day will come when the turning of humanity to God and one another is complete. God's kingdom will arrive. "On that day the Lord shall be one, and God's name one."

It was common for Jews of previous generations—and for many today—to take the words of *Aleinu* to mean that only Jews serve God faithfully and that redemption of the world will require that all humanity call upon God by the four-letter name Jews have long known (but do not say aloud). The prayer's opening lines have been read as an expression of gratitude to God for making Jews unlike any other nation and Judaism unlike any other faith. That reading, to my mind, gets in the way of appreciation for *Aleinu* as a further turning point in the Yom Kippur service. The congregation moves from atonement and the promise of forgiveness to a pledge to do the work required to fulfill God's intentions for the world. An exclusivist reading of the prayer flies in the face of Judaism's conviction that differences of language and culture (and therefore of religion) are here to stay. Diversity, though a source of perennial conflict and, tragically, even of bloodshed, incalculably enriches human wisdom and our capacity to do good. God's creation of a plenitude of species is described in the first chapter of Genesis as a source of obvious delight for the Torah and for God, Who pronounces creation, in its immense diversity, "very good."

"No Religion is an Island," Heschel declared in a speech at Union Theological Seminary in 1965. Differences in religious belief and practice pale in importance before shared experience of God and common peril from the threat of nihilism. To me, this point is what the rabbis called *p'shita*—so obvious that it needs no demonstration, although it is, of course, contradicted every day by the way the world actually works and by the intolerance and exclusivism shown by many religious communities. Human beings rarely take advantage of the varieties of knowledge, wisdom, and experience that we could bring to one another. Instead, we put up walls. *Aleinu*, against the evidence of what is, and thus far has been, the case, offers the promise of the prophet Zechariah that human beings will someday use one name for God: that is, agree on what God wants from human partners. The prayer calls upon Jews to recognize the existence of covenants with God to which they are not privy, and relationships with God to which they cannot testify. Diverse faith communities can serve the same God. Differences of creed and practice need not be a barrier to that cooperation. God hears one prayer in the many names by which human beings call out to the divine. Humanity will one day hear it too.

You may not be able to picture this yet, the liturgy implicitly advises, but you can work for it. Less inclusive visions of humanity do not offer comparable hope, and the incessant conflicts that plague humanity do not lend that hope credence. Given the catastrophic consequences of global warming looming in the near distance, it seems that human visions of the kingdom and understandings of how to bring it closer must be as far-reaching as art, science, and faith can make them. Mind, heart, and soul need to be stretched wide. One recites *Aleinu* with unaccustomed urgency. There is no time for condescension by one nation toward another or by one religion toward all the others. *Aleinu* shouts out a reminder that human beings are responsible for each other's well-being. It sounds trite, but it is the truth. Responsibility for the world is "on us" as never before.

※ ※ ※ ※ ※ ※

That said, I must add a caveat that *Aleinu* itself does not fail to note: our pluralist vision should not be so all-inclusive that it leads to moral relativism. Some ethical distinctions must not be abandoned or eliminated by leveling down. One should not blur the difference between right and wrong or truth and falsehood. Relativist claims are peddled daily in contemporary Western culture. I often heard them from students in college classrooms. A precocious fifth grader once announced to me when I visited his Jewish day school classroom as Chancellor of JTS that "there is no right and wrong, you know, just personal or group opinions about right and wrong." He agreed with me that murder and rape were wrong, but said that our shared view of the matter was just an opinion that had nothing to do with truth. There are great twentieth-century philosophers who agree with him, in opposition to the claims made by all the world's major religious traditions. "May we soon behold Your strength revealed in full glory," pleads the *Aleinu*, "sweeping away the abominations of the earth, obliterating idols, establishing in the world the sovereignty of the Almighty." Some acts *are* abominations, according to Jewish tradition. Some people do worship false gods. Even the most generous pluralism has its limits. Not every desire should be honored or fulfilled. Some objects of alleged ultimate concern are far from ultimate. Devotion to them is the definition of idolatry. We see such worship all around us.

It does not lead to greater justice or increased compassion.

There is, of course, no way to demonstrate that monotheism has made human beings more virtuous than they were when they were under the sway of pagan religions or would be again if the world's major religious traditions were to lose their hold on humanity. (I accept the argument made by some Hindu and Buddhist teachers that their religions too are monotheistic, naming as separate gods what Judaism, Islam, and Christianity would call attributes or "divine persons" or emanations of the deity.) Belief in one God, Who created all human beings in the divine image, has not stopped men and women of faith from committing atrocities against other faithful children of God who—they themselves believed—were likewise created in the divine image. Nor has that belief deterred them from asking God to bless those atrocities. Such behavior has been more common than not in the history of religions. There is no defense for it.

I suspect that the state of the world, bad as it is, would be appreciably worse if the many conflicts now raging were seen by the combatants as battles between or among various gods, conducted by armies that—as servants of foreign gods—were not entitled to respect or life. What government would accept responsibility for the well-being of its own people, let alone respect the rights of any other, if it was generally assumed that nations and their gods were subject to fate (a common pagan view) or ruled by chance? Moral decision-making would be regarded as an illusion. All hope for redemption, if such hope survived, would rest on the gods alone.

At the end of the day, one can only *witness* to the rightness of worshipping a God Who is the God of all the world, Who wants human beings to be good to one another, and Who forbids us to bow down before false gods that include money, sex, fame, power, or the self. That is not to say that the argument against idolatry lacks strong supporting evidence. Theologians and philosophers have advanced good reasons to believe in One Holy God rather than multiple gods, and there are palpable benefits that flow from that belief. A faith of truly ultimate concern, rather than service to idols, seems more likely to direct human behavior toward the good. Moral and political abominations committed in the name of false gods, or anti-gods, have wreaked devastation within living memory. Dictators and demagogues, demanding that they be treated like gods, have wielded power beyond anything that the God to whom I pray is seen to exercise. Experience teaches what happens when truth is routinely disregarded and lies become the order of the day. Devotion to popular idols of the self and the household has not been a source of justice or compassion.

I learned recently that the father of a friend of mine—a believing Christian, married to a Jew—asks the members of his interfaith family gathered at the Shabbat dinner table to say in what ways they had experienced the presence of God that week, and to tell what they had done to bring God's kingdom closer. These are the *Aleinu* questions that Yom Kippur raises for Jews and demands that we answer not only with repentance and prayer, but with righteousness. I marveled at the wisdom of posing the questions weekly with family at the Shabbat table rather than waiting for the annual introspection prompted by the Day of Atonement. There seems no better way to summon hope that next week, and next year, the world will be better because we have resolved to make it so.

Life without Fear

I approached Yom Kippur observance several years ago bearing lessons learned from a summer outing that shaped my experience of the holiday. I had gone fly fishing with my son and a very patient instructor on a river in New England. Several pieces of wisdom from that day continue to prove helpful to me when Yom Kippur draws to a close and I take stock of my success or failure at the work of *teshuvah*. I pass them on here.

First: Fly fishing is hard, very hard, and if my skill at casting in my first few dozen attempts is an indication, it is unlikely I will ever be good at it. I had, of course, taken along Norman Maclean's *A River Runs through It* and, with Yom Kippur approaching, had to agree with the narrator's observation that human beings are often a "damn mess." My effort at repentance confirmed that often it is the human beings whom "we live with and love and should know who elude us." That collection of individuals, I think, includes me. Maclean's view of humanity helps to explain why teshuvah is so difficult. As the sun sets at the end of a long day of fasting and prayer, my stomach rumbling audibly and my knees beginning to give way, it is a source of comfort to me that, for all my flaws, I am generally much better at *teshuvah* than I ever will be at fishing.

The second lesson brought back from the river is that, regardless of skill, one sometimes gets lucky. The boys' father in the novel wishes it were the case that "nobody who did not know how to fish would be allowed to disgrace a fish by catching it." I did reel in a fish that day (and promptly threw it back into the river). From this I learned the importance of facing your inadequacies but remembering that there is hope for you nonetheless. "All good things, trout—as well as eternal salvation—come by grace, and grace comes by art, and art does not come easy." That is the paradox on which *teshuvah* turns as well: if we don't work hard at seeking and receiving forgiveness from those we have harmed, God surely will not forgive us; if we do the hard work needed to merit God's forgiveness, we may, by grace, be granted it. Or we may not.

I learned a third lesson that day on the Housatonic River. It might happen that if you bend all your efforts toward a single goal, you may nonetheless fail to achieve it. But you might find that you have been vouchsafed a gift that never would have come to you otherwise and that is worth as much as—or more than—the goal for which you were striving. I set out that morning to learn to fly fish and, to be honest, to use the fishing lesson as an excuse for spending a few good hours with my son. He and I had those hours together. Remarkably, I caught a fish. And with my son close by, I experienced the joy of standing knee-deep in a sun-dappled river, surrounded by four shades of forest green, looking up at four shades of blue sky, with waterfowl gliding overhead and woodpeckers making their distinctive call—all this raised to an exponentially higher level of stunning beauty when the wind churned the water and clouds covered the sun. The show of light and shadow caused me to shudder.

Maclean concludes his story with the mystical observation that "eventually, all things merge into one, and a river runs through it." Not being a fisherman or a student of Kabbalah, those are not the words I would use to describe what I feel at the conclusion of Yom Kippur. I would search for other images of oneness and of wholeness, starting with the cadence of a Bach invention or the perfection of a late Cezanne. I'd point to my sense of Community, palpable after 25 hours of praying together in Community as at no other time in the ritual calendar, and my conviction of Meaning, which likewise seems more assured at that moment of prayer than at any other. Then I'd try to find language for the "Master of All" Whose presence in the world seems uniquely certain as we confess our sins before You, bend the knee or prostrate ourselves in recognition of Ultimate Reality, and vow to work toward the day in which "God is One and God's name is One."

For me, too, the truth of things is that "eventually, all things merge into one." I possess only inklings of this unity; no proof, but only strong intuitions, that you and I and our communities and all other communities are in fact parts of a Whole that surrounds and inspires us, without and within. This is the "Lord our God," whom Jews declare daily "is One." Transcendence and immanence fused. Distinction retained and overcome. Love given, received, and shared. Yom Kippur offers a glimpse of the far-off day when human beings will approximate that divine Oneness, with God's help: the world as we know it transformed into that world, imposed upon it like a palimpsest, morphed into it by a series of new births. We need have no fear of it, the liturgy assures us, and no fear of what transpires in the meantime. In the words of Psalm 27, which observant Jews recite daily from 40 days before Yom Kippur until 10 days afterwards,

"The Lord is my light and my salvation. Whom shall I fear?"

✳ ✳ ✳ ✳ ✳ ✳

No biblical psalm means more to me than this one. Psalm 23, far better-known to Jews and Christians alike, is a close second. It provides similar assurance in words that I first learned to recite in the King

James translation in elementary school. Psalm 23 provided invaluable strength and comfort to me at my parents' funerals and at other moments of peril to body or soul. "Though I walk through the valley of the shadow of death, I shall fear no evil, for Thou art with me." Psalm 27 seeks to make this state of being one that we inhabit all the time, not only when stalked by death or danger. Truly: If I knew that "YHWH is the stronghold of my life, of whom should I be afraid?" My personal safety would not matter very much; nor would it be important whether I expected life to end with my last breath or to continue in a world to come. Either way, if I am truly with God, and remain so, what is there to fear? I pray for this fervently. "May God shelter me from evil; hide me in the concealment of His tent."

The psalmist uses the same word in this verse, not once but twice, that the Torah uses to describe the "hiding of God's countenance." As we have seen, God is said by some texts and thinkers to hide at moments when people of faith cannot figure out how God, Who is just and merciful, could allow terrible things to happen to God's children. There are theologians who invoke the notion more broadly to describe eternal mysteries or ever-hidden matters that by their nature belong to God alone, as opposed to the things that the Torah says are revealed to human beings, especially the commandments that we must follow to fulfill God's intent for the world. I've explained why the verse in Deuteronomy that makes this foundational distinction is crucial to the faith I hold and to the ways in which I try to put that faith into practice. At some moments I accept that this is how things are and always will be. Human beings do not and cannot know all we want to know—but we have what we need to go on and to do good. On other days I bang my head against the wall that blocks the hidden things from view, frustrated at the mass of dark matter that threatens to swallow the light from the brightest stars. People of all faiths protest God's hiding in the face of fervent seeking. The world is so awful sometimes, and God is hiding. We are not sure we can bear it.

Some who do bear it find strength in the sheltering presence of God. They are well-hidden from what assails them, the psalmist would say; safely secured in a veritable divine rock-fortress. I have felt this assurance on some particularly dark days—but not always. There are moments, even in the midst of prayer on Yom Kippur, when I wonder if the world conjured up by Judaism is an elaborate myth—a great myth, to be sure, but a myth nonetheless; a picture of reality that has no basis in the way things actually are. I tell myself that even if Judaism is a myth, no better framework exists in which to live, none that offers more Meaning or inspires more good deeds. Whether Judaism is ultimately true or not, I will embrace Torah with open arms and give it all I have. On days darker still, the inner voice that Scripture calls "The Tempter" threatens to deprive me of even that modicum of meaning. It demands to know why anything matters, what the good I might manage to do amounts to, what anyone can hope to accomplish in their brief years on earth. Psalm 27 responds to the doubts that assail me with the words or assurance couched as prayer. "Please Lord, hear my voice when I call You, be gracious to me, answer me. My heart tells me to seek Your face. Do not hide Your face from me." The entire congregation voices this prayer on Yom Kippur, one by one and all together. "If only I could trust that I would see God's goodness in the land of the living."

On better days, I do stand in that trust. Vouchsafed Meaning by my tradition, joined on the path of mitzvah by my Community, "sheltered in God's presence" with other individuals and communities of faith, and "dwelling in God's sanctuary" not just on Yom Kippur but on other days as well, I rest confident that someday human beings created in the image of God will, with God's help, complete the project that I've tried to move forward during my time on earth. I pray only for the chance to do more.

At the end of Psalm 27, its author turns to each of us, in second person singular, and pleads with us to "place your hope in the Lord. Be strong. Take courage. And place your hope in the Lord."

I shall keep trying.

Epilogue
Sabbath Yearnings

Dear Ace,

I've been thinking a lot in recent weeks about what I'd like to say to you and my readers in this Epilogue. It has taken some time to decide upon the message I want to leave with readers, but it took no time at all to formulate the three things I most want to say to you: Thanks, thanks, and thanks. You've endured 42 years of marriage to me with unflagging enthusiasm and minimal complaint. Thanks for that first. Thanks for easing the aloneness of your "lonely man of faith" by teaching me more about love, the life of the spirit and relation to God than the library of books I've been studying and teaching for as long as we have known one another. And thanks for Shabbat, which you and I have celebrated together over 2,000 times so far, by my rough count. I realized while writing this essay that Shabbat means everything to me—as you do. Shabbat anchors my week, as you anchor my life. I don't know where I'd be, or who I'd be, without either of you.

Is that perhaps why Sephardi synagogues recite the Song of Songs as they usher in the Sabbath, I wonder? Poetry and melody join one love to another, expressing feelings of attachment to human and divine partners that in both cases are difficult to put into words. Ashkenazi synagogues like ours begin Sabbath prayer with Yedid Nefesh, a song of yearning in minor key that pulls us on throbbing heartstrings toward our weekly visit with a Lover Who dwells far away. "Soul mate, loving God, compassion's gentle source/Take my disposition and shape it to Your will." You are the soulmate I've been lucky enough to love up close all these years, while trying to overcome the distance that separates me from God. Without you my search for heaven could not get off the ground.

Yedid Nefesh captures two of the most important things I think I've learned while writing this essay or have come to believe more strongly than before. The first is that knowing God, insofar as that is possible, is not a matter of intellectual reasoning but of relationship between the person I am at the moment of encounter and the God to Whom I try to draw nearer. The second is that while God hides, Jews like us find numerous traces of God's presence: in rituals like Shabbat and the seder; in the study of Torah and the performance of mitzvot; in personal or communal tefillah; in natural wonders, whether daily or extraordinary; and in concentric circles of love given and received. You and I do more than get by with help from our friends and our tradition. At our best, we thrive: sharing blessings, doing good in the world, and embracing life, as Deuteronomy said we could and should.

I love this life, Ace. I love walking on the path marked out by Torah, as I know you do; I love it, in part, because we take this walk together. The mysteries remain with God, of course; that's a given, and it is frustrating; but the "revealed things" we share are so fulfilling that God's absence is not impossible to bear by any means. Honestly, I suspect that if God were not in hiding most of the time, I might be less rather than more the person you love: less courageous, creative, and thoughtful. (This might be true of human beings in general— one reason, according to theologians such as Eliezer Berkovits, that God may have chosen to keep a safe distance from us, giving us the space we need to flourish.). One thing is for sure: if God were to send down an angel to help me do more and be better, as in *It's a Wonderful Life*, the angel would be wise to consult you before getting to work. You know my strengths and shortcomings better than anyone, and you have been eliciting the best from me in my wandering through adulthood for many years—longer, it occurs to me, than the time the Israelites spent wandering in the wilderness.

2,000 Sabbaths is a lot of Friday evening candle lightings, recitals of kiddush, handwashings, blessings over challah, and singing Birkat Ha-Mazon after the meal. More synagogue services than I ever expected to attend in my life, and now feel deprived of when something keeps me away. More than half a century of reading the weekly Torah portion since I learned in my late teens to appreciate the gift of going deeper into the Torah as I grow deeper into life, and vice versa. Thirty-plus years of Havdalah ceremonies on Saturday evening since we added a family ritual to the prescribed wine, candle, and spices: me chasing our son around the dining room table and never catching him—at first because I did not want to, but soon because he was too fast for me. "Just like the years," we said, which seem to fly faster and faster as we get older; "and like the kids," we said, who snuggled deliciously on our laps when they were younger, and now live far away and ration time with us. Two more soulmates for whom we yearn. I am keenly aware of the distance love often must travel when I bless our adult children over the phone rather than in person on Friday afternoon. Yedid Nefesh expresses how I feel. "Longingly, I yearn for your embrace."

Three Sabbaths stand out in memory from the other 2,000, and together capture much of what I have tried to say in this essay. You shared all three of those moments with me, of course. See if my experiences match yours.

The first occurred in Spring 2022, soon after Passover. The seder had been different from all others that I had attended because our three-year-old grandson joined confidently in singing Dayyenu. That was indeed "enough for us," more than enough. But then came the birth of his younger brother, and still more gratitude for blessing. The bris took place just before the arrival of Shabbat. I held our newborn in my arms as we stood at the dinner table, put my hand on his head and that of his brother, and pronounced the priestly benediction. The tears flowed and would not stop. I then offered the blessing to our daughter, now a mother of two, and her husband. "May the Lord bless you and watch over you." How much "blessing" and "watching over" can a person ask or expect of the Lord? How much "light from the divine countenance" can one take in? How much peace and fulfilment? My father had given me that blessing; I now gave it to my daughter and her sons, hoping that they will pass it on long after I am gone. That is how the covenant of mitzvah is transmitted most faithfully: in love.

We both know that there's no assurance that things will work out that way—another adult truth that I probably could not have explained to the teenager in Baltimore who wanted me to tell him what is true. How do you explain to a young person how difficult it is for human beings to acquire what the philosopher Friedrich Nietzsche called "the right to make promises?" It's not easy to be as good as your word, given the drives competing for mastery inside of us and all that will change in our circumstances between the moment when we make a promise and the moment we attempt to carry it out. You must have a measure of control over events and yourself if the promise is going to be serious, and human beings generally have little control of either. Was it chance, or destiny, that caused the meeting of egg with sperm that resulted in your existence and mine? Would you and I have fallen in love if the friend whom I intended to visit the day you and I met on Amsterdam Avenue had not slept through the buzzer at the door of his building, thereby sending me forth to encounter you and the chain of events that have led to children, grandchildren, and 2,000 shared Sabbaths?

I ask you and myself: Given the role such unpredictable occurrences play in our lives, how can one possibly know what lies on the road ahead, even in broad daylight and good weather? "Think about what you are about to do," the rabbi who married us said to me when you and I were about to march down the aisle to our chuppah. "Where's Arnie going?" your mother asked, too incredulous to be irritated. "He's going off to think about what he's about to do," you answered matter-of-factly. I don't remember what thoughts crossed my mind at that moment. But I knew that I didn't have a clue, couldn't possibly have a clue, about what I was about to do. Life rarely warns us what is coming our way. No amount of thinking could enable me to leap over the unknown that opened before me that day. Love would have to get me to the other side. Perhaps that was the thought the rabbi had in mind.

Do you know what is most striking to me in the film of the wedding that your brother recently discovered? Not even one of the guests from our parents' generation who were present that day is still alive. For some reason the movie lacks sound, which makes it all the eerier to watch the procession and the dancing. Where is the march of the generations more visible than at a wedding? Your nanny walked down the aisle and was gone a few years later. My father's aunt, gorgeous and graceful on the dance floor, turned out to be celebrating for one of the last times in her long life. It hit each of us years later, when the last of our parents passed away, that you and I were next in line; we did not have that awareness of mortality when we danced at our own wedding. As you and I went round and round in the hora, faster and faster, and I left the circle momentarily, panting for breath, and someone stepped in to replace us until they themselves got winded—we did not think that the dance was giving instruction about life. The music will end someday for each of us, and others will take our places, for a time. Children will join the circle, and then grandchildren. Students and then their students. This is the way things are meant to be. And, as the Book of Genesis asserts, it is okay, even good.

Thank God for covenants of love and mitzvah to which we can bind ourselves for life despite the difficulty of keeping promises, and for the Sabbath—symbol of the covenant, and a taste of the world to come. We do our best, and fall short, and atone, and are forgiven, and try again. With the help of our community and our tradition, we proceed Sabbath by Sabbath, one Passover and Yom Kippur to another, without resolving any of the great mysteries but, hopefully, doing some good along the way. Do you think things will be different in the world to come? The older I get, the more I doubt it, and the more I hope that it is so.

✳✳✳✳✳✳

The second Shabbat that stands out in memory capped a week a couple years ago in which something truly wonderful happened. NASA released a photograph taken by the Webb telescope stationed a million miles from Earth. We looked at light that no human eye had ever seen before.

The picture showed a galaxy cluster that, according to the agency's scientists, includes "the faintest objects ever observed in infrared. Light emanating from the farthest galaxies in the photo is believed to be 13.1 billion years old." "It is beyond my wildest imagination to be alive when we get to see to the edge of black holes, and the edge of the universe," one astronomer told the *Times*. I stared at those words, not really comprehending what I was being told, and stared still more intently at the photo to which the words referred. "13 billion—let me say that again, 13 billion—years ago," President Biden gushed and stammered hours later, agape like me with wonder.

I didn't know how to process the data that was making its way into my consciousness. The color picture in my inbox had taken its place among hundreds of others there—images of the January 6 riot; photos of our grandsons; ads for hiking boots and rainproof parkas—but it seemed to have an aura all its own. I wanted to bow my head in wonder. The least I could do was sit silent for several moments to pay respect, obeying the Sabbath call to follow God's example and "cease from work and rest, refresh, and renew the soul [*vayinafash*]." It occurred to me that the author of Genesis must have written the book's first chapter out of a comparable experience of overwhelming awe, one perhaps prompted by a majestic expanse of night sky. Some philosophers and scholars have interpreted the Torah's account of creation as an implicit "argument from design" for the existence of God. But to my mind—fresh from my first sight of humanity's first sight of light from the dawn of creation—Genesis seemed an outburst of ecstasy and not an inference from evidence. The text shouts at us with exultation, awe, and wonder. "In the beginning God created! . . . God said, Let there be light, and there was light!"

The *Times* reported poetically, with scientific authority, "The universe was born 13.8 billion years ago, and even after the first stars and galaxies blazed into existence a few hundred million years later, these too stayed dark…inaccessible to every eye and instrument. Until now." I still can't take this in. My mind stalls at the sentences informing me that the edge of the universe is the edge of time, beyond which there is presumably nothing—or perhaps black holes: huge spaces of nothing that fill much of the known universe. The Kabbalah has long insisted that in the farthest reaches of divinity, God takes the form of *Ayin*: "No-Thing." As if in commentary on the creation narrative of Genesis, scientists spoke of "hints of complex carbon molecules" in the Southern Ring Nebula that "drift through space, settling in clouds that then give birth to new stars, planets, asteroids—and whatever life might subsequently sprout." That includes you and me, it seems. "We humans really are connected to the universe. We're made out of the same stuff in this landscape."

I've been asking myself for many years, as you know, what images should properly cross in front of my mind's eye during recital of the kiddush on Friday evenings. Ever since that summer Shabbat, when we peered together at photos from the Webb telescope, I've tried during kiddush to call to mind the wondrous sight of light from the edge of the universe. Stars in their billions do not cause quite as much terror, I have found, when one recognizes them as the source of the light that human beings shine upon one another in love. There is less to fear in life when one can rest confident, as Shabbat reminds us, that you and I are part of a divinely created order, summoned to "tend and steward" its creatures through acts of justice and compassion. God has pronounced this order "good," even "very good." As we light candles, recite kiddush, ritually wash hands, and say the motzi, I can believe that this is true.

✻ ✻ ✻ ✻ ✻ ✻

The final Shabbat that stands out in my mind, as I write this Epilogue in December 2023, threatened that assertion of Meaning, assailed my faith that human beings will one day form a worldwide Community, and mocked my hope that a measure of redemption will come and justice prevail any time soon, whether for Jews or for the world as a whole. I am talking, of course, about the Sabbath in early October 2023 when a brutal terrorist attack on Israeli civilians began a nightmare of war and destruction that has still not ended, as I write in late December. On the following Sabbath we read the Torah portion that recounts God's assurance that all that God had created was "good"—a claim that is hard to credit as one mourns thousands of Israeli and Palestinian dead, worries about the fate of Israeli hostages, frets over Israeli soldiers—the children or grandchildren of family and friends—who are engaged in combat, and wonders whether there will ever be peace for Israel and, if there is no peace there, what hope remains for the world. Fears of catastrophe caused by climate change have been pushed aside for the moment among Jews we know by more immediate life-and-death concerns. So much of the meaning of my life is wrapped up in the project of bringing Torah to life in the State of Israel! So many of the people I love most in the world live there! Will there never be reconciliation between Jews and Arabs in the Holy Land they share? Shabbat in Fall 2023 has seemed more a refuge from weekly cares than ever before—and, at some particularly dark moments, has felt like a flight from reality, a pleasure to which Jews far from the battle zone are not entitled, a liturgy of prayer to an absent God. It is not easy to cry from the depths for help that we do not expect will come.

The chaos on earth that seems particularly obvious these days runs counter to the vision of Heaven in which the photos from the Webb telescope led me to exalt. "May God Who makes peace in the heavens bestow peace upon us," we pray—knowing as we say these words that the image of heavenly peace is illusory, what with stars dying all the time and burning up in paroxysms of darkness and brilliant light. If there is no peace in the heavens, and creatures on earth survive for the most part by killing other creatures for food (and not only for food)— what chance is there for redemption? To which the Torah responds, I remind myself once again, that this is one of the mysteries that belongs to God alone. What does it all mean? When will the litany of death and suffering end? Will love ever prove "as strong as death?" The best answer available to us—the key "revealed thing," as the Torah calls it—may seem utterly inadequate on days of tragedy and loss, but there are the other days, when it seems the ultimate wisdom. Do as much good as you can, for as long as you live. There will be love in the world, and not just hatred, if we keep loving; there will be good, and not just evil, if we continue to perform acts of justice and compassion; there will be blessing and not just curse; there will be life fighting death, if we choose life as best we can.

This is the order of Meaning that keeps me going, thanks to help from you and the other people close to me, and with the support of a deep reservoir of faith that Judaism and Israel will be around for a long time to come. Inside this sacred order there is immense satisfaction, enormous joy, a great deal of beauty, and work enough for many lifetimes. Children and students will carry the covenants of love and mitzvah forward when the time comes, and perhaps grandchildren and students of students after them. It strikes me with renewed clarity, as I conclude this theological essay, that we don't go through life on the way marked by Torah thinking about God at every moment, much less inquiring into theology. We are not meant to spend our days and weeks that way. Rather, we live—Sabbath after Sabbath, and Passover to Passover; doing good and making mistakes; atoning when we fall short and turning together toward more good; one task, one chapter of the story, at a time.

I hope more Jews will find the Meaning that the way of Torah has afforded to the two of us, and that members of other faith communities will find comparable meaning in their traditions and, inspired by them, will do more good in the world. We all need all the help from every one of us that we can get.

May the words I have set down here and the meditations that have given rise to them prove worthy of you and of God. It's almost time to light candles and wish each other a Shabbat Shalom.

About The Author

Arnold Eisen, one of the world's foremost authorities on American Judaism, is Professor of Jewish Thought and Chancellor Emeritus at the Jewish Theological Seminary. During his tenure as Chancellor, Eisen oversaw curricular and programmatic innovations designed to give rabbinic, cantorial, and educational leaders the skills needed to cope with the unprecedented societal and spiritual challenges confronting Jews today. A popular and charismatic lecturer, Eisen has conducted frank discussions of faith, commandment, and community with hundreds of audiences at synagogues, universities, summer camps and other venues throughout North America. Those conversations form the basis of *Seeking the Hiding God*.

Eisen is the author of a widely read volume of personal reflection, *Taking Hold of Torah: Jewish Commitment and Community in America*. His scholarly publications include many dozens of articles on the contemporary Jewish situation as well as *The Chosen People in America: A Study in Jewish Religious Ideology*; *Galut: Modern Jewish Reflection on Homelessness and Homecoming*; *Rethinking Modern Judaism: Ritual, Commandment, Community*; and (with sociologist Steven M. Cohen) *The Jew Within: Self, Family and Community in America*. Eisen's op-eds and blog posts have appeared in the *Wall Street Journal*, the *Huffington Post*, *Time Magazine*, and the *Times of Israel* among other publications. His blog series, "On My Mind," has reached many thousands of readers.

Seeking the Hiding God is his first published work of theology.

Acknowledgments

This book, more than any other I have written, took shape over many years and bears the imprint of innumerable conversations, events and experiences, both momentous and mundane. Some are described in the course of the essay, but most are not. My debts are many. As Jewish liturgy puts the matter, "Were my mouth filled with song as the sea, and my lips to offer praise as limitless as the sky, I would still be unable to fully express my gratitude"—not only to God but to those who have shown me "myriad moments of kindness" in the course of my search for God. Unable to express adequately the thanks that are due, I will name only a few of those who have directly shaped this essay and shaped me.

To my teachers, not one of whom, sadly, remains alive for me to share the book with today: Van A. Harvey, Rabbi Samuel Lachs, Martin Meyerson, John J. Mulloy, Philip Rieff, Rabbi Nahum Waldman, R.J. Zwi Werblowsky, and Bryan Wilson.

To my friends, who knowingly or unknowingly engaged in theological conversation with me over the decades, and in the process—by word or deed—taught me a great deal about much more than theology: Eliav Bock, Shifra Bronznick, Mara Benjamin, Michael Bennick, Steven M. Cohen, Elliot Cosgrove, Ari Elon, Renee C. Fox *z"l*, Jonathan Friedan, Allon Goshen-Gottstein, Art Green, Serene Jones, David and Felicite Katz, David Leit, Joy Levitt, Shelly Lewis, Gideon Lewis-Kraus, David and Ruth Lindy, Danny and Anna Matt, Marc Mezvinsky, Ari Paltiel, Avi Ravitzky, Ben Resnick, Robert Rifkind, Adam Roffman, Avinoam Rosenak, Mike Rosenak *z"l*, Neal Schnall,

Eilon Schwartz, Lee Shulman, Michael and Ilana Silber, Michael Stanislawski, Michael Strassfeld, Nechama and Howie Tamler, Ellen Umansky, and Jonathan Wittenberg. Special thanks are due to my good friend David Ellenson, *z"l*, who wrote a letter in support of *Seeking the Hiding God* when that support counted the most, and whose companionship as fellow-scholar of modern Judaism, fellow-head of a Jewish institution and fellow-Jew, made me a better thinker, leader and person than I would otherwise have been. May David's memory be for blessing.

To Jill Nathanson, whose artwork appears on the cover of *SHG*, one of the magnificent paintings that she created for our joint project on the Golden Calf chapters in the Book of Exodus, entitled "Seeing Sinai."

To Mara Benjamin, Eliot Cosgrove, and of course David Ellenson, for supplying the blurbs that appear on the back cover.

To my colleagues and students over the years at Columbia, Tel Aviv, Stanford, JTS and elsewhere, from whom I have learned an immense amount about Judaism, about teaching, and about teaching Judaism in the classroom and on the page, especially Yoni Brafman, Ruth Calderon, Bill Cutter, Elliot Dorff, Bernard Faure, Eitan Fishbane, Charlotte Fonrobert, Benjy Gampel, Yitz and Blu Greenberg, Shai Held, Barry Holtz, Ken Koltun-Fromm, Noam Kornsgold, Charles Liebman *z"l*, Alan Mittleman, Danny Nevins, Wayne Proudfoot, Jonathan Sarna, Shuly Schwartz, Vered Shemtov, Ben Sommer, Claire Sufrin, Jack Wertheimer, Ethan Witkowsky, and Steven Zipperstein.

To Alan Levine and the Trustees of JTS for the generous sabbatical leave in which I began thinking and writing *Seeking the Hiding God*, and to my former assistant in the Chancellor's Office, Michelle Mehring, who helped me bringing the manuscript to completion.

To Larry Yudelson, who immediately understood the book as few others did, and has seen it through with enthusiasm and steadfast care to publication by Ben Yehuda Press, assisted by my capable and judicious editors Kira M. Schwartz and Laura Logan.

To my children, Shulie (with husband Jon) and Nathaniel, who will, I hope, understand their father better after reading this book:

just reward for having taught me more over the years than I can say about God, Torah, love, and how life should be lived. "May all your children be taught by the Lord," said the prophet Isaiah, to which the rabbis added, punning on the Hebrew word for children, "May they all be builders who increase peace in the world." Amen.

And, most of all, to Ace: How one could write about loving and being loved by human beings and by God without the experience of overflowing love that I have only known from my parents and from you, I do not know, and thanks to you (and, I believe, to God), I have not had to try. Under the chuppah, a lifetime ago, we pledged to each other words that Isaiah (64:10) pronounced in God's name almost three millennia ago, "The mountains may move, and the hills be shaken, but my lovingkindness will not move from you, nor my covenant of friendship be shaken, said the Lord, Who takes you back in love." Isaiah knew a lot about love, and thankfully so do you. I pray that we will long have the daily opportunity to study and live Torah and life together.

ENDNOTES

Preface

2. A recent article—David Novak, "What is Jewish Theology?" in *A Cambridge Companion to Jewish Theology*, ed. Steven Kepnes (Cambridge: Cambridge University Press, 2020), p. 4

2. Leap of Action—Abraham Joshua Heschel, *God in Search of Man* (New York: Harper Torchbooks, 1966), pp. 282-83.

Prologue

Note: I have given pseudonyms to all the friends mentioned in the text except for my wife Ace. The correspondent Karen is a composite persona drawn from two friends.

10. Kierkegaard—Søren Kierkegaard, "Fear and Trembling," in *Fear and Trembling and The Sickness Unto Death*, tr. Walter Lowrie (Princeton: Princeton University Press, 1974), pp. 21-132. See especially pp. 22-37.

10. The Binding of Isaac story—These paragraphs are borrowed from my book, *Taking Hold of Torah* (Bloomington: Indiana University Press, 1997), pp. 26-27.

13. Philip Rieff—Philip Rieff, "The Religion of the Fathers" in *Freud: The Mind of the Moralist* (Chicago: University of Chicago Press, 1979), pp. 257-299.

16. The sensations attributed to Cezanne—Meyer Schapiro, *Paul Cezanne* (New York: Harry N. Abrams, 1962), pp. 29, 34, 121ff.

17. "The world is twofold"—Martin Buber, *I and Thou*, tr. Walter Kaufmann (New York: Charles Scribner's Sons, 1970), p. 53. See also the slightly different translation of the opening lines of the book by Ronald Gregor Smith (New York: Charles Scribner's Sons, 1978), p. 3. This is the translation that I first encountered, and that made a lasting impression.

18. "Meet in the Eternal Thou— *I and Thou*, tr. Kaufmann, p. 123.

20. "He who speaks"—Martin Buber, *The Prophetic Faith* (New York: Harper Torchbooks, 1960), p. 164.

21. The Heschel chapter titled "Doubts"—Abraham Joshua Heschel, *Man is Not Alone* (New York: Harper Torchbooks, 1966), pp. 78-81.

21. "The hidden realm of existence"—Martin Buber, *Eclipse of God* (New York: Harper Torchbooks, 1957), p. 43.

21. The teaching of a great Hasidic master—Recounted in Arthur Green, *Tormented Master: A Life of Rabbi Nahman of Bratslav* (University, AL: University of Alabama, 1979), pp. 295-96, 302, 314, 330. Green writes of Nachman that "an overwhelming sense of wounded passion, expressed in undying yearning for an intimacy that cannot come to be, lies at the core of his religious life" (p. 304). There is this consolation: "Only in a world from which God is in some degree absent does the life of religion continue to make sense" (p. 330).

22. **The Kedushah prayer**— See, e.g., *Siddur Lev Shalem for Shabbat and Festivals* (New York: The Rabbinical Assembly, 2016), p. 161.

25. **Heschel's authoritative judgment**—Heschel, *God in Search of Man*, p. 3.

25. **"The arms of the old churches"**—Max Weber, "Science as a Vocation," in *From Max Weber*, ed. Hans Gerth and C. Wright Mills (New York: Oxford University Press, 1969), p. 153.

28. **My colleague Serene Jones**—See her book, *Call it Grace: Finding Meaning in a Fractured World.* (New York: Viking, 2019), p xxii.

30. **"Did I give birth to this people?"**—Numbers 11:12.

32. **Rosenzweig's letter to Buber**—"Teaching and Law," in *Franz Rosenzweig: His Life and Thought*, ed. Nahum N. Glatzer (New York: Schocken, 1961), p. 241.

34. **Kaplan's "God-idea"**—Mordecai M. Kaplan, *The Meaning of God in Modern Jewish Religion* (New York: Reconstructionist Press, 1962), pp. 1-14. See also Arnold Eisen, *The Chosen People in America* (Bloomington: Indiana University Press, 1982), pp. 83-91. For Kaplan's vision of Judaism "reconstructed" as civilization rather than religion, see Mordecai M. Kaplan, *Judaism as a Civilization* (New York: Macmillan, 1934).

41. **"The rabbis had the good sense"**—Mishnah Hagigah 2:1.

42. **The mysteries belong to God**—Deuteronomy 29:28.

Chapter 1: Passover and the Work of Redemption

43. **The Passover Haggadah**—See, e.g., *Passover Haggadah: New Revised Edition*, ed. Rabbi Nathan Goldberg (Jersey City: Ktav, 2007). For insight into the rabbis' reworking of the Passover holiday from Temple sacrifice to ritual performed at home, see Baruch M. Bokser, *The Origins of the Seder* (Berkeley: University of California Press, 1984).

47. **"Jews did not practice theology much"**—Solomon Schechter, *Aspects of Rabbinic Theology* (New York: Schocken, 1961), p. ix.

47. **America remains one of the most religious societies**— "3. How religious commitment varies by country among people of all ages." Pew Research Center. https://www.pewresearch.org/religion/2018/06/13/how-religious-commitment-varies-by-country-among-people-of-all-ages.

49. **My favorites lines**—Exodus 14:11-15.

51. **Joseph sincerely believes**—Genesis 45:8. See also 41:28, 39 for Joseph's references to God in his interaction with Pharaoh.

52. **Mordecai warns his cousin Esther**—Esther 4:13-14.

53. **"All is foreseen"**—Pirke Avot (Ethics of the Fathers) 3:19. Included in *Siddur Lev Shalem*, p. 247.

55. **Fackenheim's landmark essay**—Emil Fackenheim, *God's Presence in History* (New York: Harper Torchbooks, 1972), p. 32 (n. 13).

55. **He recommended**—Ibid, p. 84.

56. **"The seal of God is truth."**—Shir HaShirim Rabbah 1:9.

56. **I am not persuaded by the argument of Richard Rubenstein**—*After Auschwitz: Radical Theology and Contemporary Judaism* (Indianapolis: Bobbs-Merrill, 1966). See especially pp. 131-142, 243-264.

58. **Whatever the historical uniqueness**—For a comprehensive collection of theological responses to the Holocaust and views on its historical and theological uniqueness, see Steven T. Katz et al., eds., *Wrestling With God* (New York: Oxford University Press, 2007).

59. **Max Weber's warning**—"Social Psychology of the World Religions," *in From Max Weber*, p. 281.

59. **The Psalmist**—See for example Psalms 44:12, 14, 23-24, 73:13-14 and 74:1, 11, 22-23.

59. **Berkovits and the notion of the "hiding God"**—See Eliezer Berkovits, "Faith after the Holocaust" in *Essential Writings on Judaism*, ed. David Hazony (Jerusalem: Shalem Press, 2007), pp. 317, 316.

63. **Indeed, Berkovits argues, God always cares for us**—Eliezer Berkovits, "The Encounter with the Divine," in *Essential Essays*, p. 222.

63. **Berkovits summarizes his theory**—Eliezer Berkovits, *Faith After the Holocaust* (New York: Ktav, 1973), p. 64, cited in an insightful study of Jewish theological responses to the Holocaust by philosopher Michael L. Morgan, "The Holocaust and Jewish Theology," in Kepnes, *Cambridge Companion*, pp. 277.

60. **"Truly you are a God Who hides"**—Isaiah 45:15.

61. **This is how Buber used the phrase**—See Buber, *Eclipse of God*, pp. 20-24, 66-68, 127-129.

61. **The hiding of the hiding**—*Sefer Ba'al Shem Tov* [Hebrew] (Israel: Book Export Enterprises, Ltd., n.d.), p. 252. Commentary on Deuteronomy 31:18.

61. **Soloveitchik asserted that**—Joseph B. Soloveitchik, *Fate and Destiny*, (New York: Ktav, 1972). pp. 25-35.

62. **I prefer to state unequivocally**—Abraham Joshua Heschel, *Israel: An Echo of Eternity* (New York: Farrar Straus and Giroux, 1967), p. 130.

62. **None of us presumes to be God's accountant**—Abraham Joshua Heschel, "No Religion is an Island" in *Moral Grandeur and Spiritual Audacity*, ed. Susannah Heschel (New York: Farrar Straus Giroux, 1996), p. 246.

65. **The prayer that asks God's blessing for the State of Israel**—See, e.g., *Siddur Lev Shalem*, p. 178.

65. **The *Kedushah* prayer**—See, e.g., Ibid., p. 161.

65. **Kook's son, Tzvi Yehudah Kook**—For a brief survey of Israeli ascriptions of messianic significance to recent history and the controversy it has aroused, see Arnold Eisen, *Galut: Modern Jewish Reflection on Homelessness and Homecoming* (Bloomington: Indiana University Press, 1986), pp. 117-147. An authoritative study of this issue is Aviezer Ravitzky, *Messianism, Zionism and Jewish Religious Radicalism*, tr. Michael Swirsky and Jonathan Chipman (Chicago: University of Chicago Press, 1996).

65. **Tzvi Yehuda ride in a jeep**—see Yossi Klein Halevi, *Like Dreamers: The Story of the Israeli Paratroopers Who Reunited Jerusalem and Divided a Nation* (New York: Harper Collins, 2013). For further context see Yehudah Mirsky, *Rav Kook: Mystic in a Time of Revolution* (New Haven: Yale University Press, 2014), pp. 225-226.

67. **"Walk humbly with God"**—Micah 6:8.

67. **Jill Lepore reports**—See her recent book, *These Truths: A History of the United States* (New York: W. W. Norton, 2018), p. 20.

68. **A religious Israeli whom I respect**—Allon Goshen-Gottstein.

68. **Lincoln's Second Inaugural Address**—"Second inaugural address of the late President Lincoln." (New York: James Miller, Publisher, 1865] At https://www.loc.gov/item/2020770559/.

79. **A people with a narrative**—Laurence M. Thomas, *Vessels of Evil: American Slavery and the Holocaust* (Philadelphia: Temple University Press, 1993), p. 159.

70. **A Talmudic story about divine action and human responsibility**—Babylonian Talmud, Tractate Baba Batra 10a.

72. **Arendt on Auden**—Hannah Arendt, "Remembering W. H. Auden," in *The New Yorker*, Dec. 3, 2018, pp. 68-71.

72. **Auden on Yeats**—W. H. Auden, "Memorializing Yeats" in *Collected Poems*, ed. Edward Mendelson (New York: Viking, 1976), pp. 247-249.

73. **Auden's sober meditation**—W. H. Auden, "September 1, 1939" in *The Penguin Book of English Verse*, ed. John Hayward (Harmondsworth: Penguin, 1979), pp. 453-455. (Auden omitted the piece from the *Collected Poems* volume).

73. **"Our God is Able"**—Martin Luther King, Jr., *Strength to Love* (Philadelphia: Fortress Press, 1963), pp. 113-114.

74. **"A Knock at Midnight"**—Ibid., pp. 67-68.

74. **"Persons, not puppets"**—King, "The Death of Evil upon the Seashore," Ibid., p. 84.

75. **Ezekiel's teaching that "No more shall it be said in Israel…"**—18:1-3.

78. **Third person God-talk**—See the perceptive discussion in Novak, "What is Jewish Theology?" pp. 20-38.

78. **Heschel called it "depth theology"**—See for example *God in Search of Man*, p. 3.

78. **Neil Gillman** — *Sacred Fragments* (Philadelphia: Jewish Publication Society, 1990), pp. xv-xviii, 275-279.

79. **"The issue that emerges before us"**—Heschel, *Man is Not Alone*, p. 71.

80. **The war in Vietnam**—See Abraham Heschel, "The Reasons for My Involvement in the Peace Movement," in *Moral Grandeur*, pp. 224-226.

82. **Rousseau famously declared**—Jean Jacques Rousseau, *The Social Contract*, tr. Maurice Cranston (Harmondsworth, U.K.: Penguin Books, 1978), p. 49.

84. **Emil Fackenheim observed pointedly**—Fackenheim, *God's Presence in History*, p. 6.

84. **The 2013 Survey of American Jews**—"A Portrait of Jewish Americans." Pew Research Center. October 1, 2013, pp. 72-74. https://www.pewresearch.org/religion/2013/10/01/jewish-american-beliefs-attitudes-culture-survey/.

87. **An experiment that has not failed**—Martin Buber, *Paths in Utopia*, pp. 139-149.

87. **The "theopolitical hour"**—Buber, *Prophetic Faith*, pp. 126-154.

88. **Men trust the Lord**—Ibid., pp. 129, 135.

88. **When Gandhi proposed**—Martin Buber "A Letter to Gandhi", in *Pointing the Way*, tr. and ed. Maurice S. Friedman (New York: Harper Torchbooks, 1963),

pp. 139-147. For the complete correspondence between the two, see Martin Buber and Judah Magnes, *Two Letters to Gandhi* (Jerusalem: Reuben Mass, 1939).

88. **Buber's debates with Ben Gurion**—See David Ohana, *Meshichiyut ve-Mamlachtiyut* [Hebrew] (Ben Gurion Institute for Research on Israel, 2013), pp 74-80.

88. **The teaching by Buber that is the most important to me**—Martin Buber, *Moses: The Revelation and the Covenant* (New York: Harper Torchboooks, 1958), pp. 78-79.

91. **"Abide in the astonishment"**—Buber, *Moses*, p. 77.

Chapter 2: Covenants of Mitzvah and Love

101. **Jacob offers God a deal**—Genesis 28:10-22.

101. **"God's camp"**—Genesis 32:3.

101. **"I am unworthy"**—Genesis 32:10-13.

102. **I think this is how Leviticus sees human beings**—My view of the book is indebted to the incomparable three-volume study of the book by Jacob Milgrom, *Leviticus: A New Translation and Commentary*—Anchor Bible (New Haven: Yale University Press, 1998).

102. **God's proper name has Being at its core**—Exodus 3:14.

104. **Is the voice of God**—Exodus 19:5-19.

105. **"As a report about revelation"**—Heschel, *God in Search of Man*, p. 185.

106. **Mordecai Kaplan**—See *Judaism as a Civiliza*tion, pp. 431, 292.

106. **"The law of the state is the law"**—Babylonian Talmud, Tractate Gittin 10b and elsewhere.

107. **"Life for life, eye for eye, tooth for tooth"**—Exodus 21:23-24.

107. **I think Kaplan erred**—See *Judaism as a Civilization*, p. 431.

108. **Cracks and crevices in halakhah**—Leon Wiener Dow, *The Going: A Meditation on Jewish Law* (Switzerland: Palgrave Macmillan, 2017), p. 12.

109. **"A vote but not a veto"**—Mordecai Kaplan, *Not So Random Thoughts* (New York: Reconstructionist Press, 1966), p. 263.

109. **Kafka's *The Castle***—Franz Kafka, *The Castle*, tr. Willa and Edwin Muir (New York: Vintage Books, 1974).

110. **Moses, Aaron, two of Aaron's sons, and seventy elders**—Exodus 24:1.

111. **Moses dutifully trudges**—Exodus 33:12-23.

112. **God says no**—Exodus 33:20.

113. **Buber expressed the immense frustration**—*Prophetic Faith*, pp. 176-77.

113. **Heschel's account**—Heschel, *Man is Not Alone*, p. 78.

113. **Close resemblance to those Williams James identified**—See William James, *The Varieties of Religious Experience* (London: Collins, 1975), lectures 16-17.

116. **"I will dwell among" the people**—Exodus 25:8.

116. **I have found over the years**—Some of the those mentioned here are composites of actual congregants.

117. **Melville's paean to humanity**—Herman Melville, *Moby Dick*, ed. Alfred Kazin (Boston: Houghton Mifflin, 1956), p. 105.

118. **"And everyone who excelled"**—Exodus 35:21-29.

118. **Life-style enclaves**—The term was made famous by Robert Bellah et al., *Habits of the Heart: Individualism and Commitment in American Life* (New York: Harper and Row, 1985), pp. 71-75.

120. **A gripping account of psychological research**—Michael Lewis, *The Undoing Project. A Friendship That Changed Our Minds* (New York: W. W. Norton, 2017).

120. **Another recent study**—Jonathan Haidt, *The Righteous Mind: Why Good People are Divided by Politics and Religion* (New York: Vintage, 2012), pp. 56, 86, 93.

120. **"A part of good science"**—Lewis, *The Undoing* Project, p. 345.

121. **Plausibility structures**—Peter Berger, *The Sacred* Canopy (Garden City, NY: Doubleday Anchor, 1969), pp. 45-47; Peter Berger, *The Heretical Imper*ative (Garden City, NY: Doubleday Anchor, 1979), pp, 16-17.

122. **"I shall behold Thy face in righteousness"**—Psalm 17:15, as interpreted by Heschel, *God in Search of Man*, p. 282.

123. **A "covenant of fate"**—Soloveitchik, *Fate and Destiny*, pp. 43-54.

123. **A large number testify**—"How Much Do American Jews Pray?": https://www.pewresearch.org/religion/religious-landscape-study/ religious-tradition/jewish/frequency-of-prayer/#demographic-information; "Frequency of Prayer by Religious Group": https://www. pewresearch.org/religion/religious-landscape-study/frequency-of-prayer/; and, on belief in God among "moderately affiliated Jews," see Steven M. Cohen and Arnold Eisen, *The Jew Within: Self, Family and Community in America* (Bloomington: Indiana University Press, 2000), p. 219.

124. **Freud famously pronounced**—Sigmund Freud, *Civilization and its Discontents*, tr. James Strachey (New York: W. W. Norton, 1962), pp. 55-63.

124. **Rabbi Akiba by contrast called this mitzvah a great principle**—Genesis Rabbah 24:7.

124. **Jesus named it "the most important commandment"**—Mark 12:29-31, Matthew 22:37-39.

124. **Modern Jewish thinkers**—But see the recent study by Shai Held, *Judaism is About Love: Reclaiming the Heart of Jewish Life* (New York: Farrar, Straus, Giroux, 2023).

124. **The love that Jacob feels for Rachel**—Genesis 29:2.

125. **Love that Leviticus commands [for] the stranger**—See, e.g., Leviticus 19:34.

125. **The charged relationship of David and Jonathan**—I Samuel 18:1-3 and 20:41-42.

125. **Michal… loves David as well**—Ibid., 18:20, 28.

125. **All of Israel loves him too**—Ibid., 18:16.

125. **God is said to love the people of Israel**—Deuteronomy 4:37; see 7:7-9 for the mutual love of God and Israel.

125. **The rabbis, who spoke frequently about that love**—See, e.g., *Siddur Lev Shalem*, p. 154.

125. **Some Kabbalists saw the two loves**—See the remarkable passages quoted in Eitan Fishbane, "Emotion, Ethics and Mystical Piety: On Fear and Love in the

Reshit Hokhmah and the ShLaH," in Lawrence Fine, et al., eds., *Emotions in Jewish Mysticism* (London: Littman Library, forthcoming), pp. 9-21.

125. **Richard Elliot Friedman has demonstrated**—see his *The Exodus* (New York: HarperCollins 2017), pp. 203, 216. Friedman on the neighbor (re'a): pp. 209ff, 216.

126. **Leviticus in dialogue with Plato**—Plato, "Symposium (The Banquet)" in *Great Dialogues of Plato*, tr. W. H. D. Rouse (New York: The New American Library, 1962), l. 204e-205a.

127. **Friedman notes that love of the stranger**—*The Exodus*, p. 203.

127. **A recent book on marriage**—see Daniel Jones, *Love Illuminated* (New York: William Morrow, 2014).

130. **I am reminded of the Hasidic story**—See Martin Buber, *Tales of the Hasidim: Later Masters* (New York: Schocken Books, 1966), p. 86. The tale is attributed to R. Moshe Leib of Sassov.

131. **Akiba believed**—Babylonian Talmud, Tractate Berakhot 61b. See Abraham Joshua Heschel, *Heavenly Torah*, ed. and tr. Gordon Tucker and Leonard Levin (New York: Continuum, 2005), pp. 193-195.

131. **Ishmael believed**—See Heschel, Ibid.

131. **Rabbi Meir taught**—Pirke Avot 6:1, available in *Siddur Lev Shalem*, p. 258.

131. **The rabbis on love**—Pirke Avot 5:18, available in, e.g., *Siddur Lev Shalem*, p. 255.

131. **Rabbi Meir on love**—Ibid., 6:1, p. 258.

131. **Catherine Keller expressed it this way**—See her perceptive essay, "Returning God the Gift of Feminist Theology," in Linda Martin Alcoff and John D. Caputo, eds., *Feminism, Sexuality and the Return of Religion* (Bloomington: Indiana University Press, 2011), pp. 58-76. See especially pp. 65-72.

132. **God is the most difficult [character] to pin down**—David Stern, "Imitatio Homini: Anthropomorphism and the Character of God in Rabbinic Literature." *Prooftexts* 12 (1992), p. 151.

132. **Moses had perhaps to strike the Egyptian**—Exodus 2:11-12.

133. **The Israelites take the bones of Joseph with them**—See Exodus 13:19 and Genesis 50:24-25.

133. **This is what God does, according to Rosenzweig**—Franz Rosenzweig, *The Star of Redemption*, tr. William W. Hallo (Boston: Beacon, 1972), pp. 176-77.

134. **The Seven Blessings**—can be found, e.g., in *B'kol Echad: In Our Voice*, ed. Cantor Jeffrey Shiovitz (New York: United Synagogue of Conservative Judaism, 1999), pp. 73-76.

135. **"My God/ open windows within me"**—The poem by Miriam Baruch Halfi, "You Satisfy Each Person's Will," is quoted in *Machzor Lev Shalem*, p. 179.

136. **"Not in the heavens"**—Deut. 30:12-14.

137. **Buber said of these people**—*Eclipse of God*, pp. 36-37.

138. **We can only stammer**—Heschel, *Man is Not Alone*, p. 78.

138. **"Signals of transcendence"**—Peter Berger, *A Rumour of Angels* (Baltimore: Penguin, 1969), p. 70.

139. **The blessings recited each morning**—See, e.g., *Siddur Lev Shalem*, p. 103.

139. **The rabbis understood**—See for example Babylonian Talmud, Tractate Sotah 14a and Sifre Deuteronomy on 11:12, "To walk in His ways."

141. **Ethical commandments**—Hermann Cohen, *Religion of Reason out of the Sources of Judaism*, tr. Simon Kaplan (New York: Frederick Ungar, 1972).

141. **Ethical behavior**—Emmanuel Levinas, *Difficult Freedom*, tr. Sean Hand (Baltimore: Johns Hopkins University Press, 1990).

143. **Theologian Irving Greenberg**—See "Modern Orthodoxy and the Road Not Taken: A Retrospective View," in *Yitz Greenberg and Modern Orthodoxy: The Road not Taken*, ed. Adam S. Ferziger et al. (Boston: Academic Studies Press, 2019), pp. 52-53.

143. **A rabbi cited in the Talmud**—Jerusalem Talmud Tractate Hagiga 1:7.

143. **Adam and Eve**—Genesis 3:8-10.

144. **Journalist Michael Pollan reports**—Pollan, *How to Change Your Mind* (New York: Penguin, 2018), p. 390.

144. **"No one can tell me what I should do"**—Cohen and Eisen, *The Jew Within*, pp. 36-37.

145. **The earth is God's, not ours**—Lev. 25:23.

147. **Heschel wrote pointedly**—*Israel: An Echo of Eternity*, p. 117-128.

147. **The responsibility laid on Adam and Eve**—Genesis 2:15.

148. **"The day is short"**—Pirke Avot 2:20.

148. **"Something is very gently pulling at me"**—Denise Levertov, "The Thread," quoted in *Machzor Lev Shalem*, p. 155

149. **Moses visits Akiba's academy**—Babylonian Talmud, Menahot 29b.

150. **A related midrash**—Pesikta Rabbati, ed. Ish Shalom [Hebrew], #31. "*Va-tomer Tzion.*"

Chapter 3: Turning, Together

156. **"By the authority of the court on high"**—See, e.g., *Machzor Lev Shalem*, p. 204. (All citations from and references to the High Holiday liturgy are based on this prayerbook.)

157. **"I have forgiven"**—Numbers 14:20.

158. **"The wounds of the order-of-being"**—Martin Buber, "Guilt and Guilt Feelings," in *The Knowledge of Man*, ed. Maurice Friedman (New York: Harper Torchbooks, 1966), p. 136.

159. **As Maimonides asserted**—Mishneh Torah, Laws of Repentance, conveniently available in Twersky, *A Maimonides Reader*, pp. 76-85. See especially 5:1-4.

159. **A traditional hymn**—see *Machzor Lev Shalem*, pp. 219-220.

162. **Esau McCaulley**—*Reading While Black* (Downers Grove, IL: IVP Academic Books, 2020), pp. 76-77.

163. **Saul Bellow's protagonist**—Saul Bellow, *Humboldt's Gift* (New York: Penguin Books, 1996), p. 203.

164. **"The impalpable sustenance of me"**—Walt Whitman, "Crossing Brooklyn Ferry," in *The Best of Whitman*, ed. Harold W. Blodgett (New York: The Ronald

Press Company, 1953), pp.145-151.

164. **The Yom Kippur liturgy takes pains**—*Machzor Lev Shalem*, pp. 235-238.

164. **"We have sinned"**—Ibid., pp. 234, 237.

165. **Whitman understood**—"Crossing Brooklyn Ferry," p. 148.

166. **Charlie Citrine hides**—Bellow, *Humboldt's Gift*, pp. 7-8.

166. **If philosopher Ernest Becker is right**—see his classic study, *The Denial of Death* (New York: Simon and Schuster, 1974).

166. **"All cognition of the All"**—Rosenzweig, *The Star of Redemption*, p. 3.

167. **Maimonides lost a brother**—See the brief account in Twersky, *A Maimonides Reader*, p.4.

169. **Deuteronomy offers**—11:13-21.

169. **The *Guide for the Perplexed* daringly compares**—*Guide for the Perplexed*, 3:32, p. 521.

169. **"The Lord, the Lord"**—Exodus 34:6-7.

170. **What is hard to believe**—Ezekiel 8:9-13.

171. **Unetaneh Tokef**—*Machzor Lev Shalem*, pp. 315-316.

175. **"Turn Us Unto You, O Lord"**—Recited in the Yom Kippur liturgy at Ibid., p. 298. The source of the verse is Lamentations 5:21.

177. **I understand feminist objections**—See especially two classic pieces on this subject: Judith Plaskow, "The Right Question is Theological" in Susannah Heschel, ed., *On Being a Jewish Feminist* (New York: Schocken, 1995), pp. 223-233, and Rita M. Gross, "Female God-Language in the Jewish Context, in Carol Christ and Judith Plaskow, eds., *Womenspirit Rising* (New York: Harper and Row, 1992), pp. 167-173.

178. **"Master of all worlds....What are We?"**—*Siddur Lev Shalem*, p. 105.

178. **I find myself saying**—Compare the address to God, which I first encountered after I had written this chapter, in the beautiful essay entitled "How I Pray" in Arthur Green, *Judaism for the World* (New Haven: Yale University Press, 2020), pp. 37-39.

179. **The "Hymn of Glory"**—*Siddur Lev Shalem*, pp. 208-210.

180. **"All of them beloved"**—Ibid., p. 153.

181. **"Justice, Justice"**—Deuteronomy 16:20.

181. **Human beings are God's partners in Covenant**—On the biblical concept of covenant, see Arnold Eisen, "Covenant" in *Contemporary Jewish Religious Thought*, ed. Arthur A. Cohen and Paul Mendes-Flohr (New York: Charles Scribner's Sons, 1987), pp. 107-112.

181. **Isaiah's declaration**—58:4-8, from the prophetic reading chanted on Yom Kippur morning. See *Machzor Lev Shalem*, p. 285.

182. **Racism is a form of idolatry**—Heschel, "Religion and Race," p. 86.

182. **Hate crimes are surging**—Jeneé Osterheldt, "The Hate We Give: FBI Report Reflects the Highest Surge of Hate Crimes in 12 Years," Boston Globe, February 25, 2022, https://apps.bostonglobe.com/metro/crime-courts/graphics/2022/02/hate-we-give/. See also: "Hate Crime in the United States Incident Analysis," Federal Bureau of Investigation Crime Data Explorer (U.S.

Department of Justice).

182. **Antisemitism has increased**—"ADL Audit Finds Antisemitic Incidents in United States Reached All-Time High in 2021," Anti-Defamation League, April 25, 2022.

182. **The percentage of Americans who give charity is declining**—"Giving USA: Total U.S. Charitable Giving Remained Strong in 2021, Reaching $484.85 Billion," IU Lilly Family School of Philanthropy News (Indiana University, June 21, 2022), https://philanthropy.indianapolis.iu.edu/news-events/news/_news/2022/giving-usa-total-us-charitable-giving-remained-strong-in-2021-reaching-48485-billion.html.

182. **A prominent pundit**—David Brooks, "Why Are So Many of Us Behaving So Badly," *The New York Times*, January 14, 2020, p. A19.

182. **That verdict is confirmed**—Robert Putnam, *The Upswing* (New York: Simon and Schuster, 2021), pp. 241-242.

185. **Maimonides… makes compassion essential**—See the sources cited in Kenneth Seeskin, *Searching for a Distant God* (New York: Oxford University Press, 2000), pp. 148, 153, 160. "Loving-kindness" is part of the "perfection of man that may truly be gloried in by the person who has achieved the maximum possible apprehension of God." See the last paragraphs of *The Guide of The Perplexed*, tr. Shlomo Pines (Chicago: University of Chicago Press, 1963), Vol. 2, p. 638.

185. **Rousseau**—See Jean-Jacques Rousseau, *A Discourse On Inequality* (New York: Penguin Books 1985).

186. **I am not as certain as Heschel**—See for example Abraham J. Heschel, *The Prophets*, (Philadelphia: Jewish Publication Society, 1962, pp. 221-231).

186. **Maimonides taught a profound lesson**—See Seeskin, *Searching for a Distant God*, pp. 43-65.

187. **"The limits of reason alone"**—Immanuel Kant, *Religion Within the Limits of Reason Alone*, tr. Theodore H. Greene and Hoyt H. Hudson (New York: Harper Torchbooks, 1960).

187. **Korach leads a rebellion**—Numbers 16.

188. **Aaron will die**—Numbers 20:24.

188. **Moses "will be gathered to your kin"**—Numbers 27:13.

188. **The Children of Israel mourn him**—Deuteronomy 34:1-8.

188. **"Life of Sarah"**—Genesis 23:1.

188. **Isaac's story (*Toldot*)**—Genesis 25:19

189. **"The *toldot* of Jacob: Joseph"**—Genesis 37:2.

189. **"And we will bless the Lord"**—See, e.g., *Siddur Lev Shalem*, p.182, a refrain citing Psalm 115:18.

190. **Maimonides was particularly vehement**—For his thoughts about the world to come, see the selection from his commentary on the section of the Mishnah called "Helek," the tenth chapter of tractate Sanhedrin, in Twersky, *A Maimonides Reader*, p. 411.

191. **The brief Talmudic tale of Rabbi Chiyya**—Babylonian Talmud, Tractate

Mo'ed Katan, 28a.

191. **The long, drawn-out tale of the death of Moses**—*The Book of Legends. Sefer Ha-Aggadah*, ed. Hayim Nahman Bialik and Yehoshua Ravnitzky, tr. William G. Braude (New York: Schocken Books, 1992), pp. 101-105.

191. **Repent one day before your death**—Pirke Avot 2:15; included in *Siddur Lev Shalem*, p. 241.

192. **God's mysterious personal name**—Exodus 3:14-15.

192. **The Jewish philosopher Michael Wyschogrod**—See *The Body of Faith: Judaism as Corporeal Election* (New York: The Seabury Press, 1983), pp. 137-169. Compare the teaching of Nachman of Bratslav reported in Green, *Tormented Master*, p. 314.

192. **Protestant theologian Paul Tillich**—*The Courage to Be* (New Haven: Yale University Press, 1952). See especially pp. 40-45.

192. **"Blessed are you, Lord, for giving us the Torah"**—*Siddur Lev Shalem*, p. 172.

193. **The rabbis would say**—See, e.g., Ibid., p. 99.

193. **Max Weber argued**—"Science as a Vocation," pp. 139-140.

194. **"The sea of faith"**—Matthew Arnold, "Dover Beach," in John Hayward, ed., *The Penguin Book of English Verse* (Harmondsworth, U.K.: Penguin, 1970), pp. 344-45.

194. **Weber concluded "Science as a Vocation"**—Weber, "Science as a Vocation," p. 156.

194. **Tolstoy… labored mightily**—Leo Tolstoy, "The Death of Ivan Ilych" in *The Death of Ivan Ilych and Other Stories* (New York: New American Library, 1960), pp. 95-156.

195. **Charlie Citrine comes to the realization**—Bellow, *Humboldt's Gift*, p. 203.

197. **Spiritual regret**—The concept was articulated by my colleague Lee Yearley. See Diane Winston and Religion News Service, "New Virtues for a New World of Diversity," *Chicago Tribune*, July 7,1995, https://www.chicagotribune.com/news/ct-xpm-1995-07-07-9507070038-story.html.

198. **The Aleinu Prayer**—See, e.g., *Machzor Lev Shalem*, p. 325. I refer here to the longer version of the prayer said daily and on Sabbaths and Festivals. See., e.g., *Siddur Lev Shalem*, pp. 205-206.

199. **Heschel's "No Religion is an Island"**—In *Moral Grandeur*, pp. 236-250.

202. **I had of course taken along**—Norman Maclean, "A River Runs Through It," in *A River Runs Through It and Other Stories* (Chicago: University of Chicago Press, 1976), pp. 3, 4, 104.

204. **Psalm 27**—included in *Siddur Lev Shalem*, p. 113.

Epilogue

207. **"Lonely Man of Faith"**—I have borrowed the title from the well-known essay by Joseph B. Soloveitchik, *The Lonely Man of Faith* (New York: Doubleday, 1992).

207. **Yedid Nefesh**—*Siddur Lev Shalem*, p. 10.

209. **The priestly benediction**—Numbers 6:22-26.

210. **The right to make promises**—Friedrich Nietzsche, *On The Genealogy of Morals*, tr. Walter Kaufmann (New York: Vintage Books, 1969).

212. **NASA released a photograph**—See online and print editions of *The New York Times* July 11, 2022, p. A17; July 12, p. A18; and July 13, pp. A1 and A12-A13.

212. **"Cease from work and rest"**—Cf. Exodus 31:17, part of the *kiddush* recited over wine at Shabbat lunch.

212. **The *Times* reported**—*New York Times*, July 13, 2022.

213. **"To tend and steward" its creatures**—Genesis 2:15.

213. **God pronounced it "good," even "very good"**—Genesis 1:5, 12, 18, 21, 31.

214. **"May God Who makes peace in the heavens"**—*Siddur Lev Shalem*, p. 77.

214. **Love as strong as death**—Song of Songs 8:6.

215. **"Sacred order"**—I have borrowed the term from Philip Rieff. See index entries for "sacred order" in Philip Rieff, *The Jew of Culture*, ed. Arnold Eisen and Gideon Lewis-Kraus (Charlottesville: University of Virginia, 2008).

Recent books from *Ben Yehuda Press*

Judaism Disrupted: A Spiritual Manifesto for the 21st Century by Rabbi Michael Strassfeld. "I can't remember the last time I felt pulled to underline a book constantly as I was reading it, but *Judaism Disrupted* is exactly that intellectual, spiritual and personal adventure. You will find yourself nodding, wrestling, and hoping to hold on to so many of its ideas and challenges. Rabbi Strassfeld reframes a Torah that demands breakage, reimagination, and ownership." —Abigail Pogrebin, author, *My Jewish Year: 18 Holidays, One Wondering Jew*

The Way of Torah and the Path of Dharma: Intersections between Judaism and the Religions of India by Rabbi Daniel Polish. "A whirlwind religious tourist visit to the diversity of Indian religions: Sikh, Jain, Buddhist, and Hindu, led by an experienced congregational rabbi with much experience in interfaith and in teaching world religions." —Rabbi Alan Brill, author of *Rabbi on the Ganges: A Jewish Hindu-Encounter.*

Liberating Your Passover Seder: An Anthology Beyond The Freedom Seder. Edited by Rabbi Arthur O. Waskow and Rabbi Phyllis O. Berman. This volume tells the history of the Freedom Seder and retells the origin of subsequent new haggadahs, including those focusing on Jewish-Palestinian reconciliation, environmental concerns, feminist and LGBT struggles, and the Covid-19 pandemic of 2020.

Duets on Psalms: Drawing New Meaning from Ancient Words by Rabbis Elie Spitz & Jack Riemer. "Two of Judaism's most inspirational teachers, offer a lifetime of insights on the Bible's most inspired book." — Rabbi Joseph Telushkin, author of *Jewish Literacy*. "This illuminating work is a literary journey filled with faith, wisdom, hope, healing, meaning and inspiration." —Rabbi Naomi Levy, author of *Einstein and the Rabbi*.

Weaving Prayer: An Analytical and Spiritual Commentary on the Jewish Prayer Book by Rabbi Jeffrey Hoffman. "This engaging and erudite volume transforms the prayer experience. Not only is it of considerable intellectual interest to learn the history of prayers—how, when, and why they were composed—but this new knowledge will significantly help a person pray with intention (*kavanah*). I plan to keep this volume right next to my siddur." —Rabbi Judith Hauptman, author of *Rereading the Rabbis: A Woman's Voice*.

Renew Our Hearts: A Siddur for Shabbat Day edited by Rabbi Rachel Barenblat. From the creator of *The Velveteen Rabbi's Haggadah*, a new siddur for the day of Shabbat. *Renew Our Hearts* balances tradition with innovation, featuring liturgy for morning (*Shacharit* and a renewing approach to *Musaf*), the afternoon (*Mincha*), and evening (*Ma'ariv* and *Havdalah*), along with curated works of poetry, art and new liturgies from across the breadth of Jewish spiritual life. Every word of Hebrew is paired with transliteration and with clear, pray-able English translation.

Forty Arguments for the Sake of Heaven: Why the Most Vital Controversies in Jewish Intellectual History Still Matter by Rabbi Shmuly Yanklowitz. Hillel vs. Shammai, Ayn Rand vs. Karl Marx, Tamar Ross vs. Judith Plaskow... but also Abraham vs. God, and God vs. the angels! Movements debate each other: Reform versus Orthodoxy, one- two- and zero-state solutions to the Israeli-Palestinian conflict, gun rights versus gun control in the United States. Rabbi Yanklowitz presents difficult and often heated disagreements with fairness and empathy, helping us consider our own truths in a pluralistic Jewish landscape.

Recent books from *Ben Yehuda Press*

Reaching for Comfort: What I Saw, What I Learned, and How I Blew it Training as a Pastoral Counselor by Sherri Mandell. In 2004, Sherri Mandell won the National Jewish Book award for *The Blessing of the Broken Heart*, which told of her grief and initial mourning after her 13-year-old son Koby was brutally murdered. Years later, with her pain still undiminished, Sherri trains to help others as a pioneering pastoral counselor in Israeli hospitals. "What a blessing to witness Mandell's and her patients' resilience!" —Rabbi Dayle Friedman, editor, *Jewish Pastoral Care: A Practical Guide from Traditional and Contemporary Sources.*

Heroes with Chutzpah: 101 True Tales of Jewish Trailblazers, Changemakers & Rebels by Rabbi Deborah Bodin Cohen and Rabbi Kerry Olitzky. Readers ages 8 to 14 will meet Jewish changemakers from the recent past and present, who challenged the status quo in the arts, sciences, social justice, sports and politics, from David Ben-Gurion and Jonas Salk to Sarah Silverman and Douglas Emhoff. "Simply stunning. You would want this book on your coffee table, though the stories will take the express lane to your soul." —Rabbi Jeff Salkin.

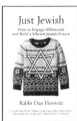

Just Jewish: How to Engage Millennials and Build a Vibrant Jewish Future by Rabbi Dan Horwitz. Drawing on his experience launching The Well, an inclusive Jewish community for young adults in Metro Detroit, Rabbi Horwitz shares proven techniques ready to be adopted by the Jewish world's myriad organizations, touching on everything from branding to fundraising to programmatic approaches to relationship development, and more. "This book will shape the conversation as to how we think about the Jewish future." —Rabbi Elliot Cosgrove, editor, *Jewish Theology in Our Time.*

Put Your Money Where Your Soul Is: Jewish Wisdom to Transform Your Investments for Good by Rabbi Jacob Siegel. "An intellectual delight. It offers a cornucopia of good ideas, institutions, and advisers. These can ease the transition for institutions and individuals from pure profit nature investing to deploying one's capital to repair the world, lift up the poor, and aid the needy and vulnerable. The sources alone—ranging from the Bible, Talmud, and codes to contemporary economics and sophisticated financial reporting—are worth the price of admission." —Rabbi Irving "Yitz" Greenberg.

Why Israel (and its Future) Matters: Letters of a Liberal Rabbi to the Next Generation by Rabbi John Rosove. Presented in the form of a series of letters to his children, Rabbi Rosove makes the case for Israel — and for liberal American Jewish engagement with the Jewish state. "A must-read!" —Isaac Herzog, President of Israel. "This thoughtful and passionate book reminds us that commitment to Israel and to social justice are essential components of a healthy Jewish identity." —Yossi Klein Halevi, author, *Letters to My Palestinian Neighbor.*

Other Covenants: Alternate Histories of the Jewish People by Rabbi Andrea D. Lobel & Mark Shainblum. In *Other Covenants*, you'll meet Israeli astronauts trying to save a doomed space shuttle, a Jewish community's faith challenged by the unstoppable return of their own undead, a Jewish science fiction writer in a world of Zeppelins and magic, an adult Anne Frank, an entire genre of Jewish martial arts movies, a Nazi dystopia where Judaism refuses to die, and many more. Nominated for two Sidewise Awards for Alternate History.

Reflections on the weekly Torah portion from *Ben Yehuda Press*

An Angel Called Truth and Other Tales from the Torah by Rabbi Jeremy Gordon and Emma Parlons. Funny, engaging micro-tales for each of the portions of the Torah and one for each of the Jewish festivals as well. These tales are told from the perspective of young people who feature in the Biblical narrative, young people who feature in classic Rabbinic commentary on our Biblical narratives and young people just made up for this book.

Torah & Company: The weekly portion of Torah, accompanied by generous helpings of Mishnah and Gemara, served with discussion questions to spice up your Sabbath Table by Rabbi Judith Z. Abrams. Serve up a rich feast of spiritual discussion from an age-old recipe: One part Torah. Two parts classic Jewish texts. Add conversation. Stir... and enjoy! "A valuable guide for the Shabbat table of every Jew." —Rabbi Burton L. Visotzky, author *Reading the Book*.

Torah Journeys: The Inner Path to the Promised Land by Rabbi Shefa Gold. Rabbi Gold shows us how to find blessing, challenge and the opportunity for spiritual transformation in each portion of Torah. An inspiring guide to exploring the landscape of Scripture... and recognizing that landscape as the story of your life. "Deep study and contemplation went into the writing of this work. Reading her Torah teachings one becomes attuned to the voice of the Shekhinah, the feminine aspect of God which brings needed healing to our wounded world." —Rabbi Zalman Schachter-Shalomi.

American Torah Toons 2: Fifty-Four Illustrated Commentaries by Lawrence Bush. Deeply personal and provocative artworks responding to each weekly Torah portion. Each two-page spread includes a Torah passage, a paragraph of commentary from both traditional and modern Jewish sources, and a photo-collage that responds to the text with humor, ethical conscience, and both social and self awareness. "What a vexing, funny, offensive, insightful, infuriating, thought-provoking book." —Rabbi David Saperstein.

The Comic Torah: Reimagining the Very Good Book. Stand-up comic Aaron Freeman and artist Sharon Rosenzweig reimagine the Torah with provocative humor and irreverent reverence in this hilarious, gorgeous, off-beat graphic version of the Bible's first five books! Each weekly portion gets a two-page spread. Like the original, the Comic Torah is not always suitable for children.

we who desire: Poems and Torah riffs by Sue Swartz. From Genesis to Deuteronomy, from Bereshit to Zot Haberacha, from Eden to Gaza, from Eve to Emma Goldman, *we who desire* interweaves the mythic and the mundane as it follows the arc of the Torah with carefully chosen words, astute observations, and deep emotion. "Sue Swartz has used a brilliant, fortified, playful, serious, humanely furious moral imagination, and a poet's love of the music of language, to re-tell the saga of the Bible you thought you knew." —Alicia Ostriker, author, *For the Love of God: The Bible as an Open Book*.

Eternal Questions by Rabbi Josh Feigelson. These essays on the weekly Torah portion guide readers on a journey that weaves together Torah, Talmud, Hasidic masters, and a diverse array of writers, poets, musicians, and thinkers. Each essay includes questions for reflection and suggestions for practices to help turn study into more mindful, intentional living. "This is the wisdom that we always need—but maybe particularly now, more than ever, during these turbulent times." —Rabbi Danya Ruttenberg, author, *On Repentance and Repair*.

Jewish spirituality and thought from *Ben Yehuda Press*

The Essential Writings of Abraham Isaac Kook. Translated and edited by Rabbi Ben Zion Bokser. This volume of letters, aphorisms and excerpts from essays and other writings provide a wide-ranging perspective on the thought and writing of Rav Kook. With most selections running two or three pages, readers gain a gentle introduction to one of the great Jewish thinkers of the modern era.

Ahron's Heart: Essential Prayers, Teachings and Letters of Ahrele Roth, a Hasidic Reformer. Translated and edited by Rabbi Zalman Schachter-Shalomi and Rabbi Yair Hillel Goelman. For the first time, the writings of one of the 20th century's most important Hasidic thinkers are made available to a non-Hasidic English audience. Rabbi Ahron "Ahrele" Roth (1894-1944) has a great deal to say to sincere spiritual seekers far beyond his own community.

A Passionate Pacifist: Essential Writings of Aaron Samuel Tamares. Translated and edited by Rabbi Everett Gendler. Rabbi Aaron Samuel Tamares (1869-1931) addresses the timeless issues of ethics, morality, communal morale, and Judaism in relation to the world at large in these essays and sermons, written in Hebrew between 1904 and 1931. "For those who seek a Torah of compassion and pacifism, a Judaism not tied to 19th century political nationalism, and a vision of Jewish spirituality outside of political thinking this book will be essential." —Rabbi Dr. Alan Brill, author, *Thinking God: The Mysticism of Rabbi Zadok of Lublin.*

Return to the Place: The Magic, Meditation, and Mystery of Sefer Yetzirah by Rabbi Jill Hammer. A translation of and commentary to an ancient Jewish mystical text that transforms it into a contemporary guide for meditative practice. "A tour de force—at once scholarly, whimsical, deeply poetic, and eminently accessible." —Rabbi Tirzah Firestone, author of *The Receiving: Reclaiming Jewish Women's Wisdom*

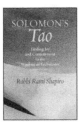

Enlightenment by Trial and Error: Ten Years on the Slippery Slopes of Jewish Mysticism, Postmodern Buddhist Meditation, and Heretical Flexidox Spirituality by Rabbi Jay Michaelson. A unique record of the 21st-century spiritual search, from the perspective of someone who made plenty of mistakes along the way.

The Tao of Solomon: Finding Joy and Contentment in the Wisdom of Ecclesiastes by Rabbi Rami Shapiro. Rabbi Rami Shapiro unravels the golden philosophical threads of wisdom in the book of Ecclesiastes, reweaving the vibrant book of the Bible into a 21st century tapestry. Shapiro honors the roots of the ancient writing, explores the timeless truth that we are merely a drop in the endless river of time, and reveals a path to finding personal and spiritual fulfillment even as we embrace our impermanent place in the universe.

Embracing Auschwitz: Forging a Vibrant, Life-Affirming Judaism that Takes the Holocaust Seriously by Rabbi Joshua Hammerman. The Judaism of Sinai and the Judaism of Auschwitz are merging, resulting in new visions of Judaism that are only beginning to take shape. "Should be read by every Jew who cares about Judaism." —Rabbi Dr. Irving "Yitz" Greenberg.

Made in the USA
Las Vegas, NV
23 December 2024

15250116R00134